CISTERCIAN STUDIES SERIES: NUMBER TWENTY-THREE

# BERNARD OF CLAIRVAUX

St Bernard de Clairvaux

les deux thèmes de sermons que Saint Bernard
de Clairvaux affectionna furent
- l'amour maternel
  Sermons sur la Sainte Vierge
- l'amour Spirituel
  Sermons sur le Cantique des Cantiques

Ces derniers sermons prennent hardiment le
texte du poème Biblique (que tant de gens
considèrent comme un chant d'amour païen)
et montrent que la femme du poème est l'Eglise
et l'homme (le bien aimé) est Dieu - et que l'amour
de l'Eglise pour son créateur s'exprime en
accents passionnés, fort naturellement

Saint Bernard a pris ce thème difficile pour
réagir contre les légèretés de son temps .

Dans ses nombreuses lettres, on trouve aussi
que ses avis spirituels sont exprimés avec des
termes d'amour violent et cela place ce sentiment
dans sa plus haute spiritualité -

Il n'est pas moins touchant dans ses commentaires
sur l'amour maternel et il étend à tous ceux
qui l'écoutent les bienfaits de l'amour maternel de
Sainte Marie - A l'entendre, chacun en est
atteint et peut compter sur l'aide de la mère
de Dieu à tout instant - On trouve dans les accents
qu'il a, le souvenir de ce que fut pour lui, sa mère,
Aleth - Une personne discrète, tendre, pieuse, vigilante
qui prépara le Saint à être ce qu'il fut -

CS 1: Thomas Merton: *The Climate of Monastic Prayer*
CS 2: Amédée Hallier: *The Monastic Theology of Aelred of Rievaulx: An Experiental Theology*
CS 3: *The Cistercian Spirit: A Symposium in honor of Thomas Merton*
CS 4: Evagrius Ponticus: *The Praktikos: 153 Chapters on Prayer*
CS 5: Adalbert de Vogüé: *The Community and the Abbot in the Rule of St Benedict*
CS 6: *The Rule of the Master*
CS 7: Jean Leclercq: *Aspects of Monasticism, Yesterday and Today*
CS 8: Bede Lackner: *The Eleventh-Century Background of Cîteaux*
CS 9: Jean-Baptiste Van Damme: *The Three Founders of Cîteaux*
CS 10: Jean Marie Déchanet: *William of St Thierry: The Man and his Works*
CS 11: Robert Barakat: *The Cistercian Sign Language: A Study in Non-Verbal Communication*
CS 12: *Rule and Life: An Interdisciplinary Symposium*
CS 13: *Studies in Medieval Cistercian History*
CS 14: Pierre Salmon: *The Abbot in Monastic Tradition*
CS 15: Bernard McGinn: *The Golden Chain: The Theological Anthropology of Isaac of Stella*
CS 16: Jean Leclercq: *St Bernard and the Cistercian Spirit*
CS 17: François Vandenbroucke: *Why Monks?*
CS 18: John J. Higgins: *Merton's Theology of Prayer*
CS 19: Jean Leclercq: *Contemplative Life*
CS 20: John Cassian: *Conferences I*
CS 21: *Contemplative Community: An Interdisciplinary Symposium*
CS 22: Ambrose Wathen: *Silence: The Meaning of Silence in the Rule of St Benedict*
CS 23: *Bernard of Clairvaux: Studies presented to Dom Jean Leclercq*
CS 24: *Studies in Medieval Cistercian History: Volume Two*
CS 25: John Morson: *Christ the Way: The Christology of Guerric of Igny*

CISTERCIAN STUDIES SERIES: NUMBER TWENTY-THREE

# BERNARD OF CLAIRVAUX

Studies presented to
Dom Jean Leclercq

CISTERCIAN PUBLICATIONS

CONSORTIUM PRESS

Washington, D.C.

1973

Cistercian Studies Series     ISBN 0-87907-800-6
This volume                   ISBN 0-87907-823-5


Library of Congress Catalog Card Number    73-8099


© Copyright, Cistercian Publications, Inc. 1973
Spencer, Massachusetts 01562

Ecclesiastical permission to publish this book was received from Bernard
Flanagan, Bishop of Worcester, June 1, 1972.

# CONTENTS

Foreword     ix

Dom Jean Leclercq, by Louis Leloir OSB     1

1 A Literary Journey: The New Edition of the Works of St Bernard     19
    Henri Rochais

2 The Friendship between Peter the Venerable and Bernard of Clairvaux     35
    Ann Proulx Lang

3 Bernard and Abelard at the Council of Sens, 1140     55
    Edward Little

4 Chrismatic and Gregorian Leadership in the Thought of Bernard of Clairvaux     73
    John R. Sommerfeldt

5 Antithesis and Argument in the *De consideratione*     91
    Elizabeth T. Kennan

6 Sacrament, Symbol and Causality in Bernard of Clairvaux     111
    William Courtenay

7 The Two St Malachy Offices from Clairvaux     123
    Chrysogonus Waddell OCSO

8 St Bernard and Eschatology     161
    Bernard McGinn

9 St Bernard and the Anglican Divines: Some Reflections on Mark Frank's Sermon for the Circumsion     187
    Benedicta Ward SLG

10 St Bernard and the Barundi on the Name of God     197
    Patrick Ryan OCSO

Bibliography of the Works by Jean Leclercq     215
    Louis Leloir OSB

# LIST OF ABBREVIATIONS

Note: For references to Sacred Scripture the abbreviations found in the Revised Standard Version are employed. Abbreviated references for the Works of St Bernard are listed separately below.

ASOC   *Analecta Sacri Ordinis Cisterciensis*, later *Analecta Cisterciensia* (Rome, 1945-    ).

Bbg   Bibliography of the Works of Jean Leclercq prepared by Louis Leloir, below, pp. 215-264.

CF   Cistercian Fathers Series (Spencer, Massachusetts: Cistercian Publications, 1970-    ).

CS   Cistercian Studies Series (Spencer, Massachusetts: Cistercian Publications, 1969-    ).

Letters   Giles Constable, *The Letters of Peter the Venerable*, 2 vols. (Cambridge, Massachusetts: Harvard University Press, 1967).

Opera   *S. Bernardi Opera*, ed. Jean Leclercq, H. Rochais, C. H. Talbot, 9 vols. (Rome; Editiones Cistercienses, 1957-    ).

Pet. Ven.   *Petrus Venerabilis, 1156-1956: Studies and Texts Commemorating the Eighth Centenary of his Death*, eds. Giles Constable and James Kritzeck, *Studia Anselmiana* 40 (Rome, 1956).

PL   *Patrologiae cursus completus, series Latina*, ed. J. P. Migne (Paris, 1878-1890).

## ABBREVIATIONS FOR THE WORKS OF ST BERNARD

Abael   *Ep. de erroribus P. Abaelardi.*
Csi   *De Consideratione libri V.*
Ep   *Epistola(e).*
Hum   *L. de gradibus Humilitus et Superbiae.*
Mal   *Sermones in Transitu S. Malachiae episcopi.*
I Nov   *Sermones in Dominica I novembris.*
Pl   *Sermo in Conversione S. Pauli.*
QH   *Sermo super psalmum Qui Habitat.*
SC   *Sermones super Cantica Canticorum.*
V Mal   *Vita S. Malachiae.*

# FOREWORD

A T A MEETING of "Cistercianologists" at Spencer Abbey a couple of years ago,[1] the monk and scholar to whom this volume is dedicated told us quite emphatically: "Don't call me 'Dom Leclercq'! Call me 'Father' or just plain John—but don't call me, 'Dom'! " And so I will.

If there is one thing Father John does lose patience with, it is pretension. He wears his own greatness graciously, simply and joyfully. And so I shall try to make this brief introduction a very simple thing.

The job of editor in preparing this volume was not an easy one. This was so not because of any lack on the part of the contributors. It was just the opposite. There were so many who wanted to join in to pay tribute to this humble monk whose indefatigable and amazingly productive labors have illuminated their work and their lives. There is potential for many other *Festschriften* and I hope they will be produced, not only for the common benefit of monks and scholars, but to unite with this one in its attempt to say some sort of "Thank you" to our friend and benefactor.

---

1. The term "Cistercianologists" was coined by Father John, somewhat in jest, yet the group which it describes has been somewhat at a loss to find a better label. The meeting at Spencer in September, 1970, was the first of a series of informal meetings which will take place periodically in Cistercian monasteries not only to foster collaboration among the interested scholars but to give those working in Cistercian studies today an opportunity to come into contact with living Cistercian communities.

Bernard of Clairvaux was chosen as the subject of this volume because we want to say "Thank you" to Father John in a particular way for the quarter of a century of ceaseless travel, search and labor that have gone into the preparation of the excellent critical edition of the works of St Bernard.[2] The final volumes of this edition are now at the press and soon all nine volumes of this valuable tool will be readily at hand for all scholars, as well as in the hands of monks and nuns as they pursue their search for God under the tutelage of the ever-living Abbot of Clairvaux.

There is another reason for the choice. As Father John said at the Second Cistercian Studies Conference:[3] "I love Bernard too much." The best way to gratify a man, especially a humble man, is to speak of his friend. Father John Leclercq and Bernard of Clairvaux are friends. This is one of the secrets of Father John's fecundity.[4]

Father Leclercq rarely speaks of himself except in jest. Indeed, he likes to speak of himself as a "jester." We would like to know more about him. And his life-long confrère and friend, Dom Louis Leloir, has now done us the favor of writing at least a few pages about his friend. Someday a full biography will have to be written of this man whose activities seem to multiply with each succeeding year. We have also wanted to know more about his work in the preparation of the *S. Bernardi Opera.* And his constant co-laborer, Henri Rochais, has been kind enough to give us a step by step account of their "literary voyage."

A few of the very many eminent scholars who have profited by Father John's articles and books and by the use of his edition of St Bernard, offer here a study in grateful tribute. The ambit

---

2. *S. Bernardi Opera*, ed J. Leclercq, H. Rochais, C. H. Talbot, 9 vols. (Rome: Editiones Cistercienses, 1957 - ).

3. Western Michigan University, Kalamazoo, Michigan, May 1 - 3, 1972.

4. One has just to peruse the Bibliography at the end of this volume to have ample evidence of this fecundity. In a recent letter to the editor, Father John wrote: "Basil, can you find some kind of pill to check this fecundity? "

of their contributions is wide — literary form, social doctrine, theology, liturgy — and gives some hint of the vast compass of Father's own work.

There are two groups who have been especially encouraged by Father Leclercq: the young and the "ladies." One of the scholars writing here likes to recall the gracious reception his first offprint received from Father John. Father has never ceased to encourage and assist with selfless magnanimity the promising labors of young scholars. And I am sure he will be gratified to find them present in this volume.

Anyone who has in recent years taken part in a conference or symposium with Father John awaits the moment when he will hear: "And now it is time we heard from the ladies." In fields that have been largely dominated by men, he ever encourages the "ladies" to speak out and make the contribution that only they can make. In this volume the ladies do speak out, both the recognized scholar and the promising young.

There are two areas of concern to which Father John has given a great deal of attention in recent years: the ecumenical movement, in the widest sense of the term, and the Third World. I did not want them to be passed by in silence and I am grateful to Sr Benedicta Ward of the Anglican Congregation of the Sisters of the Love of God and Br Patrick Ryan ocso for their contributions in these areas. The latter, one of the young scholars encouraged by Father John, has tried to portray the bridge of ideas over which Father John himself walked when he visited and dialogued with the Barundi in 1966.

To this representative tribute I would like to add my own voice. I can not adequately express what I owe to Father for his encouragement, inspiration and his constant concrete and practical assistance. He has been a most active member of the Board of Editors of Cistercian Publications, a generous contributor to our periodicals and books, an enlivening participant in our many meetings and symposia. I therefore join with all the others in expressing a very heartfelt "Thank you" to this eminent and most productive scholar who has ever remained a truly Christlike monk, humble, brotherly, ever ready to give of himself.

M. Basil Pennington ocso

St Joseph's Abbey
Spencer, Mass.
June 29, 1972

# DOM JEAN LECLERCQ

TEN YEARS AGO, February 2, 1962, Fr Jean Le-clercq was designated Doctor *honoris causa* in Philosophy and Letters by the University of Louvain. For the occa-sion, the Cistercian students of Monte Cistello had the gracious thoughtfulness to send him a card with their fifty-seven signa-tures. Since Latin was still known a bit at that time, the greet-ing was in that language: *Euge, serve bone et fidelis. Studentes Cistercienses ex omnibus tribubus, linguis et nationibus, doc-torem salutant monasticum, et ducem per amorem litterarum ad desiderium rerum aeternarum.* In sponsoring this Festschrift, the American Cistercians are giving recognition to these same qualities: they acclaim in Father Leclercq a master of monastic doctrine, whose purpose has always been to lead to God and who has endeavored to awaken the thirst for heaven and for the vision of God in all who came into contact with him. For he has never had any other ambition for himself. He has never desired nor sought human advantages or praise. He has accepted with simplicity the commendations and honors conferred upon him, but he has not sought to elicit them. Fr Leclercq's answer to his students and admirers was sent from the abbey of Mount St Bernard in England, on the feast of St Gregory.

In it Fr Leclercq referred to himself: *Nigerrimus monachorum albis fratribus amicis de Monte Cistello gratias agens et Deo.* A perpetual hyphen, because of his work, between the black monks and the white monks, Fr Leclercq saw himself as debtor of the white monks, and he very subtly explained the reason

1

for his gratitude by quoting a text of St Gregory: *Corvus profecto est quisquis praedicator qui magna voce clamat, dum pec-
catorum suorum memoriam atque cognitionem infirmitatis
propriae quasi quamdam coloris nigredinem portat. Cui quidem
in fide nascuntur discipuli . . . sed nigredinem non ostendunt.
Hi velut ad accipiendas escas os aperiunt . . . Cum enim pulli
ut satientur clamant, 'corvo esca praeparatur': quia dum verbum Dei boni auditores esuriunt, pro reficiendis eis maiora
doctoribus intelligentiae dona tribuuntur.*[1] With good reason
did Fr Leclercq attribute the merits of his teaching to the zeal
and eagerness of his hearers, and above all to the generosity
of God. The more God sees the disciples to be eager for doctrine, the more he helps their teachers to satisfy their desire
by ever new and richer lights.

### FIRST STAGES AND PREPARATION FOR THE MONASTIC LIFE

On the thirty-first of January, 1911, Jean Leclercq was born
at Avesnes, in northern France, to a family of well-to-do mer-
chants. He was the second of four children, the twin of one of
his sisters.

Avesnes is a medieval town, formerly a feudal domain dependent on the count of Chimay (a small city of Hainaut about
thirty kilometers away). The large and beautiful collegial
church dates back to the Middle Ages and the streets are
still full of indications of a past laden with history. It was thus
an appropriate setting for the blossoming of the vocation of a
medieval historian. It is, besides, the native city of Jesse de
Forest, the principal founder of New York. There is a monu-
ment to him in Avesnes.

---

1. "Every learned preacher, who cries with a loud voice, whilst he carries the
memory of his own sins and the knowledge of his own infirmity, as a kind of black
shade of colour, is doubtless a raven. To whom the disciples indeed are born in
the faith . . . (but) display not that blackness. . . . But they open their mouth, as
it were, to receive food. . . . For when the young ones cry to be filled, food is prepared for the raven; because while good hearers hunger after the word of God,
greater gifts of understanding are given to their teachers for their refreshment."
— *Morals on the Book of Job,* xxx, 33, 35, tr. John H. Newman, A Library of the
Fathers of the Holy Catholic Church (Oxford: Parker, 1850), 3:287-288.

The date 1911 also has its significance, for it was three and a half years before the beginning of the First World War. Jean Leclercq's first visual remembrance is that of the departure of his father who had been mobilized; the second, that of the arrival of the German uhlans, spear in hand, the head of a dead man on their helmets. Jean Leclercq began his studies at Avesnes and was being introduced to the piano when, during the winter 1916-1917, his family was evacuated to unoccupied France (by way of Belgium, Holland, Germany and Switzerland to avoid the front line). His family emigrated first to Paris. Then they went to Normandy, and then to Lourdes where they stayed several months. They returned to Paris, and finally returned to Avesnes at the time of the liberation, November, 1918. This transplantation from school to school during the war years explains some lacunas in Jean Leclercq's early student formation; it accounts for an almost complete ignorance of arithmetic and a permanent hostility for numbers. This allergy had practically no consequences on the future scientific life of the young scholar. He usually reconciled himself with numbers when it was a question of citing the numbering of manuscripts or of seeing to the exactness of references. As to the spiritual life, properly so-called, of Jean Leclercq, and his service of others, his incompetence in arithmetic has, on the other hand, been a blessing; when there is question of giving alms to the poor, he never calculates.

However, the war years had another very regrettable consequence; the food restrictions, the nervous shocks provoked by the alerts, the bombing and the continual uncertainties regarding the future, all these affected the physical development of Jean Leclercq, with the result that his health has always been poor.

From 1920 to 1928, Jean Leclercq pursued his studies at the College of St-Pierre-de-Fourmies, about fifteen kilometers from Chimay. His first relations with the Trappists date back to this time. He visited Scourmont toward the end of his first year at Fourmies, and he has kept a vivid remembrance of it. At fifteen, he discovered the liturgy by means of the missal. He became aware that the poetry read in chapel equaled that which he was studying in class; he decided to become a monk. At sixteen, he spoke of it to his confessor, Fr Legrand, who was on friendly terms with Dom Salmon, a monk soon to be prior of Clervaux. The two had studied together at the French Seminary in Rome. After a second visit to Scourmont, Fr Legrand and Jean Leclercq went together to Clervaux to celebrate the patronal feast of the monastery, the feast of St Maurice, September 22, 1927. Jean Leclercq asked to be admitted as a lay brother, since he did not wish to become a priest, – this explains why he later would so vigorously defend the rights of lay monasticism and would seek to re-establish it. He was told to come back later. He returned in August, 1928, and asked again to be received as a lay brother; this was refused to him and it was as a postulant for the choir, destined for the priesthood, that he was accepted.

BEGINNINGS OF HIS MONASTIC LIFE AND FIRST SCIENTIFIC ACTIVITIES

At Clervaux on the twenty-second of September, 1928, Br Jean Leclercq received the postulant's habit; on the twenty-fourth of June, 1929, the novice's cloak. He pronounced his first vows on the twenty-ninth of June, 1930. His Sub-Master as a novice was Dom Salmon, who initiated him into the liturgy and patristics. His Master of Novices was Dom Pierson, a monk who was a bit sceptical of studies but convinced of the primacy of the contemplative life. He was convinced that the first duty of a Father Master was to form his novices in humility and prayer. He had Br Leclercq read the books of Dom Vital Lehodey OCR: *Holy Abandonment* and *The Ways of Mental Prayer.* These two books, even then, nourished Br Leclercq with Cistercian spirituality. He was influenced above all by the first which fostered in him an attitude of simplicity, of holy unconcern and of very great confidence in God, events and men. Dom Leclercq always sees the beautiful side of things and of people, he loves his times and all whom he meets, he sees qualities in everyone and encourages everybody, he is a comforting person. Br Leclercq read enormously during his novitiate and, from that time onwards, acquired a broad monastic culture.

After his profession, he did two years of philosophy at Clervaux. During his first year he had as professor, Dom Jean Müller, who was soon to become a professor at San Anselmo in Rome. He taught Br Leclercq to appreciate the strong scholastic framework. During his second year he continued his initiation into philosophy under the direction of Dom Leplus, a brilliant, very well-informed professor, but also an exacting one, who corrected the assignments of his students minutely, severely and even mercilessly. He recognized Br Leclercq's exceptional gifts and formed him in precision of vocabulary, in conciseness of sentences and in the orderly and agreeable arrangement of ideas.

After his philosophy, Br Leclercq served a year of military service as a second gunner in the anti-aircraft artillery at Metz in Lorraine. Military matters held little interest for him and he was a mediocre soldier, but the contact with strangers from a bourgeois and clerical milieu taught him much. Fr Leclercq has never been intimidating, he has always remained very accessible, he has always put at their ease the lowliest persons and those whose interests were the most unrelated to his own. The contacts he made during his military service had helped him to acquire this precious quality. Then during four years, he pursued theological studies at the Benedictine College of San Anselmo in Rome—from October 1933 to June 1937. Dom Anselm Stolz, a profound theologian and a spiritual man, was his professor of dogmatics. Br Leclercq esteemed him, loved him and came under his strong and happy influence; like him, he would seek for the new formulations in theology called for by our times. He associated with Eric Peterson who was in Rome at that time and lived on the Via San Anselmo. From contact with him, he became aware of the importance of philology and of the study of vocabulary. He formed a friendship with the professor of Church history at San Anselmo, Dom Charles Poulet, a monk of Wisques and originally from Avesnes. The latter encouraged him to do some history and suggested to him, as a subject for a thesis, the treatise by John of Paris (a

disciple of St Thomas) on royal and pontifical power. Br Leclercq set to work, thus beginning his labors among manuscripts
and frequenting the libraries of Rome, especially the Vatican
library. Later, during his many travels throughout the world,
Dom Leclercq ordinarily refused to do any sight-seeing, lest he
prolong his absences which he wanted to be shorter and less
frequent. He limited his travelling occupations to those needed
for his work or for his mission. At San Anselmo however, he
took advantage of every occasion to visit one or another corner
of Italy, and his human and artistic sensitivity developed re-
markably from contact with all the beautiful things that this
marvelous country contains, as well as from the riches of its
museums.

Ordained on the nineteenth of September, 1936, Fr Leclercq
did not return to San Anselmo in October, 1937, but went to
the Institut Catholique of Paris to do his fifth and last year of
theology. There were remarkable professors on the faculty:
Fr Yves de Montcheuil for dogmatics, Fr Robert for the Old
Testament, Fr Tricot for the New Testament, Fr Arquillière for
History. At the same time, he took some courses in paleo-
graphy at the Ecole des Chartes, the courses given by Gilson
at the Ecole des Hautes Etudes, and those given by Lavelle
at the Collège de France. The redaction of his thesis on John
of Paris was almost completed when he returned to Clervaux
in July, 1938, to teach dogma for a year. At the same time he
wrote a few articles. In September, 1939, he was mobilized for
the Second World War. He was stationed with an anti-aircraft
artillery battery in northern France, in the Douai-Valenciennes
sector and he continued to read, to study and to work. On the
ninth of May, 1940, the eve of the invasion of Luxembourg,
Belgium and Holland and of the offensive against France, he
defended his thesis at the Institut Catholique of Paris. It almost
did not take place, because, too faithful to the spirituality expressed by the name of the one he was presenting — John of
Paris was named John Who Sleeps (Jean Quidort) — Fr Leclercq awoke too late from the siesta which he had taken to
prepare himself for the defense of his thesis. Happily, the in-

dulgence of Fr Lebreton, president of the jury, and the quality of the thesis and of its defense made things all right. The
next day, the tenth of May, the bombing of the railway lines
prevented Fr Leclercq from rejoining his battery where, moreover, he would have either been killed or taken prisoner like
his companions. Providence was keeping him for other tasks
and, with the sorrow caused by the news that his brother Robert had been killed in the Somme, he went to spend the rest
of the war period in the French Midi, and then at the abbey
of Ligugé. He worked there a few weeks, profiting very much
from the excellent monastic library which had grown up
around the *Revue Mabillon*. Thanks to a proposal made by
the Institut de France, Fr Leclercq was made a member of the
Ecole Francaise in Rome; this gave him the right to a three
year stay, at the expense of the State, at the Farnese Palace,
seat of the French embassy to the Quirinal in Rome. But Fr
Leclercq had already spent four years in Rome and he was
mindful of so many young French scholars who would be happy to profit from such a windfall. He gave up his rights to this
sojourn in favor of one of these. He therefore remained in
France. After a two months stay at Ligugé, the Directors of
the Bibliothèque Nationale in Paris called on him. Dom André
Wilmart had just died and Fr Leclercq was asked to continue
his catalogue of Latin manuscripts of medieval patristics and
theology. He worked on this from 1941 to 1944. At the Bibliothèque Nationale he saw much of Dom Cyril Lambot of
the Abbey of Maredsous, the editor of St Augustine's sermons.
Dom Lambot tried to interest Fr Leclercq in a study of preaching at the time of St Augustine. Fr Leclercq agreed to write
a few articles on this theme for the *Revue Bénédictine*, but,
while being very grateful to Fr Lambot and keeping his friendship for him, he returned to the Middle Ages. The field is ex-
tensive and Fr Leclercq felt himself equally attracted by scholastic thought and by monastic literature. Dom Odo Lottin
urged him toward scholasticism and Dom Bernard Capelle toward the liturgy. Obliged to make a choice, Fr Leclercq went
to seek the advice of his master, Etienne Gilson, who encour-

aged him to specialize in monastic culture. He was to become an eminent master in this field. In 1944, at the request of Fr André Combes, he prepared *Pierre de Celle* and *Jean de Fé-camp*. The printing of these two, done at Avesnes, was delayed by the liberation of the city, accomplished by the American army. *Pierre de Celle*, written in a few days at Avesnes, during the liberation, is a sort of monastic testament to which nothing will later be added. A few sentences from this book express well the major concerns of Dom Leclercq and his deep affinities with the author of whom he is treating: "The content of the sermons is not something special to monasticism, it is simply dogma and Christian morality; but the contemplative life helps the religious to know it better and to practice it more fully than can the ordinary faithful who live in the world."[2] " . . . the entire life of Christ, all the glories of Mary, the splendors of the Church, the marvels of the sacraments and, in a particular way, the Eucharist provide . . . Peter of Celles with the matter for his teaching. He rarely exhorts, he contemplates. What he has to say regarding the virtues of community life reduces itself to rare allusions. He insists rather on the essential attitude of the soul in the presence of God. He does not look at the evil and ugliness in the world, he never dwells on sin or on hell. He sees only grace and the salvation of the world, and words which speak of beauty are often found in his writings."[3] " . . . the Bible is a treasure which he does not tire of drawing upon by the handfuls. Sometimes, to be sure, he takes the precaution of specifying which of the traditional senses he intends to give to a text, and whether he is keeping to the letter or if he is being allegorical. But generally, everything is mixed up, all the senses are admitted at the same time."[4] The contemplative and ecclesial orientation of the spirituality of Fr Leclercq, his biblical and dogmatic content, the serenity, the optimism and the enthusiasm of his gaze on the marvels of grace are already perceived throughout the whole word.

2. *La spiritualité de Pierre de Celle (1115-1183)* (Paris: Vrin, 1946), p. 27.
3. Ibid., pp. 27-28.
4. Ibid., p. 29.

THE EDITION OF THE WORKS OF ST BERNARD

At Ligugé, during the summer of 1944, Dom Leclercq wrote *Pierre le Vénérable* at the request of an editor and, again at Ligugé in 1945, *St Bernard mystique,* at the request of another editor. Obliged by his doctors to take a rest, Dom Leclercq went to the Abbey of Engelberg in Switzerland for the winter of 1945-1946. He learned to ski and this sporting episode was the mainspring of his edition of the works of St Bernard, because between skiing lessons Fr Leclercq hunted through the library of the monastery. He discovered some unpublished texts of St Bernard which he published in the *Revue Mabillon,* under the title, "Inédits bernardins dans un manuscrit d'Engelberg."[5] In 1948 Fr Leclercq devoted two studies to Bernardine texts: "Deux sermons de saint Bernard selon une rédaction inédite,"[6] "Inédits bernardins dans un manuscrit d'Orval."[7] When presenting the MS Luxembourg 32, originating from Orval, Fr Leclercq said: "If chance meetings produce such results, one may ask oneself what a rich harvest would be brought forth by a systematic search."[8] That same year, after a General Chapter held in the autumn, Dom Matthew Quatember, procurator general of the Order of Citeaux, asked Fr Leclercq to carry on this "systematic search," and to prepare a critical edition of the complete works of St Bernard. A systematic exploration of libraries and, consequently, some long trips were indispensable. It was possible to bring the work to a successful issue thanks to the perfect understanding Dom Leclercq received from three successive abbots of Clervaux, to the generous financing of his work and of his travels by Fr Quatember and his successor Dom Sighard Kleiner, and to the friendly, intelligent and active help of Henri Rochais. Fr Quatember had hoped that the first volume would appear in 1953 for the eighth centenary of the death of St Bernard. This was impossible in view

5. *Revue Mabillon* 37 (1947): 1-16.
6. *Analecta monastica,* Première série, *Studia Anselmiana,* vol. 20 (Rome, 1948), pp. 124-41.
7. Ibid., pp. 142-166.
8. Ibid., p. 143.

of the complexity of the works, the necessity of studying and determining methods, of gathering and classifying material. As early as 1953, however, Dom Leclercq published a preparatory work: *Etudes sur saint Bernard et le texte de ses écrits.*[9] In it he gave, in particular, a survey on the manuscript tradition of St Bernard and a detailed study on the genesis of the sermons of St Bernard. In 1957, the first volume of the edition was published; since then, five others have followed. During this year of 1972, Dom Leclercq is finishing the preparation of the last part of the edition. Even should he disappear prematurely, the termination of the publication is assured. Already, several monasteries in Canada celebrated his funeral by anticipation at the time of the death of Msgr Jacques Leclercq, professor at the University of Louvain, with whom he was confused. Fortunately, God seems less in a hurry to take him from us. He wants to make us profit, for still a little while, from his erudition and his spiritual experience. He also wants to test and to purify his desire "to depart and be with Christ,"[10] so as, by this trial to spare him "to be in Purgatory for very long time," as he himself wrote on the occasion of this presumed death, and to enable him to merit more truly the title "the new blessed Jean," a title bestowed on him in another letter at that time.

On the eighth of December, 1952, in the presence of His Eminence Cardinal Montini, then Archbishop of Milan, Fr Leclercq was named Doctor *honoris causa* by the University of the Sacred Heart in Milan. During 1955-1956, he gave a series of conferences at the Benedictine College of San Anselmo in Rome. These were the starting point of *The Love of Learning and the Desire for God.*[11] This work bears witness to the rich contribution made by monks to western culture through their expression of their desire for God. This book was at the same time an opportunity to circulate more widely what Fr Leclercq

9. *Analecta S. O. Cist.* 9 (1953).
10. Phil 1: 23.
11. Bbg. 13. (The reference is to the Bibliography of the works of Dom Jean Leclercq to be found at the end of this volume, entry no. 13.)

had already stated in several articles regarding the existence of a monastic theology which is the continuation of patristic theology and which is distinct from scholastic theology.[12]

Fr Leclercq's research regarding the vocabulary used with reference to the monastic life and to contemplation during the Middle Ages was of the same order.[13] In these articles, he emphasized the very clear link between vocabulary and a very precise spiritual and theological vision. The studies of Fr Leclercq left no doubt as to the true meaning of the word "monk." The monk is not only someone who lives for God alone (St Augustine's conception); he is also someone who is separated from men and from the world (St Jerome's conception). The term *quies, otium, vacatio, sabbatum,* express clearly that the monastic life is a contemplative life, a life of desire for God with a strong eschatological orientation. It is quite true that owing to various circumstances during the course of their history, monks have sometimes had to engage in some pastoral duties, "however they did not say that these occupations formed a part of their vocation. This vocation remains well-defined as a call to prayer and to penance. It retains an eschatological orientation. Devotion to heaven, which is desire for God and love of the state of life where one can be completely united to him, is one of the dominant traits of this monasticism, because it is a novitiate leading to eternity."[14]

In 1959, Fr Leclercq was asked to give some courses at the Benedictine Institute of Sacred Theology located at St Benedict's Convent, St Joseph, Minnesota. He also visited St John's Abbey in Collegeville, which is close by. He returned to the BIST in 1960 and took the opportunity to visit Thomas Merton at Gethsemani. He had already been corresponding with him for ten years, and their ties of friendship were to become ever stronger over the years. From the time of his first trip to the USA, Fr Leclercq had noticed some manuscripts, particu-

---

12. See Bbg. 43, 67, 181, etc.
13. *Studia Anselmiana* 48 (1961) and 51 (1963); Bbg. 18 and 21.
14. *La spiritualité du Moyen âge* (Paris: Aubier, 1961), p. 229.

larly of St Bernard, in various libraries. It was even on the very next day after his arrival that he discovered unpublished Bernardine texts at Harvard. Henri Rochais published these in 1962 under the title: *Inédits bernardins dans le ms Harvard 185*.[15] Since 1959, Fr Leclercq has found himself in the USA once, twice, or even three times a year to give conferences at universities (Harvard, University of Pennsylvania, Bryn Mawr, Notre Dame, Catholic University, Western Michigan, etc.) and in monasteries, mostly Trappist.

Fr Leclercq was acquainted with Scourmont since his youth and became friends with Dom Anselm Le Bail and Dom Belorgey during his visits there. In subsequent years he has had the opportunity of visiting almost all the Trappist monasteries in the world. He is sometimes told that he is an "honorary Cistercian," to which he objects that he is neither "strict," nor "reformed," nor reformable, and that he is dispensed from the observance. . . . After his supposed death in 1971, he received a Scroll of Honorary Membership in the Cistercian Order from the abbot of Kopua in New Zealand. More recently, he was awarded a decoration honoring him as a member of the Trappist community of Tarrawara in Australia. But subsequently, on the door of his room in the guest house at Sept Fons, he saw his name followed by "OCSO *sine permissu superiorum.*" His Cistercian dignity was thus challenged as a usurpation. . . . In actual fact, Fr Leclercq's simplicity, his youthful spirit, his joy, his conviction of the importance of prayer and of the contemplative life, all of these draw him in a remarkable way to the Trappists. His brothers of Clervaux were welcomed during six full months at the abbey of St Remi in Rochefort when they were expelled in 1941. They were also received at Scourmont for a few weeks during the 1944 Christmas season. They all understand Dom Leclercq's instinctive attraction for the Trappists and share it with him because they have kept an unforgettable memory of these two sojourns among them. Fr Leclercq lives surrounded by Trappist souvenirs: a Chinese ink drawing sketched at Hong Kong, depicting a grasshopper and a bamboo tree and, in Chinese, the signatures of the novices of

15. *Analecta monastica*, VI, *Studia Anselmiana*, vol. 50 (Rome, 1962), pp. 53-175.

that Trappist monastery with the inscription: "To Fr Jean Leclercq, eternal youth! His spiritual sons"; a painting of a black
Virgin and Child brought back from the Trappist monastery
of Kutaba in Cameroun; a picture of Our Lady of Guadalupe
from the Abbey of Guadalupe in Oregon.

In 1951, at the request of the Camaldolese hermits of the
Congregation of Monte Corona, Fr Leclercq had written *Un
humaniste ermite: Le bienheureux Paul Giustiniani (1476-
1528)*. He emphasized how "this contemporary of Luther"
had been "the instigator, within the Catholic Church, of a
movement of reform and piety which would bear fruit in the
following generation."[16] What the world needs is not so much
monks who leave their cloister as monks who remain there
and who, like Blessed Giustiniani, take their life of prayer and
penance very seriously. In 1960, Fr Leclercq published the life
of another Camaldolese, *Saint Pierre Damien, ermite et homme d'Eglise.*[17] In it he quoted this sentence of St Peter Damian:
"Interiorly, the monk must be full of charity for all, but he
must consider it as superfluous for himself to engage in exterior
activity for the salvation of others." Fr Leclercq had introduced
the quotation with these lines, a sure indication of his conviction: "Under the pretext of winning souls, monks are seen to
be leaving their solitude in order to engage in preaching. But
is the world better because of this? And who is changing his
way of life? That is not their role in the Church, they have
not received a mission to carry out this function."[18] However,
Fr Leclercq did not hide the problem that such affirmations
posed for him, so often called upon, as he is, to leave his monastery. In his study on *Le bienheureux Paul Giustiniani,* he set
down these thoughts of the hermit, a reflection of his own
hesitations: "On the one hand, Augustine and Benedict condemned gyrovagues. On the other hand, if St Anthony, Hila-
rion, St Benedict, St Maur, and St Romuald had not travelled
throughout the world, the monastic Order would not have

16. *Un humaniste ermite: Le bienheureux Paul Giustiniani (1476-1528)* (Rome:
Editiones Camaldoli, 1951), p. 11.
   17. Bbg. 16.
   18. Ibid., p. 141.

spread."[19] This examination of conscience offered a solution. There are some — and Fr Leclercq is of this number — to whom God addresses an extraordinary call to go out far and wide and make known the monastic message they have been studying and living. They cannot escape from such a mission. With love and loyalty, Fr Leclercq strives to be such as he has described St Peter Damian: "His vocation was to be, at the same time, full of love for the Church and enamoured of the desert. There was no question of his choosing between these two attractions. He knew and he showed us that they can be reconciled; in him one was always complemented by the other. One same renunciation of self and of the world, one same total commitment to the service of the Lord enabled him to be a hermit and a man of the Church all his life."[20] "The hermit in him helped the man of the Church. He could put the leisure of his solitary life at the service of doctrine and he did not refuse to enlighten those who turned to him because of his knowledge."[21]

Fr Leclercq sometimes jokes very pleasantly about his absences. In particular, he says humorously that instead of making vows of conversion of manners and of stability of place, he must undoubtedly have made a mistake when reading his schedule of profession and promised conversion of place and stability of manners. But what is not known, I dare say, is that during these absences he frequently sends letters to his superiors, bringing them up to date, in a filial way, on the details of his trips. There are also the numerous cards sent to his confrères from every corner of the world. He remembers especially the aged, the sick, the young, the people usually overlooked but who are so appreciative of attention such as this. Dom Leclercq unceasingly carries his monastery and his brothers of Clervaux and St Jerome in his thoughts, in his heart and in his prayer, and this to the very ends of the world. He never misses an opportunity to say how much he is in their debt. This is the type of stability which God has asked of him. He is very

19. Ibid., pp. 103-104.
20. Ibid., pp. 13-14.
21. Ibid., p. 217.

faithful to it, and this fidelity, as it is more difficult for someone often living far away from his brothers, is by that very
fact the more remarkable. It is even admirable. Moreover, Fr
Leclercq has never put himself forward for the least task. He
has simply answered the appeals which have been addressed to
him whenever he could.

### AID TO MONASTIC IMPLANTATION (AIM)

In 1962, Fr Leclercq made his first visit to the monastery
of Toumlinine in Morocco. He returned there in 1964. That
same year, he was delegated by the AIM to take part in the
first meeting of the monks of Africa at Bouaké on the Ivory
Coast. At the same time he visited the monasteries of Dahomey
and of the Upper Volta. In 1965, the AIM sent him to Togo,
Cameroun, Congo-Brazzaville, Senegal; in 1966, to Uganda,
Kenya, Tanzania, Rwanda, Congo-Kinshasa, Burundi, Madagascar; in 1967, to India, Indonesia, Vietnam, Cambodia, the
Philippines. In 1968, at the time of the Congress at Bangkok,
whose chief animator he was, he visited Thailand, Japan, Hong
Kong and again Vietnam. In 1969, he went to Chile, Argentina
and Uruguay. He gave conferences and retreats also in Mexico
and Martinique. That same year, 1969, he was elected "corre-
sponding fellow" of the British Academy in London, without
having been in any way a candidate. In 1970, he returned to
Cameroun and, at the time of the Congress of the Monks of the
Far East, he stopped over in Korea, India and Japan. In 1971, he
gave conferences in the monasteries of New Caledonia, New
Zealand, and Australia and returned to Thailand. He combined
with this monastic activity outside of Europe, conferences in
European monasteries and universities in Germany, England,
Denmark, Spain, Ireland, Italy, Portugal and Switzerland. Since
1966, during the first semester of the school year (the winter
semester), while still teaching at San Anselmo, he has been
teaching at the Gregorian University in Rome. His courses are
on medieval spirituality in the Institute of Spiritual Life and
on medieval psychology in the Institute of Religious Psychology. For a few weeks during the second semester, he teaches at

"Lumen Vitae" in Brussels. His subject there is the history of the religious life in the Middle Ages. The teaching asked of him and the visits to monasteries entrusted to him have led him to concern himself with the problem of renewal in the contemplative life. He seeks to clarify them by using both his knowledge of the past and a keen and daring sense regarding the needs of the present time and the orientations of the new world which is evolving. His earlier writings had been centered mostly on the past and had usually been studies of individuals whose personalities he drew out from their writings. During these past few years on the other hand, he has produced works of synthesis in which his concern to adapt the lessons of the past to the present and the future can be seen more readily. This applied especially to his two books *Le défi de la vie contemplative*[22] and *Moines et moniales ont-ils un avenir?*[23] In this last book, Fr Leclercq poses the problem as to how the monastic life is to be lived in our day and in the days to come. He takes into account the socio-cultural context which exists now and the one which is being prepared: the greater recognition being given to women, the urban phenomenon, secularization. "The contemplative life has not lost its reason for existing. It will last and it will renew itself. . . ."[23] Historian that he is, Fr Leclercq knows that tradition is in motion and that the problems of evolution and of adaptation must be faced boldly: "a right-thinker is often a non-thinker."[24]

Fr Leclercq has passed from the more scholarly phase of his life to a stage that is more pastoral, or even, some say, journalistic. An evolution such as this necessarily brings with it debatable options and conjectures. It is easier to go astray in the midst of these than among the conclusions that were the result of his earlier scientific works. But this is still another path that Fr Leclercq did not choose himself. He accepted it with its risks in order to answer appeals made to him. He devotes to it all his spirit of service and of self-giving.

22. Bbg. 28.
23. Bbg. 29.
24. *"Un bien-pensant est souvent un non pensant."*

Fr Leclercq is a member of the Ecumenical Institute on the Spiritual Life and regularly takes part in its annual meeting. This Institute was founded during the Council and includes a few of the American non-Catholic observers, among whom is Douglas Steere. The United States has thus become his spiritual homeland, at least in the measure in which he has one more than another and to the extent that there is found there a living preview of what will eventually and progressively reach the other parts of the world.

Having journeyed alongside Father Jean Leclercq during forty years of life at Clervaux, I am very happy to pay tribute to him by means of these few pages. I have received much from him through his books and his articles, but even more through his example. I have had countless occasions to learn to appreciate his erudition and his keenness of mind, but much more still his devotion to his superiors, his love for his community, his respect for the different paths of souls, his ecclesial sense, his optimism, his faith. "You will be judged according to love," St John of the Cross has told us — that which you have had and that which you have evoked. In possessing it and in radiating it, Leclercq has sown serenity and joy wherever he has passed.

Louis Leloir OSB

Clervaux Abbey
Luxembourg

Translated by
Sr William Boudreau OCSO

# A LITERARY JOURNEY

THERE IS NO QUESTION of repeating here information already published concerning the origins of the edition of the work of Saint Bernard.[1] Rather, my purpose is to make known to future historians the conditions under which the documents preparatory to this edition were gathered. Just as the new editors searched among the papers of their predecessor, Dom Jean Mabillon, for clues on the manner in which this celebrated Maurist prepared his two editions of Saint Bernard (1667 and 1690),[2] so also scholars, careful to verify the scientific character of the new edition, will have a right to ask its authors to give an account of the materials used and of the method followed in the preparation of their work.

The materials include primarily notes, regarding manuscripts, which were written during trips made between 1948 and 1960,[3] and an abundant correspondence circulating among the various

---

1. H. Rochais, "L'édition critique des oeuvres de S. Bernard, Chronique des recherches et des travaux," in *Studi medievali*, 3 Series, 1 (1960) 701-719.

2. See "La préhistoire de l'édition de Mabillon," in J. Leclercq, *Etudes sur saint Bernard et le texte de ses écrits,* ASOC 9 (1953) 202-225. (Henceforth, *Etudes.*) See also, "Lettres de Mabillon et de Rancé sur saint Bernard" (Bbg 216). (Bbg refers to the Bibliography of Dom Jean Leclercq at the end of this volume).

3. The notes on the mss are the work of several hands. The principal contributors are:

Jean Leclercq: Rein 35, 51, 20 (= R 8). (This last indication refers to the letters and numbers assigned to each page of notes to facilitate classification.)

Dom Robert Gillet: Eton College, 39; Cambridge, Clare College, MS 10.

Dom Jean Laporte OSB, Saint-Wandrille: most of the mss of Rouen (v.g. R 112).

Miss M. M. Lebreton (then at the Institut de Recherches et d'Histoire des Textes

contributors to this immense enterprise. To these must be added such material as card indexes, films and photographs.

The method evolved as the work progressed and flowed entirely from contact with the sources and the successive discoveries we made. The genesis of the method is therefore intimately connected with the narrative of our journeys. To give an exact account of the latter, I have at my disposal two notebooks which were filled day by day and letters which have reference to work on the edition. In the present article, I will use only the notes from the journals.

When, in the spring of 1948, Dom Matthew Quatember, Procurator General of the Order of Citeaux, asked Dom Jean Leclercq[4] whether he would accept the responsibility for the preparation of a critical edition of the works of Saint Bernard, the Benedictine of Clervaux (Luxembourg) qualified his consent with two conditions: that he could see all the manuscripts wherever they might be (and therefore have the financial means to do so), and share with someone else the responsibility for the edition.[5]

---

in Paris): Troyes 1749 and many mss of sermons and sentences in Paris.

C. H. Talbot: Aberdeen 218, on small sheets.

Dom André Wilmart OSB: Arsenal 323; Engelberg 34.

H. Rochais: Rome Vat. lat. 4414(= R 52).

Some notes were typewritten on the spot by correspondents (Breslau, Cracow). Others were written out in pencil, the use of a pen being forbidden in some libraries: Lambeth Palace in London, Arquivo Nacional de Torre do Tombo in Lisbon, University of Cambridge. Others were written up from microfilms (Madrid 145) or from catalogs (Leipzig= L31 to 40).

The use of different formats (this was discontinued after a short time), writing on both sides of the page and, above all, the description of several mss on the same page (this we never stopped doing in order not to overload our baggage) were the cause of much loss of time in the frequent handling of these notes for they were impossible to classify in a suitable way.

4. For the remainder of this article I will abbreviate the name of Dom Jean Leclercq by using his initials: J. L.

5. This responsibility was shared by C. H. Talbot of London, for the first two volumes of the edition. It is also fitting to say that for the important decisions relative to the choice of mss or to the authentification of texts, J. L. asked and obtained the advice of qualified persons, among whom were his confrères at Clervaux: Dom H. de Sainte-Marie, Dom J. Winandy, Dom R. Weber, Dom J. Gribomont; scholars, such as Professor B. Bichoff of Munich, Miss Ch. Mohrmann of Nijmegen, Father P. David of Coimbra, A. H. Bredero of Utrecht, G. Constable of Harvard, J. Figuet; and those in charge in the libraries visited. It is impossible to

Between this first proposal and the official mandate of the General Chapter of the Order in the autumn of 1948, J. L. made a previously-planned study trip to Spain during the summer. The first notes on manuscripts date from this period.[6] J. L. traveled alone at this time. He did not yet have the necessary materials at hand to verify unpublished or unidentified texts. He jotted down his notes on sheets of paper of various sizes and he wrote on both sides; these proved to be difficult to classify and some had to be transcribed. The limited amount of time at his disposal was divided between looking at the mss already known attributed to Bernard and indispensable prospecting into collections which were insufficiently catalogued. At the end of some notes, more amused than irritated, he has set down his impressions on the difficulties of gaining access to certain libraries. On the whole this trip was disappointing because of its necessarily improvised character, the rather difficult working conditions and the small number of Bernardine documents encountered.[7] But it had the advantage of establishing that a trip of systematic prospecting can only be carried out if two conditions are realized: that there be instruments at one's disposal to identify the texts on the spot and that there be two to share the double task of preparing descriptions of known mss and of exploring the unknown ones. Also, it made J. L. realize the value of having a high ecclesiastical recommendation to facilitate his access to certain reserves that are guarded too jealously or are too poorly preserved. He ob-

---

mention the names of all who have contributed to those hidden but indispensable tasks required for the edition: collation of mss, typing, identification of scriptural passages, drawing up of card indexes, innumerable verifications on films, on photographs and on the originals. The editors have always received kindness, understanding and competent and devoted help from the personnel of the Latin section of the Institut de Recherche et d'Histoire des Textes in Paris.

6. See, for example, the notes of Barcelona 234 (B 17), Toledo, Seville.

7. However, J. L. brought back from this trip to Spain enough material for several articles and information for a few others: "Les mss des bibliothèques d'Espagne" (Bbg 136); "Un tratado sobre los nombres divinos en un ms de Cordoba" (Bbg 139); "S. Bernard et Origène d'après un ms de Madrid" (Bbg 142); "Un florilège attribué a un moine de Poblet" (Bbg 131); "Recherches dans les mss cisterciens d'Espagne" (Bbg 145-6).

tained a letter from Cardinal Mercati which in fact sometimes proved to be quite useful.

When J. L. received the mandate officially entrusting him with the preparation of the critical edition,[8] he already had a rather precise idea of the work to be done and of the difficulties it entailed. This was due to his first writings on the unpublished Bernardine works and also to his Spanish trip. Having learned from this experience, he decided to begin his research in southern Italy and Sicily. In order to carry it out under favorable conditions, he asked for and obtained the assistance of a Benedictine monk from the Abbey of Sainte-Marie in Paris, Dom Robert Gillet. Planning to photograph on the spot all documents judged to be particularly important, he entrusted a camera to his collaborator. But, on the very first day, when the two travellers were in Naples awaiting the hour of embarkation for Sicily, it was stolen without ever having been put to use. "It's an ill wind that blows no good." It was decided then that the necessary photographs would be ordered from the photographic services of the libraries visited. Even though later, the absence of a camera somewhat complicated the task of the editors in certain private libraries not endowed with such a service, on the whole the loss of this encumbrance saved a considerable amount of time.

However that may be, this trip has left few traces in actual documentation. The scarcity of documents and their late date account for this.

For this research in southern Italy, J. L. had prepared some lists of incipits of letters and of Bernard's published sermons and sentences. He also had photographed the passages of the *Sermones in Cantica* (SC) 24 and 71 for which Mabillon pointed out divergences in the manuscript.[9] These photographs were a great help for a preliminary classification of prime importance.

The fatigue of his travelling companion obliged J. L. to con-

8. He announced the enterprise publicly in "Une nouvelle édition des oeuvres de S. Bernard" (Bbg 134).

9. See the introduction to Vol. 1 of the *S. Bernardi Opera* (Rome, 1957), pp. xvi-xix.

tinue alone for a time. During the spring of 1949, he worked, first of all, in a few other Italian libraries.[10] Then he prospected in Denmark (Copenhagen) and in Sweden (Stockholm, Uppsala, Linkoeping, Lund).[11] In Copenhagen, he discovered the document which he published, much later, in an article on the Encyclical of St Bernard in favor of the second Crusade.[12]

After a few weeks of rest, Dom Gillet rejoined J. L. at York in England. They worked together in the libraries of Scotland and Great Britain (Aberdeen, Durham, Edinburgh, Eton, Hereford, Stonyhurst), before spending some time in London, Oxford and Cambridge

As the number of documents examined and the quantity of notes assembled increased, the magnitude of the task appeared in all its dimensions. All the problems became obvious at the same time: letters, sentences and sermons to be identified, choices to be made between different redactions of the same texts, the authenticity of the writings or passages unknown to Mabillon. Moreover, because this new effort had greatly taxed the health of his travelling companion, J. L. regretfully had to part with him. During the summer of 1949, at the end of his trip through England, J. L. was himself obliged to stop in order to reflect on the direction in which he was to continue his investigation.[13]

At the end of October 1949, he proposed to me that I accompany him and work with him. We made six "campaigns" together. These briefly are our itineraries with the dates:

(1) From November 22, 1949 to March 9, 1950, *Austria*: Innsbruck, St-Paul-in-Carinthia, Graz and Rein, Admont, Vienna, Klosterneuburg, Heiligenkreuz, Zwettl, Göttweig, Lilienfeld, Melk, Seitenstetten, Linz, Lambach, Wilhering, St Florian, Kremsmünster, Salzburg, Mattsee, Michaelbeuren. *Bavaria:* Munich, Augsburg, Eichstätt, Nuremberg, Erlangen; then the flu obliged us to retrace our steps to Munich. A fresh start was made

---

10. "Manuscrits dans les bibliothèques d'Italie" (Bbg 147).

11. "Textes et manuscrits cisterciens en Suède" (Bbg 154).

12. "L'encyclique de S. Bernard en faveur de la croisade" (Bbg 593).

13. One year after the public announcement of the edition, he made the point in a new article, "L'édition de Saint Bernard" (Bbg 151).

February 3, 1950: Nuremberg, Erlangen, Bamberg, Würzburg, Stuttgart, Tübingen, Ulm, Harburg, Hiesee. *Switzerland*: Schaffhausen, Frauenfeld, Zurich, St Gall, Aarau, Basel, Solothurn, Berne, Lucerne, Coire, Fribourg, Lausanne, Geneva. We returned to Paris by way of Dijon and Troyes.

(2) From March 15, 1950 to April 11, *Portugal:* Lisbon, Evora, Coimbra, Porto, Arouca, Braga, and again Coimbra and Lisbon.

(3) From May 15 to July 15, 1950, *Benelux*: Brussels, Liège, Louvain, Gand, Courtrai, Anvers, Beloeil, Bruges, The Hague, Leyden, Waarmond, Utrecht.

(4) From October 30 to December 15, 1950, *Germany*: Trier, Koblenz, Köln, Düsseldorf, Münster, Oldenburg, Hamburg, Kiel, Hannover, Wolfenbüttel, Paderborn, Kassel, Marburg, Frankfurt, Fulda, Fritzlar, Aschaffenburg, Darmstatt, Wiesbaden, Koblenz, Mainz, Heidelberg, Tübingen, Munich, Nuremberg, Pommersfelden, Dillingen, Ottobeuren, Friedrichshafen, Konstanz, Donaueschingen, Freiburg.

(5) From December 16, 1950 to February 15, 1951, *France:* Colmar, Montpellier, Avignon, Grenoble, Grande-Chartreuse, Paris, Alençon, Evreux, Rouen, Amiens, Cambrai, Douai, St-Omer, Boulogne, Arras, Valenciennes, Laon, Soissons, Rheims, Charleville, Troyes, Dijon, Paris.

(6) From March 27 to June 22, 1951, *Italy*: Como, Milano, Vercelli, Aosta, Torino, Alessandria, Genova, Piacenza, Cremona, Mantova, Brescia, Bergamo, Trento, Bressanone, Neustift, Buzano, Treviso, Venezia, Gorizia, Udine, Padova, Vicenza, Ferrara, Bologna, Parma, Reggio, Modena, Ravenna, Cesena, Firenze, Lucca, Pisa, Siena, Cortona, Arezzo, Perugia, Assisi, Foligno, Todi, Orvieto, Roma.[14]

In regard to the following trips I have only the dates:

1952: April 15-25: Work in Paris; September-October: trip to Oxford, Cambridge, London; November-December: Paris, Troyes, Dijon, Tamié, Aiguebelle (seat of the Historical Com-

14. It was toward the end of this trip that J. L. discovered in Trent the ms which would become known by the name of "Codex Tridentinus." He introduced it under the title, "Une ancienne rédaction des coutumes cisterciennes" (Bbg 170), the contents of which would partly renew the history of Cistercian origins, and the text of which would be published by B. Griesser, ASOC 12 (1956).

mission of the Order of Citeaux), Paris, Angers.

1963: March 22-28: Paris; August 27-28: Périgueux.

1954: January 22-February 11: Oxford, integral collation of the Merton 46 (ms. *O* of the SC) and the Rawlinson C. 118 (*R*); June-August: Paris, Clervaux, Paris.

1955: January-February: Paris, Brussels, Clervaux, Luxembourg, Paris; September-October: Clervaux, Paris, Troyes, Dijon, Lyons, Grenoble, Montpellier, Rome, Milan, Paris.

1958: September: Clervaux.

1959: April-May: Clervaux.

1959-1960: October-January: Rome, redaction of the *Enquête*.[15]

When our collaboration began, J. L. decided we would first do some prospecting in Austria. He decided this because that country has some very ancient monasteries, Cistercian and others, whose mss collections are just sufficiently known to make one suspect their riches. It was important that they be examined. Moreover, J. L. thought, not without good reason, that, in this region where the Cistercian monasteries originated from the abbey of Morimond, it was possible that the collections and the texts would be different from those which he had already seen in France or in England which came from Clairvaux.

With the approach of 1953, date of the eighth centenary of the death of Saint Bernard, J. L. was prompted to consider publishing Volume One of the edition for that year. With this in view, since it seemed to him that, among all the works of Bernard, the SC posed the fewest problems, the SC became the prime objective of our research, without however letting this priority hinder the examination of all the documents useful to the edition as a whole.

The first "campaign" was particularly fruitful, both as to the quantity and the quality of the texts examined. It enabled us to ascertain the existence of a "zone of Morimond" which preserved primitive collections and ancient redactions of Bernardine texts. This discovery was made first of all regarding

15. H. Rochais, *Enquête sur les sermons divers et les sentences de saint Bernard* (ASOC 18, 1962).

SC thanks to the photographs which I have already mentioned.

The method of describing the manuscripts developed. The more detailed notes, in which were included the rubrics, the incipit and desinit—always useful especially for texts not immediately identifiable—were soon supplemented by so-called "synthetic" notes. Every text in these was designated by an abbreviation or by a simple numerical order referring to our lists of incipits. Being shorter, these notes facilitated the comparing of collections. They showed clearly that the types of collections met with in Austria were different from those found further west. During the remainder of our research, they served as a transmission line enabling us to ascertain that a difference in the order of the texts was often accompanied by a difference in the very tenor of these texts.

During these trips, the description of long series of sentences served as the occasion for drawing up an alphabetical list of these. They were later identified in the "Miscellanea" attributed to Hugh of Saint Victor. Later, this list also greatly facilitated the identification of texts.[16]

As early as the first investigations, one of the questions that had to be faced was that of the part played by Bernard's secretaries in the redaction of the different stages of the texts, and another, the part that belonged to his contemporaries in the collections of "Bernardine" texts: Nicolas of Clairvaux, Odo of Morimond, Geoffrey of Auxerre, Gebouin of Troyes, Drogo, Guerric of Igny and William of Saint Thierry, whose personal works, often mixed in with those of Bernard, had to be made the object of particular studies based on the examination of mss.[17]

One of the most critical moments in the history of the edi-

16. From it would result the study on "Les Miscellanea et l'oeuvre de S. Bernard" in *Enquête,* mentioned in note 15, pp. 148-153.

17. "Saint Bernard et ses secrétaires" (Bbg 161): "Les écrits de Geoffroy d'auxerre" (172); "Drogon et saint Bernard" (183); "Les collections de sermons de Nicolas de Clairvaux" (231); "Gébouin de Troyes et S. Bernard" (257); "La collection des sermons de Guerric d'Igny" (259); "Deux épîtres de saint Bernard et de son secrétaire" (260); "A la découverte d'Odon de Morimond" (330). – The articles written by J. L. on St Bernard were later gathered together in the volumes entitled *Recueil d'études sur S. Bernard et ses écrits,* 3 vols. mentioned in Bbg 19.

tion was when J. L. realized that the textual tradition of the SC was in fact much more complicated than had been imagined. The successive discoveries of a redaction called "of Morimond," then of a redaction from Clairvaux anterior to Bernard's death, revised (and therefore contaminated) after his death with a view to his canonization, posed the problem in all its complexity.

After many hesitations and scholarly consultations, J. L. became certain that it would be necessary to depart from the accepted text, the one reworked at Clairvaux, and to rediscover the pure state, as it were, of Bernard's own redaction. It was in England that minute examination of manuscript collations inspired him to seek this uncontaminated text. On January 27, 1954, he cabled from Oxford asking me to join him, and we spent fifteen days there, making an integral collation of Merton 46(ms *O*), the basis of our edition, and of Rawlinson C. 118(ms *R*).[18]

The well-founded certitude we arrived at in this preparation of the SC shed light which in a remarkable way elucidated the problems posed by the edition of the other volumes (short treatises, liturgical sermons). A separate study of the Sermons on the Psalm *Qui habitat* was, in this connection, a test and a manifest confirmation.[19]

Fully aware of the privilege he enjoyed in being able to see so many manuscript collections, J. L. did not limit himself to the study of the documents directly needed for the edition of St Bernard.[20] He made good use of these trips to draw up an

18. Before appearing in the introduction to Volume One of the *S. Bernardi Opera* (1957), the history of the complex tradition and the justification for the choices it imposed were published in a series of articles entitled: "Recherches sur les Sermons sur les Cantiques de saint Bernard" (Bbg 211).

19. "Les sermons de Bernard sur le psaume Qui habitat" (bbg 186).

20. However, these documents were given foremost attention. By way of illustration, here are a few of the articles which they inspired: "Lettres du temps de saint Bernard" (Bbg 159); "Le premier traité authentique de saint Bernard" (181); "Le mystère de l'Ascension dans les sermons de Saint Bernard" (182); "Sermon pour l'Assomption restitué à Saint Bernard" (184); "Un document sur Saint Bernard et la seconde croisade" (185); "Les sermons synodaux attribués à Saint Bernard" (192); "Saint Bernard et la théologie monastique du XII$^e$ siècle" (193); "Saint Bernard théologien" (207); "Sermons de l'école de S. Bernard dans un manuscrit d'Hauterive" (226); "L'archétype claravallien des traités de Saint Bernard" (234); "Un document sur les débuts des Templiers" (241); etc.

inventory, sketchy to be sure but useful, of the Cistercian manuscripts preserved in the libraries visited.[21] He even extended his investigations to monastic literature in general, to theology, to the history of Bernard's time, to codicology. Thus, it was during these trips that he discovered the rich documentary matter which gives to his scholarly articles the attraction of novelty as well as the solidity of tradition.

He had at heart the desire to have as many scholars as possible benefit from his discoveries, by communicating, spontaneously or at their request, all kinds of information: collations of texts, descriptions of manuscripts, indications of documents pertaining to their work, etc. Only the concern for discretion prevents me from giving here the names of those to whom he thus transmitted scholarly notes throughout these trips. By way of an example, I think I may mention Dom J. Déchanet of St-André-les-Bruges and Father Saxer, who are devoting themselves, respectively, to the study of William of St Thierry and to the cult of St Mary Magdalen. For my part, I am grateful to J. L. for the liberality with which he allowed me to round off my documentation for my edition of the *Liber scintillarum* of Defensor.[22]

Between "campaign" trips, we would separate to attend to our personal work. Then J. L. would arrange to meet with me in Paris, Clervaux or Rome to put into shape some part of Bernard's work. It was during these meetings that, progressively and not without groping, the important documentation which had been accumulated was put to use.

In order to choose the manuscripts we wanted to use in view to the collations, it was first of all necessary to classify them according to date, origin, kinds of texts (SC, short treatises,

21. Mention has already been made of those of Spain (Bbg 136, 145, 146), of Italy (147) and of Sweden (154). He did the same for Portugal (153), Italy again (162), Germany (164), various libraries (214, 354, 405), the Vatican (290), the United States (324). To this should be added the following articles: "Die Verbreitung der bernhardischen Schriften im deutschen Sprachraum" (195); "L'image de saint Bernard dans les manuscrits" (191); "Pour l'histoire de l'enluminure cistercienne" (209); "Les peintures de la Bible de Morimondo" (238); "Nouvelle réponse de l'ancien monachisme aux critiques cisterciens" (247).

22. *Defensoris Locogiacensis monachi, Liber scintillarum*, ed. H. Rochais, Corpus Christianorum, Series latina, CXVII/1 (Turnhout, 1957).

liturgical sermons, sermons for various occasions, sentences and parables, letters). Using the signs drawn up for the synthetical notes, we then proceeded to make comparisons between series of sermons, sentences and letters. Such comparisons brought to light the relationships among the manuscripts and also various groupings among the sermons which sometimes corresponded to collections sent by Bernard to persons requesting his works, or at least to "partial series" which can be found in the different collections.[23] These discoveries are not without importance with regard to the history of the works of Bernard. Then came the delicate problem of identifying the texts; this made indispensable the preparation of a card index of the incipits for all the texts listed in our notes as well as the foliation and the location of the manuscripts. Without being able to rival the size of the card index of Latin incipits at the Institut de Recherche et d'Histoire des Textes, the "Bernardine" card index significantly complements it, on the theological and spiritual writings of the twelfth and thirteenth centuries. Finally, the study of the infinitely complex tradition of the various texts and sentences of Bernard and of the Bernardine school necessitated the drawing up of a "thematic card index," which would permit close comparisons and the discovery of similar ideas and developments in very dissimilar works. Imperfect though it was, this index provided an effective work tool for study in the repeated use of certain sentences.[24]

The whole formed by these notes, lists and card indexes, plus the micro-film and the photographs, constitute a first-hand documentation, not only for the edition, but, in a general way, for medieval studies.[25]

When the manuscript of volume one of the edition was ready, new problems presented themselves. The General Chapter of

23. See, for example, in "Les collections de sermons de Nicolas de Clairvaux" (Bbg 231) what is said regarding the collection of the Harley ms 3073 and even more, "La tradition des sermons liturgiques de S. Bernard" (Bbg 341).

24. For an example of what can be gained by such close comparisons, see: H. Rochais, "Remarques sur les sermons divers et les sentences de saint Bernard," in *Analecta Cisterciensia* XXI (1965): 1-34.

25. This documentation is and remains the property of the General Curia of the Order of Citeaux (Piazza del Tempio di Diana, 14, I-00153 Roma).

the Order of Citeaux decided to entrust the printing to the Catalan abbey of Poblet in Spain.[26] Then J. L. had to give painstaking consideration to the choice of paper, type, layout, etc.

Despite some hesitations very understandable in view of the international character of the edition, J. L. obtained permission that, in order to avoid the risk of inaccuracy, the text of the introductory commentaries to each volume would be written in French, while at the same time he conceded that these would be preceded by Latin summaries.

All these points, details, yet important, required much diplomacy and patience, much correspondence and travel. Busy as he was with such a variety of occupations, the question undoubtedly arises as to how, aside from work on the edition, J. L. could have found the time to write the 600 and more articles and books that are enumerated in his bibliography.[27] In spite of poor health, J. L. is a strenuous worker, with an unrivalled ability to assimilate. He also knows how to organize his files and how to add to them as he reads and as he converses with specialists. It is not a joke to say that he puts together his documentation when in bed and that he does his writing while travelling. He claims that the measured sound of the train on the tracks helps him to find the rhythm for his phrases. Actually, I have seen him writing articles or the text of conferences en route, and I know that this is a habit with him, whether he be in a railway car, in a plane or on a boat.

Responsible as he was for the use of the money put at his disposal for his study trips, J. L. always manifested a great concern that it not be wasted. When possible, we lodged in monasteries where, ordinarily, we were received gratuitously. He preferred

26. Monasterio Sta Maria de Poblet, por Espluga de Francoli (Tarragona), Spain. From the beginning, the work has been directed with much care and kindness by Fr Augustine Altisent. Starting with vol. V, which appeared in 1968, the type had to be changed. From the time that vol. IV was being prepared for printing,—it appeared in 1966—the proofreading was directed with great precision by Fr Ildefons Majoor, of Sint Beneditus Abdij, Achel, Belgium. The latter is also working on a verbal concordance of the works of St Bernard, based on the edition; he has explained his work in an article: "Une concordance des oeuvres de S. Bernard," in the periodical *IBM Information*, 45 (1967): 19-22. He has just recently handed the direction over to Fr Edmund Mikkers. His address is Kartoteek Bernard Konkordans, Achelse Kluis, Borkel en Schalt (NB), Nederland.

27. See below, pp. 215-264.

this to staying in a hotel. It permitted him to renew his contact with the monastic life to which he is deeply attached, even though his health does not facilitate his carrying out some of its observances. It also gave him the opportunity of meeting experts, who could give him useful information, and enjoying friendly conversations, which an uncommon sociability made an insatiable need for him. With the greatest ease, he had the art of passing from a scholarly exchange with serious librarians to small talk with very simple folk, even with tramps. In every encounter, he has the gift of putting the other person at his ease. For this very reason, he undertakes to speak the language of the country he is visiting. And even if he makes mistakes in grammar or pronunciation, his hearers are grateful to him for making things easier for them. This "glossolalia" was in other respects a first-class trump; because of it J. L. was able to obtain more easily much of the precise information indispensable for the edition.

But while scrupulously making sparing use of the funds entrusted to him, J. L. was also very realistic. "Fatigue costs dearly," he would say. He knew how to avoid it and how to allow himself and his collaborator some moments of relaxation after the long sessions in the libraries. In the same way, when the monastic diet abused his delicate stomach too much, he did not hesitate to frequent less austere tables. This humanness is one of J. L.'s most striking characteristics and one of the reasons for the sympathetic response he evokes in all whom he encounters.

During our trips, J. L. showed himself to be a good organizer in other respects. We rarely arrived at a library without the librarian having been informed both of our approaching visit and of the purpose of our research. This courtesy often obtained for us a prompt reception and the advantage of finding the manuscripts ready for consultation. This meant an appreciable saving of time. His gift for organization was also apparent in bringing the edition itself to realization. In spite of the complexity involved and in spite of the added difficulty of frequent trips, the work went along smoothly: collations, authentification of texts, typing, determination of variants, identification of scriptural texts and the innumerable last minute verifications.

The trips were not made without fatigue, sometimes also not without inconvenience. For instance, when we wanted to go from Graz to Vienna, then in the Soviet zone of occupation, we were twice sent back to the line of demarcation without explanation. The "westerners" could not enter Vienna except by the Salzburg-Linz line. On the other hand, having obtained Soviet passports to move about in that occupation zone, we had no difficulty with the authorities during the fifteen days of our comings and goings.

To the exactness of a good organizer, J. L. knew how to join the flexibility of a realist. When he had to draw up a plan, he always allowed for the unforeseen. "Let us not put fetters on the future," he would habitually say. Thus, always open to the unexpected, he was not disconcerted for long by delays, failures or disappointments. The fundamental optimism, which he derives from his faith, helped him to face serenely the difficulties, which were not lacking. One day we saw a squadron of tanks returning to their camp. I remember J. L.'s slightly disillusioned remarks: "If only we had at our disposal the price of just one of those useless machines, good only for scrap iron —what beautiful editions would be possible!"

It is to the honor of the Cistercian Order that it has made the sacrifices necessary to finance this enterprise, and it is to the glory of the monastery of Poblet that the writings of Bernard have been printed not only carefully but also with taste.

However, having experienced at first hand the adventure which such an edition represents, and having witnessed the dedication and sacrifices which made it possible, I cannot help expressing a regret. To be sure, the competence and the good will for this kind of work are not lacking in the Church. But the absence of organization—which seems to me to be due to the indifference of those responsible for studies in the Church —results in a considerable waste of time, of money and of work. The Church obviously needs critical editions for its studies in theology, philosophy, law, liturgy and history, yet it leaves its scholars to work at random, dependent on personal initiatives and with insufficient means. If only out of regard for justice toward the faithful who entrust it with their alms, the Church could and should give sufficient means to these men, and a suitable environment to enable them to work in respectable human conditions. In this regard it is very true that "the children of this world are more astute than are the children of light!" (Luke 16:8)

Happy the Church that, in spite of its deficiencies, can still glory in giving to the world men of light and workers who, with totally inadequate means, are capable of constructing monuments, less conspicuous than the cathedrals, but more necessary for the depth of its life.

H. Rochais

Institut Catholique de Paris


Translated by
Sr William Boudreau OCSO

# THE FRIENDSHIP BETWEEN PETER THE VENERABLE AND BERNARD OF CLAIRVAUX

PETER THE VENERABLE (1090/4-1156), abbot of Cluny, and St Bernard (1090-1153), Cistercian abbot of Clairvaux, were the outstanding monastic figures of the twelfth century.[1] During this century the Cluniac Order and the new Cistercian reform Order were in opposition to each other on almost all monastic issues, ranging from interpretation of the Benedictine *Regula*, to the definition and place of lay-brothers, to the validity of monastic tithes, and even to such trivia as the length of the pauses in the mass. The antipathy the monks of the two Orders had for each other is reflected not only in exchanges of polemical writings, but even in physical clashes between rival Cistercians and Cluniac monasteries.[2]

This antipathy and rivalry between the two Orders has sometimes been extended to include their two chief abbots, and

1. This essay is largely drawn from my unpublished honor's thesis, "The Black Abbot and the White Abbot," University of Vermont, 1969.
2. See Giles Constable's "Cluniac Tithes and the Controversy between Gigny and Le Miroir," *Rev. Bén.* LXX (1960): 591-624 for an examination of such a clash. The argument was not extended to the abbots. Indeed, St Bernard pleaded with Peter that he be clement with his monks at Gigny who instigated the attack. Twelve tracts in the Cluniac-Cistercian controversy are listed in *The Works of Bernard of Clairvaux*, vol 1, ed., M. Basil Pennington, Cistercian Father's Series 1 (Spencer, Massachusetts, 1970), p. 184. Aside from Peter's letter 28 and Bernard's *Apologia*, one of the most interesting tracts is the *Dialogus inter Cluniacensem Monachum et Cisterciensem de Diversis Utriusque Ordinis Observantiis*, in *Thesaurus Novorum Anecdotorum*, eds. Martène and Durand, V, col. 1569-1654. An English translation of this will appear in vol. 33 of the Cistercian Fathers Series.

the very different personalities of the men have encouraged such a view. However, notwithstanding a long interpretive tradition stressing their differences, there is much evidence indicating that Peter and Bernard, despite the friction between their Orders and their dissimilar personalities and viewpoints, were sincere friends. Support for this view lies in the letters between the two men, the influence each asserted on the other, and a general agreement on certain major issues of the day. Moreover, their lifelong association and their common bond of affection for Nicolas of Montiéramey, the secretary they shared, further delineates that friendship.

Peter and Bernard were similar in many ways. When, as young men, they came into their abbacies, they were nearly the same age. They both came from noble family backgrounds, both were dedicated to monastic ideals, both became major ecclesiastical figures. Their abbacies ran concurrently, and their monasteries were situated in the same area of France—Burgundy.[3] Another bond between the two men was the poor health to which they both were prey throughout much of their lives. And it has been noted that both men were greatly influenced by their mothers.[4] These similarities gave the men a common meeting ground; coming from similar backgrounds, sharing similar duties, they, in a sense, spoke each other's language, something which clearly contributed to the development of the friendship. Nonetheless, great personality differences are evident between the two men, as well as very different behavior

---

3. For Peter the Venerable's family background see Giles Constable, *The Letters of Peter the Venerable,* 2 vols., Harvard Historical Series LXXVIII (Cambridge, Massachusetts: Harvard University Press, 1967) (hereafter referred to as *Letters*), II, p. 233. Peter was a member of one of the great ecclesiastical families of twelfth century France, the Montboissiers. Bernard was related through his maternal grandfather to the Counts of Bar-sur-Seine and the Lords of Couches; his family background is discussed in Bruno Scott James' sympathetic study, *Bernard of Clairvaux, An Essay* (N.Y.: Harper and Row, 1957), pp. 17ff.

4. Constable sees Peter's mother as at least in part responsible for her son's successes in the ecclesiastical world. *Letters,* II, pp. 233-34. Bernard's relation with his mother is remarked on by his contemporaries in the *Vita Prima Bernardi,* tr. Webb and Walker (London: A. R. Mowbray & Co., 1960) and by nearly every one of his biographers since then.

patterns, undoubtedly stemming in part from the different perceptions of the world held by Cluniacs and Cistercians.

Peter was mature, reflective, something of a scholarly recluse who had considerable interest in Jewish and Arab writings in his later life, a better administrator than monk in the early Benedictine sense, lacking a certain essential religious insight, but rational and objective.[5] Peter's role as the cloistered scholar-monk was representative of the ideal monastic values of Cluny, but he also played the role of abbot, and not of one monastery, but as head of an Order of well over a thousand monasteries and priories.[6]Additionally, he had become abbot of Cluny in 1122, at a time when the great Order, disturbed by internal dissension and suffering in comparison with the vigorous Cistercian reform movement, was beginning its long, slow decline. Such an enormous monastic system as the Cluniac empire had not been anticipated in St Benedict's *Regula,* and in attending to his subordinate monasteries Peter was not an abbot in the ideal Benedictine sense, but an administrator, the source of authority and decision-making in the giant organization. This administrative role was an enormous responsibility which largely defined the nature of Peter's world view. Bureaucratic problems, demoralization at Cluny itself, internal disorder and disciplinary problems at many of the daughter monasteries, and severe financial problems engendered by the former abbot, the erratic Pons de Melgueil (1109-1122/25), unceasingly de-

5. Peter's interest in non-Christian writings was not entirely objective. He was interested in examining Jewish and Moslem texts for the purpose of refuting their heresies. See James Kritzeck's article, "Peter the Venerable and the Toledan Collection," pp. 172-201, in *Petrus Venerabilis, 1156-1956: Studies and Texts Commemorating the Eighth Centenary of his Death* (hereafter referred to as *Pet. Ven.),* eds. Giles Constable and James Kritzeck, *Studia Anselmiana,* 40 (Rome, 1956). In 1142 Peter made a trip to Spain and arranged to have the *Risalat Abdallah ibn Isma 'il al Hāshimi' ila 'Abd-al-Masih ibn Ishaq al-Kindi wa Risalat al-Kindi ila-Hashimi* translated from Arabic into Latin, a work Kritzeck describes as ". . . perhaps the most celebrated of early Christian apologetical works." Peter was also responsible for a translation of the Koran, and later produced a ". . . brief, orderly and generally accurate handbook of Islamic doctrine entitled *Summa totius heresis sarracenorum."* The Latin text of the *Summa* may be found in Constable's *Letters,* II, pp. 278-284.

6. Under Abbot Hugh (1049-1109) Cluny had 1500 monasteries under its domination.

manded Peter's attention during the thirty-four years he was
abbot. Conditioned to compromise and slow change, tied to
Cluny by his myriad duties, it is small wonder that the more
conservative side of Peter developed. An administrator-monk,
he saw his greatest service to God performed within monastery
walls.

Bernard's meteoric rise paralleled that of the Cistercian Order. He developed from the fanatically ascetic young abbot of
1115 into the powerful and influential preacher of the Second
Crusade, who wrote and spoke with authority to popes and
kings. He was at the forefront of every controversy of the day,
outspoken and opinionated, exhorting, demanding, appealing
and generally effecting change. Rarely asking advice, he often
gave it. He developed from an excessively zealous young man
to a complex, intense ecclesiastic who completely identified
himself with the Cistercian Order. His life was a combination
of the *vita activa* and mystic exaltation.[7] Throughout much
of his life Bernard attempted to set a precedent of pure and rigorous monastic principle by his own example and by verbal
correction and coercion. The character of the Cistercian Order
in the twelfth century, considerably formed by Bernard himself, gave him great opportunity and motive to enlarge his natural predilections. He faced an entirely different set of problems in his monastic, abbatial role than did Peter. At least
one-third of his time as abbot was spent outside the walls of
Clairvaux, not on monastic business, and not in the care of his
monks' souls, but as the leading reformer of Western Europe.

Because of the different roles these two men played, and because of the differences between the Cluniac and Cistercian
Orders, it has been easy for historians to be sceptical of a friendship between the two men. Joseph Lortz is suspicious of such
a friendship, and suggests that the affectionate terms in the
letters between the two men suggest nothing more than po-
liteness, rhetoric and the formal exercise of Christian brother-

---

7. A. H. Bredero in "The Controversy between Peter the Venerable and St Bernard of Clairvaux," *Pet. Ven.*, pp. 53-71, sees Bernard in his early days as "over-
zealous" and excessively rigorous, partly because of inexperience and partly because he had to justify to himself his choice of the Cistercian Order.

ly love.[8] Certainly their positions as the leading forces of their respective Orders demanded that they set an example of tolerance for their more quarrelsome monks. And, if one reads only St Bernard's side of the correspondence, one is apt to be suspicious of any love behind the façade of words. But when the letters of both men are read together, a deep friendship becomes apparent despite the differences of opinion between them. Added to the history of their relations over more than three decades, the letters delineate their growing affection and mutual regard for one another.

Although we have only twenty letters or so in the correspondence between the two men, certain phrases beyond the ecclesiastical rhetoric of the day, certain homely references to ailments, scattered bits of humor, the sense of sharing the same problems and experiences that comes through in the letters produces in the reader the very definite impression that these two men were friends beyond the official smiling masks demanded by their monastic positions.[9]

Peter refers to Bernard as his ". . . *specialissimus et sanctissimus amicus,*"[10] and says in letter 111, "For above all silver and gold, your *gratia bona,* your love, is precious to me."[11] And Bernard tells Peter, "For a long time now we have been united in the closest friendship, and an equal affection has rendered us equals. . . . [I] who love you dearly, not in mere word, but in deed and truth."[12]

A more subtle evidence of their friendship is found in a letter from Bernard to Peter, answering one of Peter's, now unfortunately lost. Bernard, whatever other virtues he possessed,

8. Joseph Lortz, *Bernhard von Clairvaux: Mainzer Kongress* (Wiesbaden, 1955), "Einleitung," p. xxxiv. "Ihre wechselseitigen Komplimente, Freundschafts— und Liebeserklärungen entflammen sich typish rhetorisch und den grossen Worten der Schrift und scheinen eher—oder doch wenigstens auch! —höfliche, vom Geist christlicher Bruderliebe getragene Überbruckungsversuche der tiefgehenden Spannungen zu sein als Äusserungen einer echten Sympathie."
9. The numbering of Peter's letters follows that of Giles Constable; Bernard's letters follow James' numbers: *The Letters of St Bernard of Clairvaux,* trans. B. S. James (London: Burns Oates, 1953).
10. Peter the Venerable, letter 192, *Letters,* I, p. 447.
11. *Ibid.,* letter 111, p. 275.
12. St Bernard, letter 308, James, pp. 378-379.

was not famous for his sense of humor. For a man to joke with Bernard was rashness, or allowed for a rather special intimacy. Peter's lost letter to Bernard was apparently jocular in tone and gist. We do not know exactly what his joke was, but from Bernard's remarks—that he had written twice to Peter and yet received no answer—it may be that Peter's levity was that he ". . . expressed, though in playful manner, some sense of neglect owing to his not having heard from Bernard. . . ."[13] We see here the strict Cistercian abbot who prided himself on answering letters punctually, who, having written twice to Peter and received no reply, is now himself chided for not having written. The image Bernard presents to us here is one of struggling manfully to maintain his dignity once he had gotten the joke. He remarks, somewhat huffily at first:

> It is thus you think fit to joke? It is all very proper and very friendly, provided only that it is not meant to take me in. It is not long ago that I wrote to salute your greatness with all due reverence, and you did not answer me a word. Not long before, also, I had written to you from Rome, and then too I did not get a single syllable. Do you wonder that on your recent return from Spain I did not introduce my nonsense upon you?

> . . . Here I am, that used to be, and am, the servant of your holiness. I am thankful that I am excellently well situated, being as you are pleased to write, an actual inmate of yourself, for if, as you charge me, I should become cold, I shall undoubtedly soon grow warm again, thus cherished by your bowels of charity.

> And now as to what you were pleased to write—I received it with outstretched hands, I read it eagerly, I love to reperuse it, and, after often reading it over, it still delights me. I confess, I love the humour of it. For it is delightful in its mirth, and serious in its gravity. I know not how it is that, in the midst of your jocularity, you do somehow manage your discourse so judiciously, that the humour has not the appearance of levity, and yet the dignity which you preserve does

13. Ibid.,

not diminish the freedom of your humour. In fact that dignity is kept up in such a way that one might fairly apply to you what was said by the holy man: "If I laughed on them they believed it not."[14]

Peter's own comment on his joke in a later letter to Bernard was:

But perhaps you will say again, "Is it thus that you think fit to joke?" Yes, I do think it fit, with you. Certainly with you, though not with others.[15]

It is difficult to interpret these passages as anything else than the expression of friendship between the two men. More directly to the point, Peter says to Bernard in another letter:

You, my dearest friend . . . While we were still young men we began to love one another in Christ; and now that we are old ones, or not far from it, shall we call in question a love so sacred and of so long standing? . . . God forbid. . . . What you wrote, therefore, in this letter, I received, I keep, I preserve. It would be easier to rob me of a thousand talents of gold, than that these things should be torn from my heart by anything that could happen—but enough of this.[16]

Lortz's opinion that the two men's friendship was rhetorical becomes more suspect when one considers that Bernard was very outspoken in his letters and his speech. If he felt he was justified he could show great anger. Since he spared neither pope nor king the lash of his tongue he should not have felt any hesitation in savaging a mere abbot, especially a Cluniac abbot. There are occasional passages in the letters where the two abbots show impatience with each other, but neither of

14. St Bernard, letter 305, S. R. Maitland's translation in his *The Dark Ages* (London: Gilbert and Rivington, 1845), p. 428.
15. Peter the Venerable, letter 111; Maitland's translation, *The Dark Ages*, p. 428.
16. Peter the Venerable, letter 149; Maitland's translation, *The Dark Ages*, pp. 430-431.

them broke into abuse. If Bernard had not been a close friend
of Peter the Venerable, he almost certainly would have written
angrily to Peter on a number of matters where Cluniacs and
Cistercians were in opposition. If we follow Lortz's denial of
a friendship between the two men we are obliged to ask ourselves the cynical question, did Bernard spare Peter his sharp
tongue in order to keep on Peter's good side so that he might
use Peter as a tool in his many diplomatic exercises? But Bernard's weapons were righteousness, wrath and outspokenness,
not sublety and guile. Only in the case of Henry of France is
Bernard's correspondence with Peter open to speculation as to
the Cistercian abbot's motives.

Henry of France was the brother of Louis VII, and, at the
time of Bernard's letter to Peter asking for his advice, a monk
at Clairvaux where he had been since 1146/47.[17] The matter
of concern was whether or not Bernard should release Henry
from monastic vows and allow him to accept his election as
bishop of Beauvais. Henry, aside from his royal connections,
had held a number of important positions in the ecclesiastical
world prior to his entry into the Cistercian Order.[18]

The fact that Bernard appealed to Peter for advice in a matter over which he himself had some hesitation and doubt is
surprising enough; Bernard's major personality traits are surety
and certainty. In this case, his appeal for advice on a matter
concerning one of his own monks from the abbot of another
Order who had had no particularly close contact with the monk
in question is so odd as to arouse our suspicion. We suspect
that what Bernard wanted was not so much Peter's advice as
a letter of support which Bernard could show to the electing
archbishops as a statement of influential support. We are not

17. Peter's answer is dated by Constable some time in the autumn of 1149, so we
may assume Bernard requested his advice shortly before. There is no exact date
and Bernard's letter no longer exists.

18. In 1125 he had been abbot of the Royal Monasteries of Notre Dame at Pois-
sy and St Mellon at Pontoise. In 1138 he was abbot of St Denis de la Chartre, and
from 1137-40, abbot of St Spire at Corbeil; between 1142-43 he was abbot of
Notre Dame at Etampes. In addition he had been archdeacon of Beauce in Orleans,
treasurer of St Martin at Tours, and had held a number of other minor ecclesiastical posts. See Constable's *Letters*, II, p. 195.

surprised then at Constable's comment that Peter's reply, ". . . when shown to the archbishops and bishops of France . . . influenced them in favor of Henry of France."[19] There does seem to be the tone of a lifted eyebrow in Peter's reply when he says:

It pleased your holiness to consult my humble self as to what seemed best to me concerning the election of brother Henry, your son; that is, whether you ought to grant assent to him or not. But consider, certainly you are filled with the spirit of wisdom and the fear of God; beyond this you do not need my counsel, nor is it necessary for you to borrow from others such as I, that which God has granted you, and which you know how* and are accustomed to provide abundantly for others.[20]

Peter goes on to extol Henry's virtues and to urge Bernard to consent to the election since the will of God has manifested itself through so many signs in favor of this election.[21]

If Bernard was using Peter here in an effort to get a good letter of recommendation rather than his advice, we see a less open and less bold side of Bernard's personality than is usually evident. In view of Bernard's great influence at this time and victorious past record in settling appointments and elections, we find his request for advice to Peter puzzling. Surely the great Cistercian spokesman did not need Peter's approval to carry through the formality of Henry's election. And without the actual text of Bernard's letter we are unsure as to whether Bernard was showing an uncharacteristic hesitancy over the matter (perhaps because he hated to lose a monk to whatever cause, perhaps because he considered Henry an ecclesiastical

19. *Letters*, 2:195.
20. *Pacuit sanctitati uestrae humilitatem meam consulere, quid michi super electione fratris Henrici filii uestri uideretur, utrum eidem assensum prebere deberetis, an non. At vos quidem plenus spiritu consilii et timoris dei, meo super hoc consilio non egetis, nec necesse uobis est, ab aliquo talium qualis ego sum mutare, quod ex collata uobis a deo gratia aliis affluenter nostis et soletis accomodare.—Letters*, I, p. 360.
*Constable comments that some scholars take this word *nostis* for *nostris*. I read it as a shortened form of *nosco*, perfect, 2nd person plural.
21. Latin text in *Letters*, I, pp. 360-361.

butterfly) or whether he was showing an uncharacteristically manipulative side of his character. There remains the possibility that he simply valued an old and loved friend's opinion, although a decade earlier he had quite ignored Peter's opinion on the bishop-elect of Langres. The question of Bernard's motive must remain unanswered without more evidence.

The so-called "*Regula* controversy" between Peter and Bernard which occurred early in their abbacies is evidence of the enmity which existed between the Cluniac and Cistercian Orders. It illuminates a monastic rivalry which has sometimes been extended to the two abbots on the basis of the three documents involved—Bernard's *Letter to Robert of Chatillon*, Bernard's famous *Apologia* addressed to his old friend, William of St Thierry, and Peter's letter 28, addressed to Bernard.[22] However, recent work has shown that the "controversy" really existed between the two Orders, not between the abbots.[23] Bernard did not aim his attack, if attack it really was, at Peter, nor did Peter take the Cistercian documents as personal attacks.

Bernard's letter to his errant monk and nephew, Robert of Chatillon, who fled the strictness of Clairvaux for the ease of Cluny, was written some years after the fact and may have been, according to Bredero, ". . . a propaganda pamphlet in favor of Citeaux, which was intended to be read by a wider public."[24] It is not known whether Peter or Robert ever saw the letter.

The crux of the problem in the controversy is the temporal relation between Peter's letter 28 and the *Apologia*. Students of these documents are generally in agreement that there is no direct relationship in the content of the two works, that is, one was not written as a direct answer to the other.[25] Tradi-

---

22. David Knowles, *The Historian and Character,* (Cambridge University Press, 1963), Chapter IV, pp. 50-75. Knowles does grant, however, that the "dispute" between Peter and Bernard ended in friendship.

23. A. H. Bredero, *Pet. Ven.* and Giles Constable, *Letters,* II, pp. 271-73.

24. A. H. Bredero, *Pet. Ven.,* p. 60.

25. G. Constable, *Letters,* II, pp. 271-72 summarizes the opinions of Charles Clemencet, Elphège Vacandard and David Knowles on the relationship between these two documents.

tionally letter 28 is seen to have been written before the *Apologia*, or at nearly the same time, 1123-1125.

But Giles Constable supports a later date for letter 28 than 1123/24, to which latter date E. Vacandard and D. Knowles hold.[26] Constable feels the letter was probably written in 1126/27 after Peter's trip to Rome in 1125/26 for the trial of Cluny's former abbot, Pons, and after Peter's slow recovery from the malaria he contracted in Rome. Constable's later date may also explain why Peter addressed his letter to Bernard, who in 1123/24 was still a relatively unimportant Cistercian abbot.

The legal head and proper recipient of a treatise like letter 28 would have been the head of the Cistercian Order, the abbot of Citeaux. There is no evidence to show that Peter was replying to some specific charges made by Bernard himself or by his monks. But by 1126/27, we are perhaps at the point in Bernard's life when he was a more important figure with greater influence than he had been three years earlier. Certainly by the later date the *Apologia* was in circulation. Additional evidence of Bernard's greater influence may be found in Bernard's letter 80 to the powerful Abbot Suger of St Denis, which James sees as written in the mid-1120's. In this letter Bernard praises Suger for having reformed both his life and his abbey. Indeed, James believes that Bernard had Suger in mind, not Peter the Venerable, when he wrote the *Apologia*.[27] Certainly this is an attractive theory, for Peter, who only became abbot of Cluny in 1122, was not the focal figure in the Cluniac world until after Pons' trial and death in 1126. Both Pons and Suger were more important representatives of the old order than was Peter the Venerable in the first half of the 1120's.

If James is right in supposing that the *Apologia* was obliquely directed at Suger, and that Bernard's letter 80 was Bernard's praise to Suger for having repaired the excesses detailed in the *Apologia*, then certainly Peter would have cause to recognize Bernard as the spear-head of the Cistercian reform movement.

26. Jean Leclercq in his introduction to the translation of Bernard's *Apologia* dates the *Apologia* 1125. *The Works of Bernard of Clairvaux, op. cit.*, pp. 5ff.

27. B. S. James, *Letters*, p. 110, n.

If such is the case, it would be logical for Peter to have addressed his letter 28 to Bernard, a letter which both defends
Cluniac policy and at the same time asks for Bernard's advice.

It becomes clear in reading the three documents that Peter
and Bernard were not attacking each other's individual beliefs,
but were defending their own Order's interpretations of St
Benedict's *Regula*. Letter 28 is clearly a defense. The Cistercian
documents, as representative of Bernard's complete self-iden-
tification with his Order, in addition to the more obvious aims
of rebuking back-biting Cistercians and excoriating Cluniac
laxity, can be construed as a justification of his personal choice
of that Order. In this light the letter to Robert and the *Apologia* can be read, not so much as attacks on Cluny, but as de-
fenses of the Cistercian view.

Peter's letter 28, whatever its relationship to the *Apologia*,
was moderate, thoughtful, full of common sense, intelligence
and reason. Peter's refusal to quarrel with Bernard is noteworthy, and in a large part responsible for allowing the friendship between the two men to begin. Bredero sees letter 28 as
having great influence on Bernard, and as having contributed
considerably to the Cistercian's growing moderation from that
point onward:

> Peter's attitude must have impressed St Bernard for, in spite
> of the overly satirical and disagreeable strain in his militant
> criticism, he seemed to be put in the right by the abbot of
> Cluny, who ever sought his friendship. For St Bernard this
> astonishing attitude led only to the conclusion that Cluny,
> which in his opinion belonged more or less to the world he
> had left, was different from what he had imagined. This ex-
> perience opened his heart again to the world, to which he
> returned and which he now accepted as a reality for the
> action of his love. From now on he could develop as a re-
> former of Church and Society.[28]

Bredero's argument for Peter's influence on Bernard is considerably weakened by his acceptance of a pre-*Apologia* date

28. A. H. Bredero, *Pet. Ven.*, p. 70.

for letter 28. For, if Peter's letter 28 led St Bernard ". . . to the conclusion that Cluny . . . was different from what he had imagined," then how is the *Apologia* explainable? We can accept Bredero's conclusion of Peter's influence on Bernard more readily if we follow Constable's later date of 1126/27 for letter 28. For if letter 28 is the last document in the "controversy," this is significant. Bernard does not write any more polemics against Cluny, and embarks on a life-long friendship with Peter.

Although it does seem likely to some extent that Peter's friendship did humanize the young Bernard, the transformation was probably nʋt the immediate result of letter 28 as Bredero hints, but a slow process over the years. There is evidence in Bernard's letter to Robert of Chattillon, presumably written before Bernard had any contact with Peter, that he was already aware of his overstrictness with others.[29] Peter's influence on Bernard was over the long passage of time where his moderate, logical manner balanced the temperamental impetuosity of Bernard.

But what of Bernard's effect on Peter? Was there one, or did Peter sail his monastic ship through the same ocean as Bernard but on quite another course? There is good evidence to show that as Bernard became less severe with his own monks at Clairvaux, and ceased his polemics against the older forms of Benedictinism, Peter became more rigorous in the administration of Cluny and her monastic subsidiaries.

Around 1146 Peter made a list of the reforms he had enacted during his rule as abbot of Cluny. At this point he had been abbot for nearly a quarter of a century. The list is a heterogeneous collection that covers both important and trivial matters. It is possible of course, that Peter might have developed his reform attitude by himself, but it is far more likely that he

---

29. St Bernard, letter 1, James, p. 2. "No doubt it may have been my fault that you left. I was too severe with a sensitive youth. I was too hard on a tender stripling. Hence your grumbles against me . . . while you were here; hence your ceaseless complaints about me even now . . . you must know that I am not the same man I was, because I do not think that you are what you used to be. Having changed yourself you will find me changed too."

was influenced by the general air of reform generated by Bernard and the Cistercian Order. Very likely he was even influenced by Bernard's *Apologia* with its thesis that the black monks were soft and corrupt in comparison with the strict, right Cistercian way. Undoubtedly he was influenced by his long friendship with St Bernard and his intimate correspondence with that abbot. David Knowles certainly sees Peter's reforms as ". . . in part, at least inspired and directed by the criticism passed upon the traditional monastic way of life in his day by St Bernard."[30]

In addition, in 1132 Peter had called a general chapter meeting of priors in order to issue some reform decrees. There is no existing copy of the decrees emanating from this meeting, but we do know that over a thousand monks attended, not all of them Cluniacs. Apparently the decrees met with anything but success in their application; rather they ". . . aroused criticism and resistance. . .and. . .were in the sequel in part withdrawn."[31]

Over the years Peter's inclination toward reform increased, despite its unpopularity in Cluniac monasteries. A letter exists to the Cluniac Priors speaking out sharply against dietary laxity ". . . in which the Bernardine influence is noteworthy."[32] This is undoubtedly letter 161, "To the Prior or Sub-priors of Cluniac Establishments," which Constable dates 1144/56.[33] In this letter Peter sternly lists forbidden foods which must be abstained from, sinful abuses which have gained footholds in the priories, and gives substitutes in cooking oils and foodstuffs for emergency use. Constable notes that this letter ". . . shows clearly both the efforts of Peter the Venerable to reform the Cluniacs and his moderate attitude toward reasonable departures from literal observance of the Rule."[34]

Knowles makes a comparison of Peter's 1146 list of reforms with his early defense of Cluniac procedures in letter 28, and

---

30. David Knowles, "The Reforming Decrees of Peter the Venerable," *Pet. Ven.*, pp. 1-20; p. 2.
31. Ibid.
32. Ibid.
33. *Letters*, I, p. 388.
34. *Letters*, II, p. 206.

in so doing, shows clearly the change in attitude and increasing strictness which has come over Peter through the years. Peter shifts ground in a number of decrees in the 1146 list dealing with food and meals. He makes an effort to control excesses in clothing and bedding, speaking

> . . . of the blameworthy, nay damnable vanity in apparel that has grown to such a pitch . . . that the monks' pride has led them to despise French catskins in favour of the cats of Spain and Italy.[35]

Four decrees dealing with the problem of keeping silence were aimed at the motherhouse of Cluny itself where the many kinds of official Cluniac business were carried on.

Peter makes some effort at curbing the Cluniac habit of admitting novices as quickly as possible—a serious and indefensible infraction of the *Regula*. Peter had defended immediate admittance in letter 28. Now in statute 35 admittance is restricted; in statute 36 twenty-one is set as the minimum age for admittance; in statute 37 the period of novitiate is set at least (!) one month.

As is well known, Cluny was geared to liturgy, masses, meditation and reading rather than to manual labor in the fields. In letter 28 Peter had answered the Cistercian charges of evasion of the *Regula's* strictures on this point by declaring that for monks to labor would be both impossible and indecent. In 1146, however, he finds it good that monks work since so many of them were given to dozing in corners and gossiping into the late hours at night.[36] Further statutes dealt with restricting the lighting of the famous chandelier at Cluny to the more important feast days and in easing the injustices toward Cluny's oblate children who were doomed to fruitless careers in scholastic areas.

In his examination of Peter's statutes Knowles sees Peter as ". . . an administrator rather than a legislator; a man of practical remedies rather than of first principles, and one who is of-

---

35. D. Knowles, *Pet. Ven.*, p. 9.
36. It is possible that he was referring to the Cluniac *conversi* rather than to the choir monks in this statute.

ten curiously unable to see the compelling spiritual reasons for a course of action."[37] And for the most part Peter's reforms were largely ineffectual and ignored; they were also unpopular, indicating that for Cluniacs customs and a way of life that had for so long prevailed constituted not laxity but the very essence of Cluny. In such a situation a reformer will meet with little success. The Bernardine influence on Peter produced little real change.

The friendship between Peter the Venerable and St Bernard is sometimes only seen by reading between the lines of events. Generally the two men agreed on many of the major issues of their day—both supported the election of Henry of France as bishop of Beauvais, both supported Innocent II during the schism, both supported the Second Crusade. But in 1138-1139 they found themselves on opposing sides in the confusing cloak-and-dagger affair of the episcopal election at Langres.

The election in question concerned the bishopric of Langres, an extremely important position which exerted enormous influence over much of Burgundy.[38] The authority of the bishop of Langres lay over Molesme, Morimond, and, most important, over Clairvaux. Constable's careful examination of both Peter's and Bernard's correspondence concerning the election shows that by their own accounts of events the abbots were drawn into the fracas by opposing factions within the Cathedral Chapter of St Mamas at Langres. Neither of them entered the controversy voluntarily, but rather at the request of men more intimately involved. And neither abbot was at first aware of the other's participation.

The bishop-elect,[39] although supported by Dean Robert and Canon Ulric of the Cathedral Chapter, Archbishop Peter of the Metropolitan Chapter in Lyons, the Bishops of Autun and Ma-

---

37. D. Knowles, *Pet. Ven.*, p. 19.

38. G. Constable, "The Disputed Election at Langres in 1138," *Traditio* XIII (1957), pp. 119-120. Late in the twelfth century the holder of this bishopric became a count and the king's tenant-in-chief ". . . for all his lands and powers" and shortly thereafter attained the rank of duke ". . . and was recognized as the third ecclesiastical peer of the realm, taking precedence over his own metropolitan, the archbishop of Lyons, at the coronation of the king."

39. His identity is not sure, but Constable believes he may have been William of Sabran.

con, the King of France, the Abbot of Cluny and probably the Duke of Burgundy, was nevertheless defeated at the penultimate moment, largely because of Bernard's bitter opposition.[40]

What is important here for us is that despite the opposite opinions they maintained on the character of the Cluniac candidate, and the desire each had to see his own Order holding this powerful position, the friendship between the two men is evident as soon as they learn of each other's participation in the election. Peter quickly writes a cordial and reassuring letter to Bernard explaining his own part in the matter and defending the character of the Cluniac bishop-elect. He begs Bernard to reconsider his stand. Bernard, whose busy pen was writing no less than eight letters damning the supposedly wretched candidate, neither turned sharply on Peter nor railed at him for prolonging the affair. He simply disregarded Peter's rational appeal and pursued what he, Bernard, felt—an unmovable antipathy to the Cluniac candidate. But the friendship, which might well have foundered on this rock, was maintained.

Bernard as the great Crusade preacher is one of the most familiar figures of the medieval period. Peter the Venerable's role in the Second Crusade has too often been presented negatively. Virginia Berry's "Peter the Venerable and the Crusades" has corrected the view that Peter was disinterested in the Second Crusade.[41] This view, part of the traditionally black and white contrast between the two abbots, came about through a number of related factors: Peter is not mentioned in the contemporary twelfth-century crusade literature, he was absent from the Assembly of Chartres supposedly without good reasons, and his interest in ". . . Jewish and Moslem dogma" aroused suspicion.[42] Berry refutes this view and states flatly that Peter was

. . . consistently sympathetic to the crusade throughout his

---

40. Curiously enough, Bernard never directly examined the candidate as did Peter, but referred vehemently if vaguely to the stories circulating about the man's character, stories so awful Bernard could not bring himself to repeat them.

41. Virginia Berry, "Peter the Venerable and the Crusades," *Pet. Ven.*, pp. 141-162.

42. *Ibid.*, p. 141.

life, and . . . participated in the preparation for the Second Crusade and the attempt to launch a third crusade as much as his other ecclesiastical responsibilities and his status as a monk allowed.[43]

Peter supported the Second Crusade with letters (especially letter 130 to Louis VII in 1146), perhaps a donation of money, and at least one crusade sermon.[44] And, according to Berry, he was even among the small handful of people who were enthusiastic about a proposed third crusade. Certainly the two friends agreed on the importance of the Second Crusade.

Both men saw the Second Crusade primarily as a means of salvation for lay persons; beyond the opportunity it presented for fighting God's foes, their concept of the crusade was rather naive.[45] Neither apprehended the political facets of the crusade, nor did either see the defense of the Latin States in the East as the main point of the expedition. Instead, both saw the Second Crusade as a "good work," a way to individual salvation for men unable to serve God in the best way—as monks. If this mutual sympathy for the crusade by the two abbots does not precisely delineate the friendship between Bernard and Peter, it nevertheless shows an accord where there was once believed to be disagreement.

In conclusion, it seems possible to discern a certain responsiveness between the two abbots early in their careers in spite of the hostility between the Cluniac and Cistercian Orders. This responsiveness and the early friendship probably developed from their similar personal backgrounds, and from Peter's rational, open letter 28 to Bernard in the *Regula* controversy. As the years went by, the men were bound closer by mutual friends and experiences, and, if the requests for advice in their letters can be believed, developed something of a dependence on one another. The close relationship between the men led to a mutual influence. We have seen that on many of

43. *Ibid.,* pp. 141-142.
44. Berry mentions his crusade sermon, *De laude Dominici sepulchri, Pet. Ven.,* p. 152.
45. G. Constable, "The Second Crusade as Seen by Contemporaries," *Traditio* IX (1953), p. 247.

the major issues of the day the two men were in agreement. On matters such as the election at Langres, where the two abbots disagreed, both were careful not to strain the friendship. The intimate tone of the correspondence between Peter and Bernard clearly indicates that what has sometimes been taken for the usual rhetoric between high ecclesiastics, was in reality the expression of a sincere, strong friendship. In this brief examination of some of the evidence of that mutual affection we have seen that there was not so wide a gulf between the two abbots as there was between the Cistercian and Cluniac Orders. The fragile bridge of friendship that Peter and Bernard constructed is especially noteworthy against the background of changing monastic values and the complex metamorphoses of twelfth-century society.

Ann Proulx Lang

Sir George Williams University
Montreal, Canada

# BERNARD AND ABELARD AT THE
# COUNCIL OF SENS, 1140

FROM THE VIEWPOINT of the existing literature on the Council of Sens, 1140, and on the relations of Bernard and Abelard, our picture of neither of these two great men at that council is a very good one. The reason is not far to seek. The deep, and sometimes bitter, controversy at Sens has been carried on through many of the intervening centuries. As a result most of the literature is polemic. Some has been more so than other, but it has been very difficult in any case to look at this meeting without some measure of special pleading creeping into the account. Abelard has been too good a foil for the rebel or the modernist, and Bernard, for the traditionalist. Arno Borst's fine article on "Abälard und Bernhard"[1] in 1958 represents the beginning of escape from this situation, and so does Joseph Lortz' remark that "a dusting off of the picture of Bernard as a saint, and the elimination of a sweetness, strange and false to this hero, are still necessary."[2]

These were two great men. That is to say that they were great and they were men. Even saints are men and women. There is little need to pause and expatiate upon the greatness of them and of their contributions. That is fairly obvious. But we need to be reminded that they were men (as Otto of Freising re-

1. *Historische Zeitschrift*, vol. 186 (1958): 497-526.
2. *Eine Entstaubung des Heiligenbildes Bernhards und die Uberwindung einer diesem Heros fremdem, falschen Süszigkeit sind noch immer fällig.* Quoted from *Bernhard von Clairvaux, Mönch und Mystiker*, ed. Joseph Lortz (Wiesbaden: Franz Steiner Verlag, 1955), p. xxiv.

minded us),[3] men subject to the failings of the flesh as all are. For all his heroic appeal, one cannot escape the impression that Abelard was a very difficult person to have around. He could be combative and querelous to a fault. His own correspondence is evidence of this. Likewise one cannot escape the impression that Bernard at Sens carried his great and deep sincerity and conviction just one small step too far. It is the paradox of life that it was precisely his sincerity and conviction, his faith and his sense of rightness that made him do it. And in a way, if it was culpable, it was felicitous, because it proved him one of us, and he may be forgiven, just as Abelard was forgiven. In fact, as far as the sources that remain to us from that time are concerned, Abelard was forgiven more than Bernard, whose part in the proceedings at Sens seems to have remained to haunt him at Reims in 1148, where he met some resistance from the cardinals and the pope.[4]

But what do we really know about what happened at Sens? Let us set aside not only Berengar's hardly impartial account,[5] but also Otto's[6] and Geoffrey's,[7] and confine our attention to the immediately contemporary documents of people who were there. The documents are few, but precious. Some, being official, were probably fairly carefully written: the reports of the archbishops, Henry and Samson. There are also letters of Bernard.[8] It is clear from these, especially the first, that some sort

3. Speaking of Bernard, Otto wrote: *Utrum autem praedictus abbas Claravallensis in hoc negocio ex humanae infirmitatis fragilitate tamquam homo deceptus fuerit, vel episcopus* [Gilbert of Poitiers, whose trial at Reims is under consideration] *tanquam vir litteratissimus propositum astute celando ecclesiae iudicium evaserit, discutere vel iudicare nostrum non est. Gesta Friderici Imperatoris,* I, 57, in *Monumenta Germaniae Historica. Scriptores,* vol. 20. p. 384. A little earlier, in his account of the Council of Sens, he had described Bernard as *ex habitudinali mansuetudine quodammodo credulus,* and Abelard as *arrogans.* Ibid., p. 376.

4. John of Salisbury, *Historia pontificalis,* viii-ix, ed. Marjorie Chibnall (London: Thomas Nelson and Sons, 1956), pp. 15-21.

5. Berengarius Scholasticus, *Apologeticus contra Beatum Bernardum,* in Migne, PL 178:1857-70.

6. Otto of Freising, *op. cit.,* I, *cap.* 47-49.

7. Geoffrey of Auxerre, *Vita prima,* III, v, 13, PL 185:310-12.

8. Letters 337, 191, 193, 333, 334, 335, and 338 in the collection of Bernard's letters, PL 182:357-59, 538-43. The new critical edition, soon to appear, will supersede this convenient collection based upon Mabillon's edition. Abelard's extant letters were written before the council. E. Buytaert, "Thomas of Morigny and the Apologia of Abelard," in *Antonianum* 52 (1967): 45-64.

of a meeting was held the day before the great session in the cathedral.[9] This is the most likely explanation for Abelard's diffidence and departure.[10] Geoffrey of Auxerre's explanation is hearsay with nothing else to substantiate it;[11] Otto's is possible;[12] Dr Jeannin's hypothesis that Abelard was suffering from Hodgkin's disease seems to force the evidence a bit too far.[13]

We know for sure that the previous day's meeting took place, although what went on there is not easy to determine with any certainty. We know that Abelard broke off the session of Monday in the face of Bernard's charges in the cathedral. We have the comment of John of Salisbury[14] on the similarity of the caucus at Reims with the one at Sens. We may be sure that both the principals were contending hard after their characteristic fashions. That is all we may be certain of. It is regrettable that discussion could not have been continued long enough for explanations. But it was not, and that fact cost the schools and the clergy some long years of controversy that might have been avoided. Perhaps that would have been expecting too much. In any case from this distance we had best divide the responsibility. If we assign a share of humanity to Bernard, it is not just to follow the judgment of Otto of Freising;[15] it is to say that this is just what makes Bernard a believable and a grand person withal. As for Abelard, there is little question that he could be downright irritating at times. Both men wanted to be right to a fault.

Another point: it is not correct to contrast Abelard as the equivalent of what we call a "liberal" or "progressive," and Bernard as a "conservative," and so forth. Both of these men were radical innovators, the one in the schools and the other

9. PL 182:542B.

10. *Ibid: visus diffidere et subterfugere.*

11. PL 185:311C: *Nam et confessus est postea suis, ut aiunt, quod ea hora, maxima quidem ex parte memoria ejus turbata fuerit, ratio caligaverit, et interior fugerit sensus.*

12. *Mon. Germ. hist., Script.* vol 20, p. 377: *seditionem populi timens.*

13. J. Jeannin, "La dernière maladie d'Abélard," in *Mélanges saint Bernard* (Dijon: M. l'abbé Marilier, 1953) pp. 109-15.

14. Op. cit., p. 19.

15. See note 3, above.

in the monasteries. What is more, both could be very traditional too, and to make more complications, both appreciated something of the other's world: Abelard, reformed monasticism, and Bernard, intellectual life. At the same time it would be a mistake to consider Bernard in the least bit a scholastic. His intellect is intuitive (accurately intuitive in some of his criticisms of Abelard), not analytical, not making the fine distinctions that were being made in the schools. Both these men were the leaders of great changes in their time; their difference lies in the changes they were leading and in the way they went about them.

When we consider the nineteen *capitula* associated with the council, some evidence for some of the above remarks will be seen. These propositions were the heart of the controversy.[16]

Let us make clear a couple of assumptions, however, before proceeding to consider the *capitula*: (1) Let us assume that these propositions were Bernard's (recognizing of course that they were suggested in part by the thirteen propositions of William). Father Leclercq has contested this assumption, and we have presented our views to one another for discussion, which is a special, and indeed important matter that deserves separate treatment.[17] Let me simply declare this assumption, for the time being. (2) Let us assume also that all nineteen propositions are relevant to the controversy, that is to the council too, even though it has become pretty clear from the researches of Fathers Leclercq and Grill that probably only a limited number, perhaps five, were in some fashion acted upon by the council and/or forwarded to the pope.[18] What then do

16. The nineteen *capitula* associated with the council proper, and the thirteen of William of St Thierry are listed in an appendix at the end of this article.

17. Jean Leclercq, "Les formes successives de la lettre-traité de saint Bernard contre Abélard," in *Revue bénédictine* 78 (1968): 105, where the consideration is textual. Whatever the textual status of this list appended to Bernard's *Letter 190*, there is evidence to support the association of these propositions with Bernard. For example, in his *Apologia Ne juxta Boetianum,* Abelard lists the nineteen propositions and names Bernard as his accuser.

18. Jean Leclercq, *Études sur saint Bernard et le texte de ses écrits,* ASOC 9 (1953): 101-105; Leopold Grill, "Die neunzehn Capitula Bernhards von Clairvaux gegen Abälard," in *Historisches Jahrbuch der Görresgesellschaft* 80 (1961): 230-39; Jean Leclercq, "Les formes successives . . .," pp. 87-105.

these nineteen *capitula* yield us in way of knowledge of Bernard and Abelard, and of their controversy?

Summarily, in the cases of seven of the *capitula* Bernard seems to have failed to understand Abelard and further explanation was in order. These were numbers 1, 2, 3, 5, 7, 16, and 18 (since there have been several numbering systems, it must be noted that the order of the propositions found in those MSS of Bernard's *Letter 190*, where they exist, is being followed here; it may be found more conveniently in Leopold Grill's and in Dom Leclercq's articles just referred to, and in the appendix below). In these cases Abelard was justified in his countercharge that he had been misunderstood, or that he had not said (i.e. meant) such things. Four of these seven are of the five he denied having said (i.e. meant) in the *Apologia Universis Ecclesiae*.[19] But Bernard may also be excused in some cases for failing to see right away the subtleties of Abelard's distinctions.

In the case of eight of the *capitula*, Bernard seems to have understood Abelard correctly: Abelard's meaning was reasonably close to what Bernard meant. There were appropriate, substantive issues joined in the cases of *capitula* 4, 8, 9, 10, 11, 13, 15, and 19. In some of these cases Abelard seems to be simply exploring difficult, paradoxical questions (4, 8, and 10), but in others (9, 11, 13, 19) he seems to be quite consciously advancing bold and unusual views: for example, his doctrines of sin, of ecclesiastical powers and of the attributes. Here he was most vulnerable to Bernard's attack. Bernard, for all his failure to see Abelard's distinctions, demonstrates skill at reaching the heart of Abelard's doctrine in these areas.

In the cases of four of the *capitula*, whether Bernard understood Abelard seems either doubtful (6), questionable (14, 17) or not too clear (12).

These are all analyzed in detail in a dissertation submitted by the present writer to the University of Montreal in Sep-

---

19. PL 178: 105-108; 180: 329-32; and MSS, noted by Leclercq in *Études sur saint Bernard . . .* , p. 15, note 5 and p. 103, note 5.

tember, 1969,[20] but for the sake of example it might be in
order to look at a few of them briefly.

From the first group, proposition 5 is an illustrative and especially knotty example: *Quod neque Deus et homo, neque
haec persona quae Christus est, sit tertia persona in Trinitate.*
By the way, *tertia persona in Trinitate*, as you may be aware
(this writer was not, and perhaps many of us are not) was a
manner peculiar to that time and earlier times (it may be traced
back to Isidore of Seville)[21] of referring to him whom we call
the second person of the Trinity, Christ. This confusion has
not been helpful for us. But no matter, this was to William and
Bernard (the latter seems to have added the *haec persona quae
Christus est*) the Nestorian heresy, the radical separation of the
human person, Jesus Christ, from the Son of God, second (as
we say) person of the Trinity. And we must confess that it certainly looks like just that. What was Bernard missing here?
What did Abelard mean? Quite the opposite, or better, two
opposite doctrines. With the phrase *neque Deus et homo* standing for the human nature, he was endeavoring to distinguish
the natures of Christ in the hypostatic union, *salva proprie-
tate utriusque naturae.*[22] This is no trick. There are a good
many passages in the *Theologia Scholarium*, III, vi,[23] and the
*Apologia Ne juxta Boetianum* (Thomas of Morigny's frag-
ments)[24] to support this. It is hardly surprising however that
William and Bernard missed it. It had been a long struggle on
the way to Chalcedon, and the words easily become under-

20. *The "Heresies" of Peter Abelard, Thèse présentée en vue de l'obtentation du
grade de Philosophiae Doctor en sciences médiévales, Institut d'Etudes Médiévales,
Faculté de Philosophie, Université de Montréal,* September, 1969. In subsequent
preparation of this dissertation for anticipated publication, the explanation of
proposition eleven has been changed, and it has been classified with the first of
the three groups summarized here.

21. Isidore of Seville, *De fide catholica contra Judaeos*, I, iv 6-7; *Quaestiones
in vetus testamentum. In Exodum*, XL, ii, *Sententiarum*, I, iii, PL 83:458C-459A,
308D and 543A respectively. Translations of all of the *capitula* are given below
in the appendix.

22. "Saving the property of each nature," the phrase of Tertullian, *Adversus
Praxean*, 27, made famous by Pope Leo the Great, in his letter to Flavian, bishop
of Constantinople, *Lectis dilectionis tuae* (Tomus ad Flavianum), 3, in the Nestorian controversy.

23. PL 178:1106-1109.

24. PL 180:300D-301B, 316B-D, 322B.

stood in senses contrary to those which were intended.

But this leaves us with the knottier half of the problem: *neque haec persona quae Christus est sit, tertia persona in Trinitate.* This looks plainly Nestorian. Or is it? The difficulty can be traced back at least as far as Anselm of Canterbury *(Epistola de incarnatione verbi,* known also as *De fide trinitatis).*[25] It seems to have begun with the impact of Boethius on the late eleventh century intellectual world, and of his famous definition of *persona* in (ironically) *Contra Eutychen et Nestorium: naturæ rationabilis individua substantia.*[26] The word *persona* had assumed a new meaning: *omnis homo individuus esse persona cognoscitur* (Anselm).[27] This created a problem which Anselm wrestled with, and so did Hugh of St Victor,[28] and probably many others. We may be sure that Abelard did, and that he was endeavoring to distinguish between the Boethian notion of *persona* and the *persona trinitatis*: it was as though he were saying, *neque haec persona Boetiana quae Christus est sit tertia persona in Trinitate.*[29] It had become a school problem, which Bernard seems not to have appreciated. The evidence for Abelard's part in this is plain in the sentence books of his students, especially *Sententiae Hermanni* xxiv.[30]

We can also see what might have been avoided, had this all been made clear at Sens in 1140, instead of eight hundred years later: one of the inferences apparently of the argument that *haec persona Boetiana* (this Boethian concept of person) was not the third (or, as we say second) person in the Trinity, was that conversely the person of the Trinity was not *haec persona Boetiana*, or by extension not (in Boethius' sense) *aliquis*, i.e.

25. Anselm, *Opera omnia,* ed. F. S. Schmitt (Edinburgh: Thomas Nelson 1946-61), 2:1-35.

26. "Individual substance of a rational nature," Boethius, edd. H. F. Stewart and E. K. Rand (*The Theological Tractates,* Cambridge, Mass.: Harvard University Press, and London: William Heinemann, 1962; Loeb Classical Library), p. 84.

27. "Every individual man is recognized to be a person." Anselm, *op. cit.,* pp. 21-25.

28. Hugh of St Victor, *De sacramentis christianae fidei,* II, part 1, chapters 9-11, PL 176:393-411.

29. "Nor is this person, as Boethius conceives of it, the 'third' person of the Trinity." We put it this way, in Latin, to show how close we are to the formula of the proposition 5, under consideration.

30. PL 178:1732-33.

someone! A famous student of Abelard put this very plainly, that Christ, *secundum quod homo non sit persona, et ut verius loquamur nec menciamur, nec aliquid.*[31]

After the council of Sens the discussion of all this context of the statement that Christ was (or was not) *aliquid* seems to have been shut off. When Peter Lombard later in the decade referred to the *aliquid* question, it was without the context.[32] He may have assumed that his immediate readers were aware of it, but many of the next generation seem to have forgotten it. Bereft of its context the statement that Christ is not *aliquid* is a rather stark assertion, obviously difficult to accept. The *aliquid* controversy became a raging one in the 1160's. One gets a bit of the flavor of it from Walter of St Victor's *Contra quatuor labyrinthos Franciae*[33] and John of Cornwall's *Eulogium ad Alexandrum III papam quod Christus sit aliquis homo.*[34] Alexander III, the former Roland, seems to have had enough of it so that he put an end to it. In fact, he reversed his own position, at a council at Tours in 1163,[35] and again in letters to archbishop William of Sens (later Reims) in 1170 and 1177.[36] The matter was set aright by the encyclical letter *Sempiternus Rex* in 1951,[37] not however before a great deal had been written about the *aliquid* controversy, and about the *assumptus*, subsistence and *habitus* theories that grew out of it (without the context) as a result of the famous distinction of Peter Lombard. Bernard was not the only one to fail to see the original, and typical, school problem that Anselm, Hugh of St Victor and Abelard wrestled with.

The seventh proposition has also been placed in the first

31. "Christ, as man, is not a person, and (that we may speak more truly and not lie) not something." *Sententiae Rolandi,* ed. Ambrosius M. Gietl, *Die Sentenzen Rolands nachmals Papstes Alexander III,* Freiburg i. Br.: Herder'sche Verlagshandlung, 1891), pp. 176-77.

32. *Sententiarum lib. III, dist.* vi. *(Ad Claras Aquas: Collegium S Bonaventurae,* 1916), pp. 573-79.

33. Ed. P. Glorieux, *Archives d'histoire doctrinale et littéraire du moyen âge* 19 (1953): 187-335.

34. Ed. Nicholas M. Häring, *Mediaeval Studies* 13 (1951): 253-300.

35. *Annales Reicherspergensis,* in *Mon. Germ. Hist., Script,* vol. 17, p. 471.

36. Denzinger-Schönmetzer, *Enchiridion symbolorum* 33rd ed. (Freiburg i. Br.: Herder, 1965), p. 239.

37. *Ibid.,* p. 782.

group (those which Bernard failed to understand and for which especially further explanation was needed): *Quod ea solummodo Deus possit facere vel dimittere, vel eo modo tantum, vel eo tempore quo facit, non alio.* This appears right away like a restatement of the old problem of reconciliation of the power and the goodness of God, related to the problem of evil: if God could have arranged things better, and did not, it seems like a derogation of this goodness; if he could not have done so, of his power. In fact Abelard does raise this very question explicitly in *Theologia Scholarium, III,*v,[38] and Professor Lovejoy's interpretation in this matter, in *The Great Chain of Being,* is very persuasive.[39] There is little doubt that Abelard's apparent selection of one of the horns of this dilemma, defending God's goodness to the detriment of his power, was what shocked Bernard. But in this particular proposition, which Bernard drew almost verbatim from Abelard's text, Abelard seems to have had something else in mind. Just what it was, is elucidated by an alteration to his text in the fifth and final redaction of *Theologia Scholarium,* where he stated *quod fieri bonum est, dimitti bonum esse non potest, quia bono non nisi malum contrarium est . . . si igitur cum bonum sit aliquid fieri, non est bonum ipsum dimitti.*[40] So in the passage from which Bernard quoted propositon 7,[41] the argument is not that God lacks the power to do what he wishes or what is good,[42] but that good is the contrary of bad, and *dimittere* and *dimitti* are the contrary of *facere* and *fieri*; thus whatever it is good to do or to forego doing, it is bad to forego doing or to do, etc. One can

38. PL 178:1093D-94A.

39. Arthur O. Lovejoy, *The Great Chain of Being* (New York: Harper and Row, 1960), p. 71.

40. *Balliol MS. 296,* ff. 49V-50R: "What it is good to be done, it cannot be good to be foregone, because nothing but bad is contrary to good . . . therefore when it is good for something to be done, it is not good for the same to be foregone."

41. PL 178:1101D.

42. To be sure, Abelard has recognized this problem, quoting Augustine, *Quaestionum,* lxxxiii, 83: *Si enim voluit, et non potuit, infirmus est; si potuit et noluit, invidus est.* "For if he would, and could not, he is infirm; if he could, and would not, he is envious." *Theologia Scholarium,* III, v, PL 178:1094C. This is of course the classic dilemma, recapitulated in the concise and balanced style which Augustine was often capable of, and which was so effective. Abelard, it cannot be doubted, knew the formula well, but he substitutes other balanced periods of his own.

only do one *or* the other; only one *or* the other is good. It is the presence of contraries and the disjunctive *vel* that is the basis of Abelard's argument. Bernard did not see it this way.

We may do well to ask, especially since the particular words quoted above were added to the final redaction after the attack upon him by Bernard: was this an evasion on Abelard's part? It could be, but it does not seem so: (1) It is the sort of *sprach-logik* and fine grammatical distinction for which Abelard was famous. (2) It fits the rest of the argument very well: his final solution is based upon the gulf between human and divine natures, in light of which this statement, based upon the logic that governs human affairs, is not applicable to the divine and is therefore no derogation of the transcendent power of God (*si more hominum dicamus eum etiam posse uno tempore etiam aliquid quod alio non possit . . . nulla ejus in hoc impotentia vel potentiae diminutio est intelligenda.*[43] Although directed to a particular phase of the solution, these words well express the sense of the whole). (3) This is not at all an unusual analysis; it is in fact to be found again a little further on in the earlier redaction of *Theologia Scholarium,*[44] where Abelard discusses the distinction of copulative and disjunctive conjunctions. The problem is traditional, and may be traced back quickly through Abelard's *Logica Ingredientibus,*[45] to Boethius' commentaries on Aristotle's *Peri hermeneias* and to the *Peri hermeneias,* ix, itself. (4) Finally, the same sort of argument as the one Abelard added in the fifth redaction after Bernard's accusation is already to be found in the fourth redaction (*quod justum est fieri, injustum est dimitti*)[46] in an abbreviated form.

Perhaps it appears pedantic to go to such lengths to determine whether Abelard's response to Bernard was an *ad hoc* evasion or not, but the point seems rather important, because it is such a good example of the distinction of the psychologies and the

---

43. *Ibid.,* 1104A: "if, after the manner of men, we say that he can indeed do at one time even something that he cannot at another . . . no impotence or diminution of power is to be understood in this."

44. *Petri Abaelardi opera,* edd. Victor Cousin and Charles Jourdain (Paris: Aug. Durand, 1849-59), 2:144.

45. Ed. Bernhard Geyer, *Beiträge zur Geschichte der Philosophie und Theologie des Mittelalters* 21, Part 3 (1927): 442-43.

46. PL 178:1095C: "What is just to be done, it is unjust to forego."

outlooks of these two men, clarifying each by contrast.

Proposition 2 is a simpler example of misunderstanding. This is revealed by Bernard's alteration of the preposition *ex*, in William of St Thierry's original formulation, to the preposition *de*, along with his omission of part of William's formulation. William's words reveal Abelard's meaning better: *De Spiritu sancto, quod non sit ex substantia Patris et Filii, sicut Filius est ex substantia Patris.* In brief: procession is not generation.[47] Bernard overlooked the point.

In other instances, in the second group, Bernard hit the nail on the head. He and William fixed on solid objections to Abelard's doctrine. The fourth proposition is a good example, especially as a foil for the seventh, which has just been examined. Here too the problem has to do with the power of God, not *vis-à-vis* his goodness, as Bernard read the seventh, but *vis-à-vis* the necessity of the incarnation: *quod Christus non assumpsit carnem, ut nos a jugo dyaboli liberaret.* This time, in contrast to the seventh (if the seventh were to be understood as Bernard understood it), Abelard could not brook any limitation on God's power, and his solution of the dilemma was a form of exemplarism: *in nos tam verbo quam exemplo instituendo usque ad mortem perstitit.*[48] It was of course unacceptable.

The best example is perhaps the thirteenth. It may be recalled that the first two *capitula* had been taken over by Bernard from William's list, and that they were concerned with Abelard's doctrine of the Trinity, which was after all the point of origin of his theology. Unfortunately for any clear and substantial issue, the first was quoted out of context and the second was altered by Bernard, providing the word-conscious schoolman (whose life-long concern had been exact meanings) with a defense against these charges.[49] However, Bernard got right to

---

47. *Theologia Scholarium, Balliol MS 296*, ff. 39R-40R.

48. PL 178:836A: "He persisted even unto death in teaching us by word and by example."

49. Paul Ruf and Martin Grabmann, "Ein neuaufgefundenes Bruchstück der Apologia Abaelards," in *Sitzungsberichte der Bayerischen Akademie der Wissenschaften, Philosophisch-historische Abteilung*, 1930, pp. 13-18; *Theologia Scholarium, Balliol MS. 296*, ff 39R-41R; H. Ostlender, "Die Theologia Scholarium des Peter Abaelard," in *Beiträge zur Geschichte der Philosophie und Theologie des Mittelalters*, supplementary volume 3 (1935), pp. 276-78.

the heart of the matter in the thirteenth proposition, which was his own contribution to the list, not William's: *Quod ad Patrem, qui ab alio non est, proprie vel specialiter attineat omnipotentia, non etiam et sapientia et benignitas.* One of the foundations of Abelard's doctrine of the Trinity was his doctrine of the attributes, *potentia, sapientia* and *benignitas*, as the basis of the distinction of the persons.[50] There is no answer to Bernard's charge to be found in Abelard's writing. It is a substantive issue, and historically Abelard's theology on this point was rejected.

The conclusion then is that detailed examination of the *capitula* reveals the distinction between Abelard the schoolman, steeped in grammar and logic, concerned with fine distinctions, and Bernard. What was Bernard? It seems clear from the above details that he was not a schoolman in the sense that Abelard and others were, but that his powerful intellect was of a different sort: he was intuitively right on some points.

The others incidentally seem to include to some extent William of St Thierry. Comparison of the *Disputatio* of William[51] and the *Letter 190* of Bernard, reveals that William has much more of the scholastic quality than Bernard. William had spent some time in the schools at Laon, before he entered the abbey of Saint Nicaise at Reims in 1113.[52]

The above presentation itself has been scholastic, that is Abelardian, in character, engaging in some word analysis and all that goes with it. There is a place for some intuitive, Bernardine insights, too. It would not be fair to judge Bernard by Abelardian standards alone. A complete picture may be gained by judging both men by both standards. After all both men and both of the institutions that they stood for and renewed, the schools

50. *Theologia Scholarium*, I, viii-x, PL 178:989-995: power, wisdom and goodness.

51. William of St Thierry, *Disputatio adversus Petrum Abaelardum*, PL 180: 249-82.

52. The fact that William of St Thierry studied at Loan and entered St Nicaise in 1113 has been fairly commonly held by writers following Déchanet, but it was seriously challenged in a recent thesis passed at the Catholic University of America: S. Ceglar, *William of St Thierry: The Chronology of his Life.* . . . (Ann Arbor: University Microfilms, 1971). [Ed.'s note.]

and the monastic orders, have made enormous contributions to the western world in the second millenium. We hardly need to be reminded how these institutions are threatened at this time. Renewal will bring change, no doubt. What happened at Sens cannot be undone, but we may at least learn a lesson from it that there may be truth and fecundity in diverse views, that it pays to continue discussions, and that there is a place for both logic and intuition.

Edward Little

Claremont, California

## APPENDIX

There are many versions of the list of nineteen *capitula* associated with the Council of Sens. The result is obviously much confusion. Of the council itself there are no formal records. The reports of the archbishops of Sens and Reims are the nearest thing to them, and contain no lists. In fact it now seems possible that the council never formally considered the full list of nineteen propositions.[53] All these points, and those that follow, are discussed in detail in this writer's 1969 dissertation in Montreal.[54]

The list that follows seems to have a claim to priority over all others, because it is the earliest, if not the original one. It is the list appended to Bernard's *Letter 190,* given as Leopold Grill gives it from *MS. Heiligenkreuz 226,* in his article "Die neunzehn Capitula. . . ."[55] Jean Leclercq's edition of the list, from other MSS, of *Letter 190,* differs only in these barely significant details: proposition 4, read *i* for *j* and *y*; 6, read *aliquod* for *aliquid*; 7, read *possit Deus* for *Deus possit*; 8, read *contraximus*; 9, read *adscribendum*; 11, read *etiam* for *et*; 12, read *nec melior nec peior* and add *homo* at end; 15, read *i* for *y* in *diabolus,* and read *sive* for *vel.*

The list given in Abelard's *Apologia Ne juxta Boetianum,*

53. See note 18.
54. See note 20.
55. See note 18.

which was followed by J. Rivière and preferred by Denzinger-Schönmetzer, differs slightly in its text and arrangement. Since this Apology of Abelard appears to be a response to *Letter 190* (containing a nearly *verbatim* quotation of the closing words, as edited by Grill), it seems appropriate to follow the prior text, giving the accusations in the words of the accuser.

### THE NINETEEN PROPOSITIONS

1. *Quod Pater sit plena potentia, Filius quaedam potentia, Spiritus Sanctus nulla potentia.* That the Father is full power, the Son a certain power, the Holy Spirit no power.

2. *Quod Spiritus Sanctus non sit de substantia Patris aut Filii.* That the Holy Spirit is not of the substance of the Father or the Son.

3. *Quod Spiritus Sanctus sit anima mundi.* That the Holy Spirit is the world-soul.

4. *Quod Christus non assumpsit carnem, ut nos a jugo dyaboli liberaret.* That Christ did not assume flesh to liberate us from the yoke of the devil.

5. *Quod neque Deus et homo, neque haec persona quae Christus est, sit tertia persona in Trinitate.* That neither God and man, nor this person which Christ is, is the third person in the Trinity.

6. *Quod liberum arbitrium per se sufficiat ad aliquid bonum.* That free choice by itself suffices for something good.

7. *Quod ea solummodo Deus possit facere vel dimittere, vel eo modo tantum, vel eo tempore quo facit, non alio.* That God can do or forego only those things, or only in that manner, or at that time, in which he does, not in another.

8. *Quod non traximus culpam ex Adam, sed poenam tantum.* That we did not contract guilt from Adam, but only penalty.

9. *Quod non peccaverunt, qui Christum ignorantes crucifixerunt, et quod non sit culpae ascribendum quidquid fit per ignorantiam.* That they did not sin, who, ignorant,

crucified Christ, and that whatever is done through ignorance is not to be ascribed to guilt.

10. *Quod in Christo non fuerit spiritus timoris Domini.* That
in Christ there had not been a spirit of fear of the Lord.

11. *Quod potestas ligandi atque solvendi apostolis tantum
data sit, non et successoribus eorum.* That the power of
binding and loosing was given only to the apostles, and
not to their successors.

12. *Quod propter opera nec peior nec melior efficiatur.* That
on account of works neither better nor worse is brought
about.

13. *Quod ad Patrem, qui ab alio non est, proprie vel specialiter attineat omnipotentia, non etiam et sapientia et benignitas.* That to the Father, who is not from another,
properly or specially belongs omnipotence, not however
wisdom and goodness.

14. *Quod etiam castus timor excludatur a futura vita.* That
also chaste fear is excluded from future life.

15. *Quod dyabolus immittat suggestiones per appositionem
lapidum vel herbarum.* That the devil instigates suggestions by the application of stones or herbs.

16. *Quod adventus in fine saeculi possit attribui Patri.* That
the advent at the end of the world can be attributed to
the Father.

17. *Quod Deus nec debeat nec possit mala impedire.* That
God neither ought nor can prevent evil.

18. *Quod anima Christi per se non descendit ad inferos, sed
per potentiam tantum.* That the soul of Christ itself did
not descend to Hell, but only through its power.

19. *Quod neque opus neque voluntas neque concupiscentia,
neque delectatio quae movet eam, peccatum sit, nec de-
bemus eam velle extingui.* That neither the deed nor the
will nor the desire, nor the delight which moves it, is a
sin, nor ought we wish to extinguish it.

Bernard's nineteen propositons are a re-working of a list of
thirteen, which William of St Thierry had included in a letter
he had written to Bernard and to Bishop Geoffrey of Char-

tres.[56] Bernard took some of William's propositions unchanged
(William's no. 3, 5); he altered some (William's no. 4, 6, 7, 8,
10, 11, 13); he omitted some (William's no. 1, 2, 9, 12); he
added some of his own (Bernard's no. 7, 10, 11, 12, 13, 14,
16, 17, 18). *Haec sunt ergo capitula ex opusculis ejus collecta,
quae vobis offerenda putavi.* "These therefore are the propositions culled from his little works, which I think are to be
offered to you:"

### WILLIAM OF ST THIERRY'S THIRTEEN PROPOSITIONS

1. *Quod fidem definit aestimationem rerum quae non vi-
   dentur.* That he defines faith as an opinion of things that
   are not seen.

2. *Quod impropria dicit esse in Deo nomina Patris, et Filii,
   et Spiritus sancti, sed descriptionem hanc esse plenitudinis summi boni.* That he calls improper in God the
   names of Father and Son and Holy Spirit, but this description is of the fullness of the highest good.

3. *Quod Pater sit plena potentia, Filius quaedam potentia,
   Spiritus sanctus nulla potentia.* That the Father is full
   power, the Son a certain power, the Holy Spirit no power.

4. *De Spiritu sancto, quod non sit ex substantia Patris et
   Filii, sicut Filius est ex substantia Patris.* Concerning
   the Holy Spirit, that he is not out of the substance of
   the Father and the Son, as the Son is out of the substance of the Father.

5. *Quod Spiritus sanctus sit anima mundi.* That the Holy
   Spirit is the world-soul.

6. *Quod libero arbitrio, sine adjuvante gratia, bene possumus et velle et agere.* That from free choice, without as-
   sisting grace, we can will and do well.

---

56. *Letter 326,* PL 182-532A-C. This point, the authorship, has been subject
to further discussion by Father Leclercq and the present writer, to be reported in
a later publication, "The Source of the *Capitula* of Sens (1140)," a paper
delivered at the Conference on Medieval Studies, May 1-3, 1972, at Western
Michigan University, Kalamazoo, Michigan.

7. *Quod Christus non ideo assumpsit carnem et passus est ut nos a jure diaboli liberaret.* That Christ did not for this reason assume flesh and suffer, to liberate us from the law of the devil.

8. *Quod Christus Deus et homo non est tertia persona in Trinitate.* That Christ, God and man, is not the third person in the Trinity.

9. *Quod in sacramento altaris in aere remaneat forma prioris subtantiae.* That in the sacrament of the altar the form of the prior substance remains in air.

10. *Quod suggestiones diabolicas per physicam dicit fieri in hominibus.* That he says diabolical suggestions are brought about in men by natural science.

11. *Quod ab Adam non trahimus originalis peccati culpam, sed peonam.* That from Adam we do not get the guilt of original sin, but the penalty.

12. *Quod nullum sit peccatum, nisi in consensu peccati et contemptu Dei.* That there is no sin, except in consent to the sin and in contempt of God.

13. *Quod dicit concupiscentia, et delectatione, et ignorantia nullum peccatum committi; et hujusmodi non esse peccatum, sed naturam.* That he says in concupiscence, delight, and ignorance no sin is committed; and things of this sort are not sin, but nature.

# CHARISMATIC AND GREGORIAN LEADERSHIP
# IN THE THOUGHT OF BERNARD OF CLAIRVAUX

**B**ERNARD OF CLAIRVAUX is surely one of the most outstanding figures in the history of western civilization. As Achille Luchaire says: "To recount his life would be to write the history of the monastic orders, of the reform, of orthodox theology, of heretical doctrines, of the Second Crusade, of the destinies of France, Germany, and Italy, for a period of almost forty years."[1] Bernard's central role in the life of his time poses an obvious problem: how was his leadership reconciled with the leadership of the pope?

The very fact that in his treatise *On Consideration* Bernard ventured to criticize the life of the pope and his court and to prescribe what should be done to remedy what he felt to be an unsatisfactory situation is of great significance. Indeed, Professor Haydn V. White concludes that with Bernard one can recognize a reaction against the Gregorian concept of ecclesiastical leadership and the assertion of a monastic concept of leadership fundamentally at odds with it. Professor White sees an incompatibility between the Gregorian concept of ecclesiastical leadership, in which the power of the pope inheres in his office, and the charismatic doctrine of leadership, accord-

---

1. A. Luchaire, *Les premiers Capétiens (987-1137)* (*Histoire de France*, ed. Ernest Lavisse, II/2; n.p., 1911), p. 266. This enthusiastic statement is supported by recent scholars, at least to the extent that it is ". . . ohne viel Übertreibung. . . ." See Adriaan H. Bredero, *Bernhard von Clairvaux im Wiederstreit der Historie* (Institut für europäische Geschichte, Mainz, *Vorträge*, 44; Wiesbaden, 1966), p. 14.

ing to which power is conferred in virtue of the moral suprem-
acy of the leader.[2]

Indeed, the epistemological presuppositions apparently inherent in Bernard's treatise *On Consideration* would seem to
bear out Professor White's thesis. Bernard apparently intended
through this treatise to impose upon the pope the mystical
method of attaining truth; he seems to have urged Pope Eugenius III to adopt an epistemology more like that of a monk than
the intellectualism associated with the Gregorian prelate.[3] Bernard would have the pope practice the monastic exercise of
consideration because:

> The creature of heaven already possesses the means through
> which he can contemplate invisible things. He sees the Word,
> and in the Word he sees what has been made through the
> Word. He has no need to beg knowledge of the Maker from
> the things which have been made. Nor does he descend to
> them even in order to know them, for he sees them there
> where they are far better then they are in themselves. Con-
> sequently, he does not require the medium of a bodily sense
> to reach them; he is his own sense and he senses them them-
> selves. The best kind of vision occurs when you are self-
> sufficient and need nothing in order to know everything you
> wish to know. . . . Is not the heart of God to be seen there
> [in the temple of the Lord]? Is it not shown there what is
> the good, the acceptable, the perfect will of God—good in
> itself, pleasing in its effects, acceptable to those enjoying it,
> perfect to those who are perfect and who seek nothing be-
> yond it? His heart of mercy lies open, his thoughts of peace
> lie revealed, the riches of his salvation, the mysteries of his
> good will, the secrets of his kindness, which are hidden from

2. Haydn V. White, "The Gregorian Ideal and Saint Bernard of Clairvaux," *Journal of the History of Ideas*, 21 (1960): 321-48. See also the same author's *The
Conflict of Papal Leadership Ideals from Gregory VII to Bernard of Clairvaux
with Special Reference to the Schism of 1130* (Diss. University of Michigan, 1955),
*passim.*

3. White, "The Gregorian Ideal . . . ," p. 346.

mortals and beyond the comprehension of even the elect.[4]

From this, it would seem that ecclesiastical leadership would depend upon the attaining of the loftiest sort of insight not by the Gregorian program of education, study of the liberal arts, practice in the rules of curial life, and experience in diplomatic and military affairs.[5] Rather, the insights necessary for leadership were to be obtained by a life of monastic piety.

Jean Leclercq has explained this apparent appeal to the pope to practice a monastic exercise by reference to the fact that Eugenius had been a Cistercian monk before his election to the papacy;[6] Bernard was simply urging him to continue the contemplative life.[7] However, there is another and more complete explanation of Bernard's purpose; for Bernard did not define the mystical act of contemplation and consideration in the same way, although he often used the words interchangeably. He gave Eugenius this definition of consideration:

First of all, consider what it is I call consideration. For I do not want it to be understood as entirely synonymous with contemplation, because the latter concerns more what is known about something while consideration pertains more to the investigation of what is unknown. Consequently, contemplation can be defined as the true and sure intuition of the mind concerning something, or the apprehension of truth without doubt. Consideration, on the other hand, can be defined as thought searching for truth, or the searching of a mind to discover truth. Nevertheless, both terms are customarily used interchangeably.[8]

4. Csi, 5, 1, 1 and 5, 4, 9. PL 182:788-89 and 793. Also found in the edition by Jean Leclercq et al., *Opera* (Romae, 1957-), III, 467-68, 474. I am indebted to Professor Elizabeth T. Kennan who has allowed me to use her translation of the *De consideratione* soon to be published in the *Cistercian Fathers Series*. I have not always followed her translation, and any errors are thus mine not hers.

5. White, "The Gregorian Ideal...," p. 331.

6. See Horace K. Mann, *The Lives of the Popes in the Early Middle Ages* (2nd ed., London and St Louis, Mo., 1925-1932), 9, 131-34.

7. Jean Leclercq, *Saint Bernard mystique* (Bruges, 1948), p. 198.

8. Csi, 2, 2, 5. PL 182:745. *Opera*, III, 414.

Bernard saw consideration as an application of reason rather than as a revelation of truth; he regarded consideration as an intellectual process, not an intuitive grasp of reality. Consideration was then not strictly a monastic method and it was thus not inconsistent for Bernard to recommend it to the pope. On the other hand, Bernard did not completely identify consideration with the application of reason to theological propositions as it was carried on in the schools; for it should be noted that he distinguished three types of consideration:

> If it is acceptable, let us call the first consideration dispensive, the second estimative, the third speculative. . . . Consideration is dispensive when it uses the senses and sense objects in an orderly and social manner to win God's favor. Consideration is estimative when it prudently and diligently scrutinizes and ponders everything to discover God. Consideration is speculative when it recollects itself and, insofar as it is aided by God, frees itself in order to contemplate God.[9]

It would seem that the last type of consideration, the speculative, is identical with contemplation; this view is borne out by Bernard's choice of the ecstacies of St Paul to exemplify speculative consideration.[10] However, when one remembers that Bernard defined consideration in terms of a process or action rather than as an experience of attaining knowledge, this argument loses some of its force. Yet perhaps the difficulty can be solved by examining the context of the foregoing quotation; Bernard prefaced his explanation of the different types of consideration with this remark:

> Moreover, these three [steps toward invisible things] occur together when consideration, even in the place of its exile, is strengthened by the efforts of virtue and the assistance of grace and either restrains sensuality so it does not grow haughty, or constrains it so it does not stray, or flees it so it cannot corrupt. In the first instance, consideration is more

9. Csi, 5, 2, 4. PL 182:789-90. *Opera*, III, 469.
10. Csi, 5, 2, 3. PL 182:789. *Opera*, III, 469.

powerful, in the second more free, in the third more pure: indeed, that flight is made with the wings of purity and of ecstacy.[11]

It would seem that Bernard regarded speculative consideration as that activity of the intellect which aimed at purifying the soul in preparation for the mystical experience;[12] indeed, it should be realized that the first step of knowledge in Bernard's mystical epistemological system was humility, which he thought to be a result of a process of rational self-examination.[13] Consideration was thus a necessary part of the mystical path to knowledge—it helped supply the wing of purity with which the flight of the spirit was made—but it was not the same as contemplation—the wing of ecstasy was necessary too. Bernard saw consideration as a tool in the spiritual life which could be used by monks, secular clergy, or laity;[14] the monk was to use consideration as a necessary preliminary to contemplation, while the lay person, priest, or prelate living with the cares and distractions of the world was to maintain his contact with heavenly things through consideration.

However, to say that consideration was not exclusively a monastic practice is not to say that there were not serious implications for the society of Bernard's time in his admonition to the pope to spend his time in consideration. Bernard knew consideration was not an activity then common in the Roman curia; Bernard wrote:

What is more servile and more unworthy, especially for the Supreme Pontiff, than every day, or rather every hour, to sweat over such affairs [hearing lawsuits] for the likes of these. Tell me this, when are we to pray or to teach the people? When are we to build up the Church (I Cor 14:4) or

11. Ibid.
12. An example of how consideration was valued by Bernard in the mystical life is to be found in I Nov 1, 2. PL 183:345. *Opera,* V, 305.
13. Hum, 7, 21. PL 182:953. *Opera,* III, 32.
14. It would seem that Bernard admonished Melisande, queen of Jerusalem, to practice consideration in his Ep 289, 2. PL 182:495.

meditate on the law (Ps 1:2)? Oh yes, every day laws resound through the palace, but these are the laws of Justinian, not of the Lord.[15]

If Bernard considered that the study and use of canon law were inappropriate for a pope and his court (as this quotation would seem to imply), what was to be the pope's source of knowledge of those things which were necessary to the proper discharge of his office? Bernard had the following answer:

Now concerning justice, one of the four virtues, is it not a fact that consideration guides the mind into conformity with this virtue? For the mind must reflect upon itself to deduce the norm of justice which is not to do to another what one would not wish done to himself, nor deny another what one wishes for himself (Mt 7:12). In these two rules the entire nature of justice is made clear.[16]

Justice was here simplified to its barest and most basic principles, which apparently made a complicated legal system, and the study of it, unnecessary; the pope, it would seem, could be a judge without any education beyond that of the moral training necessary to his own spiritual perfection.

If this attitude toward the attainment of knowledge about justice expresses Bernard's general educational theory with regard to the papacy—if the *On Consideration* was indeed a *speculum paparum*[17]—then the key to Bernard's concept of the proper qualifications for a pope emerges clearly. If the pope's epistemological method (and, hence, his training) was to be linked to holiness rather than to reason—if his insights were a result of spiritual self-examination rather than dialectical exposition—then Bernard's pope would be a pious man rather than a learned one.

Bernard's role in the schism of 1130 gives us an insight into his position. At the Council of Étampes, called by Louis VII,

15. Csi, 1, 4, 5. PL 182:732. *Opera*, III, 398-99.
16. Csi, 1, 8, 10. PL 182:737. *Opera*, III, 405.
17. This is the phrase used by White in his *The Conflict of Papal Leadership Qualifications...*, p. 546.

king of France, to decide the question of the disputed papal election,[18] Bernard made his views known. Significantly, Suger, abbot of Saint Denis, reported that the purpose of the council was to debate the worthiness of the two pretenders rather than the canonicity of their elections.[19] If this was the Leitmotif of the council, the twelfth-century pope was to be judged on the basis of his spiritual proximity to God, and his power would flow from charismatic gifts rather than from his apostolic office. Did Bernard subscribe to this apparent denial of the papal office as the source of a pope's power? Bernard's position is quite clear since he was instrumental in formulating the decision of the council.[20] Bernard's letters persuading others to adopt the position of the council and acknowledge Innocent as pope repeatedly contrasted the virtue of Innocent and the bad conduct of his rival Anacletus; he referred to Innocent's "better reputation,"[21] and the witness of his "pure life," [22] whereas Anacletus was referred to as a "man of sin":

And who else can he be but that man of sin who . . . invaded the holy place which he wanted, not because it was a holy place, but because it was the highest place. He invaded it, I say, and he invaded it with arms, with fire and with bribes, not by the merits and virtues of his life. And he has arrived there and he stands there by the same means that brought him there. [23]

Thus it seems that Bernard, in choosing a pope on the strength of his moral character and spiritual attainment rather than on

18. See Hefele-Leclercq, *Histoire des conciles* (Paris, 1907-1949), 5, première partie, 681.

19. Suger, abbot of Saint Denis, *Vita Ludovici regis VI,* 21. PL 186: 1330-31.

20. See Arnold of Bonneval, *Vita prima, Liber secundus,* 1, 3 (PL 185:270), who represented the council fathers as having completely delegated their authority to Bernard. However, one cannot accept Arnold's position uncritically since "Suger, who was also present, does not ascribe such influence to him." See Elizabeth Kennan, "The 'De consideratione' of St. Bernard of Clairvaux and the Papacy in the Mid-Twelfth Century: A Review of Scholarship," *Traditio,* 23 (1967): 92, n. 80.

21. Ep 125, 2. PL 182:270.

22. Ep 124, 2. PL 182:269.

23. Ep 126, 8. PL 182:276.

the basis of the canonicity of his election, ignored the power and knowledge—apostolic authority—conferred on the pope by virtue of his legally valid attainment of the office of the papacy. Such an attitude would, of course, make the papacy dependent on charismatic power and mystical knowledge and hinge the authority of the papacy on the virtue of the pope. If this were the case the Church would either be run by monks —the men whom Bernard considered to have taken the straightest path to God—or by a pope whose life was monk-like because his leadership hinged on his sanctity. Support for this interpretation lies in the fact that it was a monk who at Étampes chose, or was instrumental in choosing, the true recipient of the papal dignity; Arnold of Bonneval wrote:

> Bernard came to Étampes fasting, having already spent some time in prayer. On arriving there, he found that the king and all the bishops were unanimous in deciding that he should be their spokesman. And although he was loath to do so, he was persuaded by the unanimity of so many good men to do as they wished. He therefore led the discussions, investigating the merits of Innocent and the manner of his election, opening his mouth so that the Holy Spirit might fill it. As the mouthpiece of that assembly, Bernard decided for Innocent. The whole council acclaimed Innocent as rightful pope forthwith, and hymns of praise were sung to God. All subscribed to the election of Innocent and swore their obedience to him.[24]

However, all this is incomplete; Bernard had a more complex standard by which to judge the case. This standard included a recognition of legal as well as moral considerations. In a letter to the bishops of Aquitaine, Bernard spoke of Innocent's virtues, but he also spoke of the requirements of canon law:

> Then if you examine the elections you will at once see that ours is the more honest, more creditable and the first in time. The two first points are proved by the virtues and dignities

24. Arnold of Bonneval, *Vita Prima, Liber secundus*, 1, 3. PL 185:270.

of the electors, and the last is obvious. You will find, I cannot doubt, that the election was made by the more reputable
of the electors. There are the cardinal bishops and priests
and deacons and those who are especially concerned with
the election of a pope in sufficient number to render it valid
according to the decrees of the Fathers. But what about the
consecration? Did we not have the bishop of Ostia to whom
the consecration of a pope especially appertains? Since then
the person elected is the more worthy, the election more
honest and regular, what reason or what pretext have these
people to try to depose him and, against the will of the
Church of God, to set up another over and above him?[25]

Bernard's appeal to the virtue of both the electors and the
elected was associated with his insistence that Innocent's claim
was legal because the form of his election was canonical. This
apparently was Bernard's definitive basis for his selection for
it was constantly repeated, in his letter to Geoffry of Loretto,
for example:

> The Church supports him [Innocent] with good reason, for
> it has learned that his reputation is more fair and his election
> more sound in that his supporters prevailed both in numbers
> and in excellence.[26]

Even in Bernard's description of Anacletus' wickedness quoted
above, the criticism of the anti-pope's taking possession of the
see of Rome by force was based on the opinion that Anacletus
had done it ". . . notwithstanding that a Catholic had been
canonically elected by Catholics. . . ."[27] Bernard continued in
the same place:

> That election of his [Anacletus'] supporters of which he
> makes so much was not an election but a faction, a mere

25. Ep 126, 13. PL 182:280.
26. Ep 125, 2. PL 182:270. White's contention that Bernard was untruthful
in claiming for his candidate a majority ("The Gregorian Ideal . . . ," p. 338) is
at least open to doubt. See Horace K. Mann, *Lives of the Popes,* 9, 9, n. 2. At any
rate, it is clear that Bernard understood that his claimant had a majority, and this
is what is important for the argument.
27. Ep 126, 8. PL 182:276.

shadow and excuse, a cover for his malice. It could be called an election, but to do so would be impudent and a lie. The authentic decree of the Church still holds; after the first election there cannot be a second. When the first election has taken place a second is not an election at all, it is completely null. Even if the first election did take place with less solemnity and order than the second, as the enemies of unity contend, how can anyone presume to hold a second without first discussing the manner of the former and suppressing it by judgment. For this reason whoever hastens to thrust himself forward and rashly lay hands upon a usurper, in spite of the Apostolic injunction, "Do not inconsiderately lay hands on anyone," they, I say, have the greater sin, they are the authors of the schism, they are the principals of this great mischief.[28]

Even in his opposition to calling a general council to settle the schism, Bernard made an appeal to the legality of his case and only obliquely to the virtue of his candidate:

Let us grant, for the sake of argument, that God may change his decision, call a council together from the ends of the earth, and suffice to have the matter judged twice over. Whom, in such a case, would they choose as judges? All have taken sides in the matter and would not easily agree upon a judgment. Such a council would be rent by faction and lead to even more quarrelling rather than to peace. Then I should like to know to whom that schismatic would entrust Rome which, after having desired it for so long, he has at last got into his clutches at great labor and expense and which he possesses with such great pride and would be so ashamed to lose. If he should lose his suit and not his city the whole world would have assembled for nothing. Why otherwise should he who has been despoiled of everything [Innocent] enter upon this cause? Neither the laws nor the canons oblige him to do so. I say this not because I distrust the justice of our cause, but because I distrust the cunning of our adversaries.[29]

28. Ibid.
29. Ep 126, 12. PL 182:279-80.

If, however, Bernard considered that the canonical argument was valid, why did he resort to the argument regarding the virtue of the two candidates? Surely, a consideration of the virtue problem would provide material out of which Bernard could forge conviction in the minds of his audience by using the hammer of his explosive rhetoric:

> Innocent, the anointed of the Lord, has been set up for the fall and rise of many. Those who are of God have freely chosen him; but he who stands over against him is either the Antichrist or his follower.[30]

It might be asked, however, whether this is a sufficient reason for Bernard's insistence on the virtue of his candidate. Bernard Jacqueline presents a theory which would seem to clarify this question still further. According to Jacqueline, Bernard knew Yvo of Chartres' answer to the problem of a contested election, namely, that the merits of the competitors should be taken into account.[31] It has not been proven that Bernard actually was aware of this opinion.[32] Yet it seems most probable that Bernard had read Yvo, for he did make reference to another principle of canon law in such cases also found in Yvo's work, namely, that when one election has been held, a second is invalid.[33] In addition, Yvo held that the question of a simoniacal election (which Bernard insisted had been the case with Anacletus) was not only a moral question, but was also one on which the canonicity of an election depended.[34] If Jacqueline is correct in his analysis, then Bernard's consideration

---

30. Ep 124, 1. PL 182:268.

31. See Ivo of Chartres, *Panomiae*, 3, 6. PL 161:1130. See Bernard Jacqueline, "Bernard et le schisme d'Anaclet II," *Bernard de Clairvaux* (Commission d'histoire de l'Ordre de Cîteaux, [*Etudes et documents*], III; Paris, 1953), pp. 349-54. The difficulty of deciding a papal election strictly on the basis of procedure seems to have been apparent to Suger who mentioned the problem of the Roman mob as a reason for deciding the issue on the question of the virtue of the candidates. Suger, abbot of Saint Denis, *op. et loc. cit.* (above, note 19).

32. Yvo attributed this opinion to St Leo the Great. Jacqueline, *op. cit.*, p. 351.

33. Yvo of Chartres, *Decreti*, 5, cap. 359. PL 161:432. Again there is no reference by Bernard to this work; it is simply that the doctrines are the same.

34. Yvo of Chartres, *Decreti*, 5, cap. 75. PL 161:351.

of the virtues of Innocent and Anacletus was itself an attempt to judge canonically and no conflict of charismatic and Gregorian qualifications for leadership is implied. But, as I have said, this argument is not absolutely conclusive.

Bernard did make clear his position on the power of the pope; indeed he used the expression *"plenitudo potestatis."*[35] The pope was, of course, to use his power to promote the spiritual welfare of his flock. But what if the pope failed to meet his obligations: if the pope's power were based on his moral superiority, would he not have to be deposed? By whom? How does one know who is morally superior? All of these questions are crucial in a society with charismatic leadership.

Was it Bernard's position that the pope exercised power because of his moral superiority or that the pope's power was rooted in the office itself? Bernard answered this question explicitly in writing to Innocent II about the errors of Abelard:

The danger and scandals which are coming to the surface in the Kingdom of God, especially those which touch the faith, ought to be referred to your apostolic authority. For I judge it fitting that there most of all, the losses suffered by the faith should be repaired, where faith cannot suffer defect. This, truly, is the prerogative of your see. For to what other person has it ever been said, "I have prayed for you, Peter, that your faith fail not"? Therefore that which follows is required from the successor of Peter: "And when you are converted, strengthen your brothers." The time is come, most loving Father, for you to recognize your primacy, to prove your zeal, to do honor to your ministry. In this plainly you fulfill the office of Peter whose seat you occupy, if by

35. See Ep 131, 2. PL 182:286-87. Other references to the extent of papal power are found in Csi, 3, 2, 6 (PL 182:761; *Opera*, III, 435); Csi, 2, 6, 10 (PL 182: 748; *Opera*, III, 417); Csi, 4, 3, 7 (PL 182:776; *Opera* III, 454); Ep 156, 1-2 (PL 182:463-64); and Csi, 2, 6, 13 (PL 182:749; *Opera*, III, 420). For an excellent discussion of the literature on the meaning of *plenitudo potestatis* and Bernard's view of papal power, see Kennan, "The 'De consideratione' . . . ," pp. 95-99. Professor Kennan's own views are found on pp. 114-15, and I find them thoroughly convincing.

your admonition you strengthen the hearts that are wavering in the faith.[36]

Thus Bernard thought that the pope could not err in matters of faith because of his descent from Peter, and that it was because he held the office of Peter that he was able to avoid error.[37] Bernard clarified his position on the means by which the pope received his power in asking Eugenius:

Who are you? The high priest, the Supreme Pontiff. You are the prince of the bishops, you are the heir of the Apostles; in primacy you are Abel, in governing you are Noah, by patriarchate you are Abraham, by order you are Melchisedech, in dignity you are Aaron, in authority you are Moses, in judgment you are Samuel, in power you are Peter, by anointing you are Christ. You are the one to whom the keys have been given, to whom the sheep have been entrusted. It is true that there are other doorkeepers of heaven and other shepherds of flocks; but you are more glorious than all of these, to the degree that you have inherited a name more excellent than theirs. They have flocks assigned to them, one flock to each; to you all are assigned, a single flock to a single shepherd.[38]

In analyzing these statements one is presented with two different attributes of the papal dignity, the pope's power and the pope's knowledge. In each of these cases, Bernard thought the source of the attribute was Apostolic succession from Peter, not the pope's proximity, by reason of his moral purity, to God, the source of the knowledge and power. This is definitely a "Gregorian" concept.[39] Bernard preached the same doctrine to his monks:

36. Abael, *praefatio*. PL 182:1053-54.
37. This directly contradicts White's contention that Bernard would have the pope not so much a second Peter as a second Paul. See "The Gregorian Ideal . . . ," p. 343.
38. Csi, 2, 8, 15. PL 182:751. *Opera*, III, 423.
39. The appropriateness of the adjective "Gregorian" is open to doubt; I have used it because of White's practice. See Kennan, "The 'De consideratione' . . . ," p. 106.

And without the Key, how could anyone dare attempt to enter, rather say, to intrude into the divine treasure of wisdom and knowledge? "He that enters not by the door, he is a thief and a robber." Peter, therefore, shall enter because Peter has received the keys. Yet not alone shall he enter, for, if he pleases, he may introduce me with him as he may also exclude another, according to his pleasure, by the wisdom and authority bestowed on him from above. And what are these keys, my brothers? They are the power of opening and the power of shutting and the power of discriminating between those who are to be excluded. It is not in the serpent that the "treasures of wisdom and knowledge" are laid up, but in Christ. Therefore the serpent could not communicate the wisdom which he did not himself possess; but it was truly communicated by him by whom it was truly possessed. Neither was the serpent possessed of power, since he had not received it. It was given by Christ and given to Peter.[40]

Hence Peter's authority was not only to be felt and acknowledged in the world, but it was to be acknowledged even by those who had in mysticism their own source of knowledge and in charisma their own source of miraculous power.

How is it possible that Bernard the mystic could have acknowledged the apostolic source of the pope's knowledge and power and have at the same time been true to his mysticism? It seems quite clear that just as Bernard acknowledged the efficacy of both mysticism and reason as epistemological tools,[41] so too he could recognize the different but parallel sources of power in charisma and apostolic authority. Bernard was quite explicit in his recognition of these two sources of power;

40. SC, 69, 4-5. PL 183:1114. *Opera*, II, 204-205.

41. See my "Abelard and Saint Bernard of Clairvaux," *Papers of the Michigan Academy of Science, Arts, and Letters*, 46 (1961), 493-501; "Bernard of Clairvaux and Scholasticism," *ibid.*, 48 (1963), 265-77; "The Epistemological Value of Mysticism in the Thought of Bernard of Clairvaux," *Studies in Medieval Culture*, I (1964), 48-58; and "The Social Theory of Bernard of Clairvaux," *Studies in Medieval Cistercian History Presented to Jeremiah F. O'Sullivan (Cistercian Studies*, 13; Spencer, Massachusetts, 1971), pp. 35-48.

in listing those who had supported Innocent against Anacletus
he wrote:

> It [the legitimacy of Innocent's claim] is recognized as the
> judgment of God by Archbishops Walter of Ravenna, Hil-
> degar of Terragona, Norbert of Magdeburg and Conrad of
> Salzburg. It is known and accepted as the judgment of God
> by Bishops Equipert of Münster, Hildebrand of Pistoia, Ber-
> nard of Pavia, Landulf of Asti, Hugh of Grenoble, and Ber-
> nard of Parma. The singular prestige, the outstanding sanc-
> tity and authority of these prelates, respected even by their
> enemies, have easily persuaded me, who occupies a lower
> position both in office and in virtue, to follow them whether
> right or wrong.[42]

With due allowance for Bernard's humility regarding his virtue,
it can be seen that he placed himself below these men on two
accounts. Thus he must have recognized the existence of two
hierarchies within the Church, the charismatic hierarchy of
virtue and the hierarchy of office. As a consequence, even if
Jacqueline is wrong in identifying as canonical Bernard's appeals to the virtue of the candidates in deciding the schism of
1130, it still follows that Bernard recognized both arguments
as valid—the appeal to one not excluding the efficacy of the
other.

In view of this, how is it possible that Bernard could have
written the *On Consideration* to urge the pope to retreat to
the quiet of consideration and in this way to attain the knowledge requisite to the proper discharge of his function in society? The answer becomes clear when one also remembers that
Bernard had written to Cardinal Robert Pullen urging him to
apply his experience to the supervision of the newly-elected
Cistercian pope, Eugenius III.[43] The tone of the letter leads one
to conclude that in addition to his Apostolic authority and
knowledge and the knowledge obtained in spiritual practices,
Eugenius was to receive advice on the practical matters of being

42. Ep 126, 9. PL 182:277-78.
43. Ep 362. PL 182:563-64.

pope from one who through experience had gained a knowledge of the affairs of the curia. Bernard's insistence that the
pope employ consideration in order to discover the principles
of justice upon which to base his decisions did not, therefore,
mean that intellectual preparation for the pope and his curia
and the use of canon law in the activites of the papal court
were prohibited. Bernard meant to balance the value of the
study of canon law and experience in the practical affairs of
the papal court with the insights, gained by meditation, into
the principles upon which the law of the Church should be
based. Bernard would have had the pope retire from the every-
day business of the papal court[44] to ascertain the bases upon
which he and his officials would make decisions about this business; Bernard's criticism of the pope's way of life did not mean
that consideration was to be the exclusive training of the pope,
but rather that this spiritual element needed strengthening.
There is consequently no question of any conflict in Bernard's
mind between apostolic authority, charisma, and experience;
but rather one supplemented and enhanced the other, remem-
bering always that succession to the office of Peter was the essential attribute of the pope and his primary source of power.[45]
The charismatic and ecclesiastical hierarchies were then ideal-
ly to correspond as closely as possible; the pope was to be a
virtuous man. But the authority and power of the pope were
not conditioned by his virtue; he could be an evil man and
still command obedience; Bernard remarked on this subject:

"The successor of the Apostles," they [the heretics] say,
"are all sinners, archbishops, bishops, and priests, and therefore are not fit to administer sacraments or receive them."
Are, then, these two things, to be a bishop and to be a sin-

44. Bernard did not mean to have the pope retire from his activities as judge but
rather to judge only those cases which were so important as to demand his attention. See Csi, 1, 7, 8. PL 182:736. *Opera*, III, 402-404.
45. Bernard's *Life of St Malachy* is filled with incidents illustrating the com-
plementary nature of his episcopal and charismatic powers. For example, compare
V Mal, 14, 32 with 15, 33. PL 182:1092-93. *Opera*, III, 339-40. White is able to
see only one side of Bernard's view of Malachy; see White, "The Gregorian Ideal
... ," pp. 346-47.

ner, so incompatible that they can never be found in the same person? That is not the case. Caiphas was a high-priest, and how great a sinner was he who pronounced the sentence of death upon the Lord? If you deny that he was a high-priest you contradict the testimony of St John who declares that he was high-priest for that year and that he prophesied. Judas Iscariot was an apostle, having been chosen by Christ himself, in spite of his avarice and sinfulness. Surely you can entertain no doubt of his apostolate, considering that it was the Lord who elected him. He himself said: "Have I not chosen you twelve and one of you is a devil?" Here you are told that one who was a devil has been called to the apostolic office. And do you still deny that it is possible for a sinner to be a bishop? "The Scribes and Pharisees have sat on the chair of Moses," and all that refused to obey them as is due to ecclesiastical superiors were accounted guilty of disobedience to the Lord himself, who gave a command, saying: "Whatsoever they shall say to you, do and observe." It is clear, therefore, that although they were Scribes, although they were Pharisees, although they were the worst of sinners, nevertheless, because they "sat on the chair of Moses," to their authority also must be understood to apply these other words of Christ, "He that hears you hears me, and he that despises you despises me."[46]

Thus, it is clear that Bernard thought that the power of God could be obtained both through succession to office or directly from him.

But what of our original question? How could Bernard's leadership of twelfth-century society and culture be reconciled with papal authority. What happens when the hierarchy of office culminates in a man, the pope, who is not the charismatic leader as was Bernard? In speaking of the Roman rebellion against Eugenius III, Bernard answered this question:

The trouble is in the head, and, for this reason, there is no member of the body so small or so insignificant that it is not affected by it, not even myself. This very great trouble af-

46. SC, 66, 11. PL 193:1100. *Opera*, II, 185-86.

fects even me although I am the least of all, because what affects the head cannot but affect the body of which I am a member. When the head is suffering does not the tongue cry out for the members of the body that the head is in pain, and do not all the members of the body confess by means of the tongue that the head is theirs and the pain too?[47]

It seems that this was an accurate description of Bernard's role in early-twelfth-century society. Although he was the leader of so very many aspects of that society, he disclaimed headship. The legal or coercive practices which a man supports should be a relatively objective index to his values; here it is interesting to note that, in the case of Abelard, the trial was brought about through the agency of Bernard, but the actual condemnation and punishment Bernard considered quite properly pertained to the pope.[48]

Bernard could be the "tongue" for such a large part of early-twelfth-century society because his penetrating analysis of the anatomy of that social body enabled him to express so well the ideals of such a large group. Bernard's extraordinary influence on the society of his time can perhaps be explained by the fact that he not only was a member of the element of society which best expressed the Christian values of so great a part of that society, but he also presented to his contemporaries a rationale for the existence of all other significant elements of that society. Bernard was thus a most powerful spokesman for his age and, therefore, the study of his writings is of immense value for the understanding of his age. But it must be understood that, contrary to Professor White's thesis, Bernard considered that his leadership in no way compromised that of the pope and that he agreed wholeheartedly with the "Gregorian" concept of papal leadership.

John R. Sommerfeldt

Western Michigan University
Kalamazoo, Michigan

47. Ep 243, 2. PL 182:438.
48. See above, pp. 84-85.

# ANTITHESIS AND ARGUMENT IN THE
## *DE CONSIDERATIONE*

S AINT BERNARD is occasionally referred to as the last of the Fathers by historians who wish to capture the conservative nature of his thought in the face of the new dialectical mode of the early scholastics who were his contemporaries. It is clear that Bernard proceeded in his reasoning by a method which was pre-dialectical. He shared with St Augustine and St Gregory the determination to enunciate truth as it pertained to the existential situation. Although his interest in the absolute but somewhat removed truth of theology was acute, his writing was most often practical and immediate. He dealt with the realm of human behavior where paradox is most evident and absolute prescriptions rare. His aim was to define the norm of righteous behavior in the welter of experience. His first task was discovery of right. But beyond this, as a moralist rather than a philosopher, he had a second task: he must persuade his audience so that they would not simply *know* righteousness but would *will* it. In both these tasks, discovery and persuasion, Bernard found the tools of rhetoric more useful than dialectic.

Of the various devices of rhetoric: antithesis, balance, rhythm, appeal to emotion, it was antithesis which was most useful to Bernard in casting the argument of the *De consideratione*. Ironic antithesis was commonly used by classical and medieval writers to heighten the interest of a sentence or of an image. Bernard's choice dictum on flatterers, "It is not the face of the scorpion that you should fear; he stings with his tail," is a

neat example of the method.[1] But in the *De consideratione*
antithesis plays a far larger role than simple dramatic shading
of a sentence. The work, at least insofar as the first four books
are concerned, is a homily on virtue as exercised in the papal
office. And virtue, as a practical matter, is exactly the discovery
and maintainence of the mean between extremes.[2] In his search
for righteousness, then, Bernard will use the rhetorical technique of antithesis to chart human experience, pinpointing
one extreme and then its opposite as he moves to discover the
mean between them. And, once the mean has been discovered,
he will frequently use ironic antithesis to advance it.

Antithesis structures the argument of the *De consideratione*
because it offered Bernard a method almost perfectly suited
to a discussion of virtue. But the peculiar circumstances in
which the treatise was written made the technique doubly useful. St Bernard was addressing himself to an existential situation which was almost unbearably paradoxical. The pope to
whom he wrote was Eugene III, a former monk at Clairvaux.
Bernard's business was to instruct Eugene in the double task
of maintaining his own Cistercian sanctity while generously
fulfilling the demands of the papal office. Yet the demands
generated by the two roles were contradictory. As a Cistercian,
Eugene had been—and still was—dedicated to the perfection
of his own spiritual life. His being was to be centered in prayer,
in study and in contemplation of God. Attainment of the New
Jerusalem was the urgent and all-consuming goal of the monks
trained in St Bernard's monastery. But the papacy overwhelm-
ed its incumbent with business. The office might assume holiness in its holder, but it scarcely fostered it. The pope was

1. St Bernard of Clairvaux, *De consideratione* 4, 9 (J. Leclercq and H.M. Rochais,
ed., *S. Bernardi Opera III: Tractatus et opuscula* [Roma 1963]) 456: *Scorpioni non
est in facie quod formides, sed pungit a cauda.*
2. Bernard does not accept this point as a truism but develops it at length in the
second book. Csi 2, 19. *Opera*, III, 426: *Proinde si consideras quantus es, cogita
etiam qualis, et maxime. Haec te sane consideratio tenet in te, nec a te avolare
sinit, non ambulare in magnis, neque in mirabilibus super te. In te consistito. Non
infra deici, non attolli supra, non evadere in longius, non extendi in latius. Tene
medium, si non vis perdere modum. Locus medius tutus est. Medium sedes modi,
et modus virtus. Omnem extra modum mansionem, sapiens exsilium reputat.*

responsible (or wished to be) for the government of Rome, for the administration of the busiest court in Europe, for the regulation of the entire European hierarchy, for the protection of monastic houses, for the safety of the Holy Land, and for the health and well being of all God's unfortunate: the poor, the widowed, the orphaned. Sheer pressure of work engulfed Eugene and denied him both time and strength to pursue the New Jerusalem. Within the contradictions of this situation, Bernard had to find a right rule for both the man and the office. He did so by examining opposite possibilities, not as Gratian or Abelard did in the hope of flawing one or the other by logic, but in the hope of submerging both in the enunciation of a workable mean between them.

Bernard's argument depends on his description of opposite possibilities for each aspect of the papal office and behavior. He gives elaborate care to establishing the contradictory poles of each situation, for it is in the tension between them that the mean of right action is to be found. The danger for the modern reader, remote from the modes of balance and antithesis in rhetoric, is that he might overlook Bernard's solution in his fascination with the extremes which surround it. Indeed, most of the historians and political analysts who have dealt with the *De consideratione* have fallen into just this error. With peculiar self-confidence, eminent historians have chosen a single set of poles in Bernard's antitheses and advanced these as his "unique view" of papal office. Predictably, interpretations have been as opposite as the poles which engendered them. The *De consideratione* has been called both Gregorian and anti-Gregorian, hierarchical and egalitarian, other worldly and power oriented. At least one noted historian was so confused by Bernard's use of antithesis and contradiction that he dismissed the whole treatise as hopelessly muddle headed.[3]

Even if one recognizes Bernard's use of antithesis, however, his middle ground must be carefully plotted. Arguments in the *De consideratione* are seldom presented systematically. Op-

3. Elizabeth T. Kennan, "The '*De consideratione*' of St Bernard of Clairvaux and the Papacy in the mid-Twelfth Century: A Review of Scholarship," *Traditio* 23 (1967) 73-115, for a discussion of the historiography.

posites are occasionally juxtaposed with no immediate solution offered. Often Bernard's statement of one pole of an antithesis is so impassioned that the reader is drawn to affirm it without waiting for the entire argument to unfold. Sometimes one pole will simply be assumed with the consequence that the discussion becomes lopsided and the median more difficult to trace. Yet each time, Bernard ultimately adopts a moderate position which he accepts, by definition, as virtuous.[4]

At the same time, it must be recognized that Bernard was not interested simply in establishing a theoretical virtue. For an action to be righteous it must be moderate, but it must also be effective. "I seek not gifts but fruit," says the Apostle, and it is the fruit, or the outcome of one's actions, which test whether they are truly virtuous. The *De consideratione* was a work intended for immediate application. The mean must be discovered, seized, acted upon. Only the results could tell whether true moderation and appropriate vigor had been applied.

There were a variety of problems which demanded prompt, righteous action from Eugene. First of these was an understanding of his role among the new temptations and pressures of power. Here Bernard presents in its most classic form the discovery of right by a scrutiny of opposites. "Who are you?" Bernard asks Eugene.

> You are the high priest, the Supreme Pontiff. You are the prince of the bishops; you are the heir of the Apostles; in primacy you are Abel, in governing you are Noah, by patriarchate you are Abraham; by orders you are Melchisedech; in dignity you are Aaron; in authority you are Moses; in judgment you are Samuel; in power you are Peter; by annointing you are Christ.[5]

But, once Eugene's glory in his office is established, Bernard presses the point in a different direction.

---

4. Csi. 1, 11. *Opera*, III, 406.
5. Csi 2, 15. *Opera*, III, 423: *Quis es? Sacerdos magnus, summus Pontifex. Tu princeps episcoporum, tu heres Apostolorum, tu primatu Abel, gubernatu Noe, patriarchatu Abraham, ordine Melchisedech, dignitate Aaron, auctoritate Moyses, iudicatu Samuel, potestate Petrus, unctione Christus.*

You were born a man; you were elected a pope, you were not transformed into a pope . . . . Consider yourself naked, for you came forth naked from your mother's womb. Were you born wearing the mitre? Were you born glittering with jewels or florid with silk, or crowned with feathers, or covered with precious metals? If you scatter all these things and blow them away from the face of your consideration like the morning clouds which quickly pass and rapidly disappear, you will catch sight of a naked man who is poor, wretched, miserable. . . .[6]

Does Bernard mean the pope to be exalted in his office only by the naked sanctity of his own spirit, stripped of the trappings of glory? Yet what greater glory is there than, by unction, to *be* Christ, a claim imitated on a lesser scale by secular rulers who described themselves as "vicars of Christ"? The conceits are opposite, yet they are reconciled by Bernard's rhetoric. By unction, the pope has received the highest office. In it, he is an apostle; he is virtually Christ on earth; yet despite it, he is a man whose sin even the legitimate insignia of office cannot hide. His glory and his power are purely functions of his office.

And what is the office? Is the pope a ruler? Bernard offers another antithesis when he urges,

Glorify your hand and your right arm and deal out vengeance on the nations and punishment on the peoples; bind their kings in chains and their nobles in fetters of iron.[7]

and then warns,

6. Csi 2, 17, 18. *Opera*, III, 425: *Denique illud natus es, mutuatus hoc, non in hoc mutatus. . . . nude nudum consideres, quia nudus egressus es de utero matris tuae. Numquid infulatus? Numquid micans gemmis, aut floridus sericis, aut coronatus pennis, aut suffarcinatus metallis? Si cuncta haec, veluti nubes quasdam matutinas, velociter transeuntes et cito pertransituras, dissipes et exsuffles a facie considerationis tuae, occurret tibi homo nudus, et pauper, et miser, et miserabilis. . . .*

7. Csi 2, 13. *Opera*, III, 420: *Glorifica manum et brachium dextrum in faciendo vindictam in nationibus, increpationes in populis, in alligando reges eorum in compedibus et nobiles eorum in manicis ferreis.*

There is no poison more dangerous for you, no sword more deadly than the desire to rule.[8]

Bernard urges the pope to wield power in an overwhelming metaphor, yet forbids him to rule. The antithesis is clear. But resolution is offered in a compromise. Papal office, Bernard states, is a ministry, not a rule.[9] Dominion, or rule, implies the imposition of personal will. This is the function of princes who can make law by the very force of their wills. By contrast, ministry is severely limited: it is service to explicit charges. Bernard insists that the two concepts are exclusive:

Therefore, go ahead and dare to usurp the office (of pope) as a lord, or as an apostle usurp dominion. Clearly, you are forbidden to do either. If you want to have both of these at the same time, you will lose both. Moreover, you should not think that you are excluded from those about whom God complains, "They have reigned but not by me; princes have arisen but I did not recognize them." . . . Let us listen to the decree which says, "Let the one who is greater among you become lesser, and let the one who is foremost become as a servant."[10]

Ministry is essentially unlike kingship. It is best described in the figure of the teacher or the steward:

Go out into the field of your Lord and consider how even today it abounds in thorns and thistles in fulfillment of the ancient curse. . . . Go out into it not as a lord, but as a stew-

---

8. Csi 3, 2. *Opera,* III, 432: *nam nullum tibi venenum, nullum glrdium plus formido, quam libidinem dominandi.*

9. Csi 2, 10, 11. *Opera,* III, 417, 418.

10. Csi 2, 11. *Opera,* III, 418: *I ergo tu, et tibi usurpare aude aut dominus apostolatum, aut Apostolicus dominatum. Plane ab alterutro prohiberis. Si utrumque simul habere voles, perdes utrumque. Alioquin non te exceptum illorum numero putes, de quibus queritur Deus sic: "Ipsi regnaverunt, et non ex me; principes exstiterunt, et ego non cognovi eos!" . . . audiamus edictum: "Qui major est vestrum," ait, "fiat sicut iunior, et qui praecessor est, sicut qui ministrat."*

ard (*villicus*) to oversee and to manage that for which you must render an account.[11]

The steward has no authority of his own, but derives his position from the power and precepts of his lord. Like the overseer, the pope is bound by the charges of his Lord given in the New Testament. He serves without reference to his own will. Yet his power over the fields entrusted to him is absolute. There is no appeal from it, except to the Lord; no other human agency can approach it. Bernard calls it a *plenitudo potestatis,* a power without bounds.

> The power of others is bound by definite limits; yours extends even over those who have received power over others. If cause exists, can you not close heaven to a bishop, depose him from the episcopacy and even give him over to Satan?[12]

But St Bernard will not rest with this description of absolute papal power. He insists that it must be limited by the pope's own self-restraint. Papal power in action must represent the true mean between personal rule and no rule at all. It must be the exercise of total power entirely without reference to personal interest:

> "Are you greater than your Lord who says, "I have not come to do my will? . . ."" What can be so unworthy of you as your holding everything, yet not being content with it, unless you can strive in some way to make your own the trifles and insignificant elements of all that has been entrusted to you—as if they were not yours already? In this connection also, I want you to recall the parable of Nathan about the man who had a hundred sheep and yet desired one which belonged to

11. Csi 2, 12. *Opera,* III, 419: *Exi in agrum Domini tui, et considera quantis hodieque de veteri maledicto silvescat spinis ac tribulis. . . . Exi in illum, non tanquam dominus, sed tanquam villicus, videre et procurare unde exigendus es rationem.*

12. Csi 2, 16. *Opera,* III, 424: *Aliorum potestas certis artatur limitibus; tua extenditur et in ipsos, qui potestatem super alios acceperunt. Nonne, si causa exstiterit, tu episcopo caelum claudere, tu ipsum ab episcopatu deponere, etiam et tradere Satanae potes?*

a poor man. On this point also, remember the deed, or rather the crime of King Achab, who possessed supreme power but strove to obtain a single vineyard. May God spare you what Achab heard, "You have slain and you have taken possession."[13]

At issue was a practical consideration: the papacy, acting by virtue of its plenitude of power, had made a practice of exempting established monasteries from diocesan supervision and subjecting them to itself alone, thus disrupting the hierarchy and interrupting regular discipline. The results to the monasteries in Bernard's eyes were horrific: loss of virtue, loss of protection, anarchy. Such application of power, even though legal, was proven unrighteous by its results. The pope simply could not tamper with the established hierarchy without bringing the Church into confusion. Thus, in practice, his power was limited by the exact forms of the hierarchy which, after all, had their exemplar in heaven.[14]

The pope's error in issuing blanket exemptions, however, did not stem from the inclusive definition of papal power, but from the intemperate use to which it was put. Bernard makes the point in his conclusion. "What," Eugene is made to ask, "Do you forbid me to dispense?" "No," Bernard answers, "but to *dissipate.* . . ."[15] He goes on to elaborate the moderate position:

Where necessity demands, a dispensation is excusable; where utility requires it, a dispensation is praiseworthy. But this

13. Csi 3, 15. *Opera,* III, 442-443: *"Tune maior Domino tuo, qui ait: 'Non veni facere voluntatem meam?".* . . *Quid item tam indignum tibi, quam ut, totum tenens, non sis contentus toto, nisi minutias quasdam atque exiguas portiones ipsius tibi creditae universitatis, tamquam non sint tuae, satagas, nescio quo modo, adhuc facere tuas? Ubi etiam meminisse te volo parabolae Nathan de homine qui, centum oves habens, unam, quae erat pauperis, concupivit. Huc quoque veniat factum, immo facinus regis Achab, qui rerum summam tenebat, et unam vineam affectavit. Avertat Deus a te quod ille audivit: 'Occidisti, et possedisti.' "*

14. Csi 3, 17. *Opera,* III, 445.

15. Csi 3, 18. *Opera,* III, 445: " *'Quid?'* inquis, *'Prohibes dispensare?'* Non, sed dissipare."

utility must be common to all, not the property of one.[16]

Bernard has returned to his original vision of the papal mean: ministry is exercise of power in the service of all, never in the interest of one.

Papal office and power were by institution spiritual. But in practice, it has often been useful for popes to employ secular tools in the service of that office. The question of their right to do so was particularly exacerbated just at the time Bernard was writing the *De consideratione* by the presence in Rome of Arnold of Brescia who bitterly denounced all the papacy's temporal connections as diabolical.

Bernard himself felt compelled to treat the problem in the context of the morality of office. He began with the difficult question of papal wealth, which was to plague the Church in reform *pronunciamentos* for centuries to come. Initially, he appears to concur with the extreme reform position:

> What else did the holy Apostle leave to you? . . . I am sure of one thing: It is neither gold nor silver; for he himself says, "I do not have silver or gold."[17]

Bernard never really considers the antithesis to apostolic poverty: the absurd notion that popes might rightfully appropriate wealth and enjoy it for its own sake. But even so, he bypasses Arnold's position and characteristically offers a compromise. He envisions a righteous solution which rests once again on the concept of ministry or selflessness in office:

> If you happen to have (gold and silver), use them not for your own pleasure, but to meet the needs of the time. Thus you will be using them as if you were not using them.[18]

16. Csi 3, 18. *Opera,* III, 445: "*Ubi necessitas urget, excusabilis dispensatio est; ubi utilitas provocat, dispensatio laudabilis est. Utilitas, dico, communis, non propria.*"

17. Csi 2, 10. *Opera,* III, 417: "*Nam quid tibi aliud dimisit sanctus Apostolus? . . . Unum scio: non est aurum neque argentum, cum ipse dicat: Argentum et aurum non est mihi.*"

18. Csi 2, 10. *Opera,* III, 417: "*Si habere contingat, utere non pro libitu, sed pro tempore. Sic eris utens illis, quasi non utens.*"

When the initial distinction between the papal office and its holder is maintained, tools in the service of the office, even such potentially dangerous tools as wealth, are morally neutral. Indeed, the productive use of them is a positive good.[19] It is only when the officeholder appropriates them or solicits them, or yearns over them, that they become dangerous.[20]

The same rule holds for the insignia of power with which twelfth-century popes awed, or hoped to awe, the Roman crowds: the crown, the white horse bearing the pontiff, the entourage of attendants. These too were no inheritance from the Apostles. In a famous phrase which has often been taken as a sneer, Bernard compared the contemporary pope with the founder of his office.

> This is Peter, who is known never to have gone in procession adorned with either jewels or silks, covered with gold, carried on a white horse, attended by a knight or surrounded by clamoring servants. . . . In this finery, you are the successor not of Peter, but of Constantine.[21]

The passage probably does sneer, but it does not make an ideological pronouncement, for Bernard goes on to observe that,

> I suggest that these things must be allowed for the time being, but are not to be assumed as a right.[22]

Saint Bernard was convinced that the times in which he and Eugene were living were fraught with exceptional danger for the Church.[23] He was unwilling, therefore, to take a doctri-

---

19. Ibid.
20. Ibid.: *"abusio mala, sollicitudo peior, quaestus turpior."*
21. Csi 4, 6. *Opera,* III, 453; *"Petrus hic est, qui nescitur processisse aliquando vel gemmis ornatus, vel sericis, non tectus auro, non vectus equo albo, nec stipatus milite, nec circumstrepentibus saeptus ministris . . . In his successisti, non Petro, sed Constantino."*
22. Ibid.: *"Consulo toleranda pro tempore, non affectanda pro debito."*
23. Csi 1, 13. *Opera,* III, 408: *"alius inolevit mos, dies alii sunt et alii hominum mores, et tempora periculosa non instant iam, sed exstant. Fraus et circumventio, et violentia, invaluere super terram."*

naire stand on the means by which popes might combat the enemy. As long as the tools were applied to winning the legitimate, God-given aims of the office, and as long as they were useful, then let them be used!

But even in times of peril, would he countenance military force to do the work of Christ? Historical interpretation of Bernard on this point is very vexed.[24] It all hinges on his discussion in the *De consideratione* of the two swords possessed by the Church. The discussion is cryptic, for it is not a major concern in the work. It is set in the larger treatment of Eugene's relationship to his special flock, the people of Rome. His role as their pastor and governor had been distorted beyond recognition by rebellion in the city which had finally driven him into exile. Clearly, only force could restore the shepherd to his flock. Then force them to submit, Bernard urges, but force them with the sword of the word, with the imprecations and anathema of the Lord.[25] If that should fail, however, is there another sword? Can the pope rightfully call out an army? Bernard recoils: "Why would you try to use that sword a second

---

24. A. Fliche, "Bernard et la société civile de son temps," *Bernard de Clairvaux.* Commission d'Histoire de l'Ordre de Citeaux, Abbaye N.D.d'Aiguebelle (Paris, 1953), pp. 355-378; Edouard Jordan, "Dante et saint Bernard," *Bulletin du Jubile.* Comite Français Catholique pour la célébration du sixième centenaire de la mort de Dante Alighieri (Paris, 1921), pp. 267-330; A. J. Carlyle, "The Development of the Theory of the Authority of the Spiritual over the Temporal Power from Gregory VII to Innocent II," *Tijdschrift voor Rechtsgeschiedenis* 5 (1923): 33-44; H. X. Arquillière, "Origines de la théorie des deux glaives," *Studi Gregoriani* 1 (1947): 501-521; J. Leclercq, "L'argument des Deux Glaives dans les controverses politiques du moyen âge: ses origines et son développement," *Recherches de science religieuse* 21 (1931): 299-339; Etienne Gilson, *La philosophie au Moyen Age* (2nd ed. Paris, 1947) pp. 348ff; Gerhart B. Ladner, "Aspects of Medieval Thought on Church and State," *Review of Politics* 9 (1947): 403-422; Id., "Concepts of 'Ecclesia' and 'Christianitas' and their Relation to the Idea of Papal 'Plenitudo Potestatis' from Gregory VII to Boniface VIII," *Misc. Hist. Pont.* 17 (October 1953): 49-78; A.M. Stickler, "De ecclesiae potestate coactiva materiali apud Magistrum Gratianum," *Salesianum* 4 (1942): 2-23; Id., "Il 'Gladius' negli atti dei concili e dei RR. Pontifici sino a Graziano e Bernardo di Clairvaux," *Salesianum* 13 (1951): 414-445; Hartmut Hoffmann, "Die beiden Schwerter im hohen Mittelalter," *Deutsches Archiv für Erforschung des Mittelalters* 20, 1 (1964): 78-114.

25. Csi 4, 7. *Opera*, III, 454: "*Propter hoc, inquam, magis aggredere eos, sed verbo, non ferro.*"

time which you were once ordered to place in its sheath?" he asks.[26] But then, apparently, he equivocates:

> Both the spiritual and material swords . . . belong to the Church, but the latter is drawn for the Church and the former by it. One by the hand of the priest, the other by that of the soldier; but the latter surely is used at the bidding of the priest and by the order of the emperor.[27]

Bernard then does not take the extreme position of denying resort to force. Armed might could be authorized by a pope, but it must be executed by the emperor. Yet in the years between 1145 and 1152, imperial power was mired in Germany and unavailable for any campaign around Rome. In 1149, despairing of help from Germany, Eugene collected an army himself and led it in an assault on Rome which temporarily reestablished him within the walls. It is this drastic solution which Bernard seems to be rejecting here.[28] If anathema will not break the resistance of the Romans and if the emperor cannot subdue them, then the pope must abandon Rome, sacrificing his ministry in the city for the world.[29]

Whether in Rome or in exile, the pope had one truly universal power in society, the power of appellate jurisdiction. It was a power which arose *de jure* from his authority over the Church and *de facto* from the widespread demand for a disinterested,

26. Ibid.: *"Quid tu denuo usurpare gladium tentes, quem semel iussus es reponere in vaginam?"*

27. Ibid.: *"Uterque ergo Ecclesiae, et spiritualis scilicet gladius, et materialis, sed is quidem pro Ecclesia, ille vero et ab Ecclesia exserendus: ille sacerdotis, is militis manu, sed sane ad nutum sacerdotis et iussum imperatoris."*

28. Cf. Gerhoh of Reichersberg, *Ep. 17 ad Alexandrum papam* (PL 193, 568-69 ): *"Cum essem Viterbii apud sanctae recordationis papam Eugenium et ille familiari alloquio mihi retulisset de sua vexatione, in qua Tiburtinis contra vices Romanos favens multas pecunias expenderat, et tandem satis miseram pacis compositionem fecisset, ego respondi: Licet sit misera pretio multo coempta pax ista, melior tamen est quam pugna vestra, quia cum Romanus pontifex praeparet se ad bellum per milites conductos agendum videor mihi videre Petrum evaginantem gladium ferreum. Sed cum ei sic pugnanti vel pugnaturo, non bene cedit, videor mihi audire Christum. . . . Petro dicentem 'Mitte gladium tuum in vaginam.' "*

29. Csi 4, 8. *Opera*, III, 455: *"Puto nec paenitebit exsilii, orbe pro Urbe commutato."*

competent court. Bernard himself had been a frequent appellant in the curia and his comments in the *De consideratione* bespeak an intimate knowledge of its conditions. It was, indeed, one of the spheres of papal activity in which he most urgently pressed for reform.

It was also one of the areas of papal responsibility which he regarded as most equivocal. He gives prominent place to Paul's disparagement of the office of judge.

But listen to what the Apostle thinks about this, "Is there no wise man among you who can judge between brothers?" And he adds, "I say this to shame you; set them to judge who are most despised in the Church." According to the Apostle you, as a successor of the Apostles, are usurping a lowly, contemptible office, which is unbecoming of you. This is why a bishop instructing a bishop said, "No one who fights for God entangles himself in secular affairs."[30]

So keen was Bernard's appreciation of this condemnation that in the first book of the *De consideratione* he toyed with the extreme possibility of abolishing papal justice entirely. Such a solution would solve many of the pope's existential problems. It would remove the pressing weight of distracting business in Rome which, Bernard implies, was mainly derived from court.[31] It would clear the palace of ambitious, parasitical persons who sought to subvert justice to enhance their own ends.[32] It would make it possible for the pope to withdraw and devote himself to the spiritual exercises necessary to protect his inner life and to clarify his perspective on the problems of the Church.[33] How idyllic the papal office might be without the curia! But the idyll was no more than that.

30. Csi 1, 7. *Opera*, III, 401: "*Audi tamen Apostolum, quid de huiusmodi sentiat: 'Sic non est inter vos sapiens,' ait ille, 'qui iudicet inter fratrem et fratrem?' Et infert: 'Ad ignominiam vobis dico: contemptibiliores qui sunt in Ecclesia, illos constituite ad iudicandum.' Itaque, secundum Apostolum, indigne tibi usurpas tu, Apostolice, officium vile, gradum contemptibilium. Unde et dicebat Episcopus, Episcopum instruens: 'Nemo, militans Deo, implicat se negotiis saecularibus.'*"
31. Csi 1, 4. *Opera*, III, 397.
32. Csi 1, 13, 14. *Opera*, III, 409 ff.
33. Csi 1, 4. *Opera*, III, 397; 1, 5 (398f); 3, 5 (434).

But let that be; a different custom has developed. The times and the habits of men are different now. Dangers are no longer imminent, they are present. Fraud, deceit and violence run rampant in our land. False accusors are many; a defender is rare. Everywhere the powerful oppress the poor. We cannot abandon the downtrodden; we cannot refuse judgment to those who suffer injustice. If cases are not tried and litigants heard, how can judgment be passed?[34]

The antithesis is clear: between current practice and abolition of papal justice a mean must be found. And that mean must somehow resolve the question of jurisdiction. In the current practice of the curia, civil cases were regularly brought before ecclesiastical judges. Laws echoed in the palace, in Bernard's famous phrase, yet they were not God's laws, but Justinian's.[35] Would it be possible to eliminate these civil actions completely from the papal court and still preserve its unique role in society? It is clearly a possibility:

It seems to me that a person is not very observant if he thinks it is shameful for Apostles or Apostolic men not to judge such things (civil cases) since judgment has been given to them in greater matters. Why should those who are to pass judgment in heaven even on the angels not scorn to judge the paltry worldly possessions of men? Clearly your power is over sin and not property, since it is because of sin that you have received the keys of the heavenly kingdom, to exclude sinners not possessors.[36]

34. Csi 1, 13. *Opera*, III, 408: "*Sed esto: alius inolevit mos, dies alii sunt et alii hominum mores, et tempora periculosa non instant iam, sed exstant. Fraus et circumventio, et violentia, invaluere super terram. Calumniatores multi, defensor rarus, ubique potentiores pauperiores opprimunt: non possumus deesse oppressis, non negare iniuriam patientibus iudicium. Nisi agitentur causae, audiantur partes, inter partes iudicare quis potest?*"

35. Csi 1, 5. *Opera*, III, 399.

36. Csi 1, 7. *Opera*, III, 402: "*Mihi tamen non videtur bonus aestimator rerum, qui indignum putat Apostolis seu apostolicis viris non iudicare de talibus, quibus datum est indicium in maiora. Quidni contemnant iudicare de terrenis possessiunculis hominum, qui in caelestibus et angelos iudicabunt? Ergo in criminibus, non in possessionibus potestas vestra, quoniam propter illa, et non propter has, accepistis claves regni caelorum, praevaricatores utique exclusuri, non possessores.*"

But in one of the nicest phrases of the *De consideratione*, Bernard admits that this course is not practical:

> However, I spare you, for I speak not of the heroic, but the possible. Do you think these times would permit it if you were to answer in the Lord's words those men who sue for earthly inheritance and press you for judgment: "Men, who set me as a judge over you?" What kind of judgment would they soon pass on you?"[37]

In some form or other, concern with earthly inheritance and civil injustice will remain with the curia, partly because more radical reform, though theoretically righteous, would never be effective. The best one could hope for would be partial restraint. The pope must recognize the separate competence of civil courts and must respect their jurisdiction in most cases. But, where human suffering or rank injustice were involved, the papal court must still take action.

> Why do you put your sickle to someone else's harvest? Not because you are unworthy, but because it is unworthy for you to be involved in such affairs since you are occupied by more important matters. On the other hand, where necessity demands it, listen not to me but to the Apostle: "If this world will be judged by you, are you unworthy to judge the smallest matters?"[38]

Bernard, then, would resolve the problem of papal jurisdiction by confining it to spiritual matters except in the case of extraordinary need. Adjudication of civil causes would be the strict exception to the rule. But even if jurisdiction were re-

37. Csi 1, 7. *Opera*, III, 401: "*Ego autem parco tibi. Non enim fortia loquor, sed possibilia. Putasne haec tempora sustinerent, si, hominibus litigantibus pro terrena hereditate et flagitantibus abs te iudicium, voce Domini responderes: 'O homines, quis me constituit iudicam super vos?' In quale tu iudicium mox venires?*"

38. Csi 1, 7. *Opera* III, 402: "*Quid falcem vestram in alienam messem extenditis? Non quia indigni vos, sed quia indignum vobis talibus insistere, quippe potioribus occupatis. Denique ubi necessitas exigit, audi quid censeat non ego, sed Apostolus: 'Si enim in vobis iudicabitur hic mundus, indigni estis, qui de minimis iudicetis.'*"

formed along these lines, procedure remained a grave question.
Current procedures were, in Bernard's eyes, so debased that the
court actually thwarted justice by its processes and spawned
contempt for law and equity in its reckless decisions.[39]
Judges tended to favor appellants to foster appeals.[40] Cases
were decided not on the merits but on the strength of money
or persons involved.[41] Delays were allowed, sometimes for an
entire lifetime, so that the appellant could enjoy his illicit circumstances.[42] Venal judgments had turned the appellate court
from a refuge for the oppressed into a subterfuge for oppres-
sors.[43]

Abuse so pervasive demanded reform root and branch. Trust-
worthy judges must be found to whom most cases could be
delegated.[44] Defendants on appeal must be prevented from
appealing to forestall lower court decisions or to gain time
against their execution.[45] Defendants on appeal should be pro-
tected from harrassment: Bernard shrewdly suggests that appellants be forced to pay their expenses.[46] Finally, appellate jurisdiction, although universal in definition, must not be thought
of as universal in practice. Restraint above all must be exercised
in agreeing to hear individual cases. Only cases which are genuinely vexed at law, or which involve clear Christian issues
such as the protection of widows and orphans should be coun-
tenanced in the curia.[47] All the rest could be decided, finally,
in the lower courts.

Restraint in selecting cases to be tried, strict impartiality in
reaching a decision, these are the reforms which Bernard ad-
vocates for the court. After the excoriating scorn he poured
on the abusers of papal justice and the violent denunciations
he made of the practices of the court, these measures seem

39. Csi 3, 10. *Opera,* III, 437.
40. Csi 3, 8. *Opera,* III, 436f.
41. Csi 4, 4. *Opera,* III, 451.
42. Csi 3, 11. *Opera,* III, 438.
43. Csi 3, 7. *Opera,* III 436.
44. Csi 3, 12. *Opera,* III, 439.
45. Csi 3, 7-3, 8. *Opera,* III, 436f.
46. Csi 3, 9. *Opera,* III, 437.
47. Csi 3, 10. *Opera,* III, 437f; 1, 13 (408-09); 3, 5 (434).

tame enough. Indeed, they sometimes seem to be aimed not so much at the moderate as the possible.

In his discussion of reform of the papal office Bernard was consistently guided by norms of moderation and effectiveness. But could a Cistercian pope ever be moderate without betraying his vocation? Was it not the essence of monasticism —and especially of early Cistercian monasticism—to reject compromise with the world? How, then, could Bernard advise Eugene in the personal dilemma of adjusting a monk's life to the business of office?

He began, simply, by bewailing the existential situation:

I ask you, what is the point of wrangling and listening to litigants from morning to night? And would that the evil of the day were sufficient for it, but the nights are not even free! Your poor body scarcely gets the time which nature requires for rest before it must rise for further disputing. One day passes on litigation to the next; one night reveals malice to the next, so much so that you have no time to breathe, no time to rest and no time for leisure.[48]

The situation is uncomfortable, but why is it dangerous? Only because business can so easily become a habit which dulls the sensibilities and erases that monastic compunction which alone makes a man aware of self and sin. The end of such stupor is a hard heart.

To encompass all the evils of such a heart in a single phrase: it is a heart which neither fears God nor respects man. This is indeed the state to which these cursed demands can bring you if you continue, as you have begun, to devote yourself to them, leaving no time or energy for yourself. You are wasting your time, and, if I may be a second Jethro, you

---

48. Csi 1, 4. *Opera,* III, 397: "*Quaeso te, quale est istud, de mane usque ad vesperam litigare aut litigantes audire? Et utinam sufficeret diei malitia sua! Non sunt liberae noctes. Vix relinquitur necessitati naturae, quod corpusculi pausationi sufficiat, et rursum ad iurgia surgitur. Dies diei eructat lites, et nox nocti indicat malitiam: usque adeo non est respirare in bonis, non est alternam capessere requiem, non vel rara interseri otia.*"

also are exerting energy foolishly on these things which are nothing but a spiritual disturbance, a mental drain and a squandering of grace. What do all these things produce but spiders' webs?[49]

In describing the extreme outcome of papal business, Bernard has opened the way for compromise. Preoccupation with routine is evil insofar as it creates dullness, then hardness, of heart. A close reading of the passage shows, however, that this happens only if the pope leaves "no time or energy" for himself beyond the fulfillment of duty. Reform, then, lies not in rejection of one's duties, but in moderation of one's work habits. Bernard makes this argument explicitly. He allows Eugene to ask, "And what do you want me to do?" Bernard answers:

Spare yourself these demands upon you. You may say this is impossible, that it would be easier to bid farewell to the papal throne. You would be correct if I were urging you to break with them completely, rather than to interrupt them.[50]

Again, urging that the evils of the time are an extenuating circumstance in the paradoxical situation of the monk-pope, Bernard asks only a partial disengagement from business:

It is one thing to rush headlong into these affairs when there is an urgent reason, but it is another, entirely, to dwell on them as if they were important and worthy of this kind of papal attention. . . . But since these are evil days, it is enough to have warned you not to give yourself completely or con-

---

49. Csi 1, 3. *Opera*, III, 396f.: "*Et ut in brevi cuncta horribilis mali mala complectar, ipsum est quod nec Deum timet, nec hominem reveretur. En quo te trahere habent hae occupationes maledictae, si tamen pergis, ut coepisti, ita dare te totum illis, nil tui tibi relinquens. Perdis tempus et, si licet nunc alterum me tibi exhibere Iethro, tu quoque in his stulto labore consumeris, quae non sunt nisi afflictio spiritus, evisceratio mentis, exinanitio gratiae. Nam fructus horum quid, nisi aranearum telae?*"

50. Csi 1, 5. *Opera*, III, 399: "'*Et quid vis me facere?*' *inquis. Ut tibi ab his occupationibus parcas. Impossibile forsitan respondebis, facilius cathedrae valedicere posse. Recte hoc, si rumpere et non magis interrumpere ista hortarer.*"

tinually to activity and to lay aside something of yourself —your attention and your time—to consideration.[51]

That is all. The press of business is the inescapable result of the dangers besetting the Church in Eugene's time. In the face of constant peril, even a Cistercian pope could "be still and know God" only temporarily. In accepting this, Bernard shows himself a realist. His conclusion may seem an anticlimax after his argument. And yet the argument itself with its dramatic use of antithesis gives life and persuasive power to a conclusion which might otherwise seem a truism.

Elizabeth T. Kennan

The Catholic University of America
Washington, D. C.

---

51. Csi 1, 8. *Opera*, III, 402-03: "*Sed aliud est incidenter excurrere in ista, causa quidem urgente, aliud ultro incumbere istis, tamquam magnis dignisque tali taliumque intentione rebus . . . . Nunc autem quoniam dies mali sunt, sufficit interim admonitum esse, non totum te, nec semper dare actioni, sed considerationi aliquid tui et cordis, et temporis sequestrare.*"

# SACRAMENT, SYMBOL, AND CAUSALITY
# IN BERNARD OF CLAIRVAUX

THE AUTHORITY OF BERNARD OF CLAIR-
VAUX holds an unique place in the late medieval discussion of sacramental causality. His was the only pre-
thirteenth-century name consistently associated with the view
that the sacraments cause grace on the basis of an ascribed
rather than an inherent virtue or power, a view usually termed *sine qua non* causality and generally in disrepute since the
Council of Trent. The association of Bernard and *sine qua non*
causality in the sacraments was based on a passage from Bernard's sermon *In cena domini* in which he suggested that the
sacraments are signs of the investiture of grace and compared
their action to the way a canon is invested into office through
a book, an abbot through a crozier, and a bishop through a
crozier and ring.[1] The early opponents of sacramental causality based on ascribed virtue alone (for example, Peter of Tarantasia or Thomas Aquinas) claimed the Bernard was misin-
terpreted on this issue. But several supporters of ascribed virtue in the fourteenth century (for example, John of Bassoles
and Durand of St Pourçain) continued to enlist the authority
of Bernard on their side. Opponents of ascribed virtue accepted the association of Bernard with the denial of effective cau-

---

1. V HM 2 (5, 68-69): "*Sicut enim in exterioribus sunt diversa signa et, ut coepto immoremur exemplo, variae sunt investiturae secundum ea de quibus investimur, —verbi gratia, investitur canonicus per librum, abbas per baculum, episcopus per baculum et anulum simul—, sicut, inquam, in huiusmodi rebus est, sic et diviones gratiarum diversis traditae sunt sacramentis.*"

111

sality in the sacraments and simply rejected what they mistakingly regarded as Bernard's view.

To the modern historian of medieval thought it is apparent that both sides in this discussion were interpreting the passage from Bernard in light of the more highly developed sacramental theology of the late thirteenth and fourteenth centuries. The limited late medieval understanding of the development of dogma and of the broader twelfth-century milieu in which Bernard was writing made a balanced interpretation of the Bernard passage difficult. However, the disagreements over Bernard's meaning do provide the later historian with considerable material on how later generations of theologians interpreted him on this issue, a topic interesting in itself. Perhaps with the increased understanding of twelfth-century thought and of the development of sacramental theology in the high and late Middle Ages we are now in a better position to evaluate the Bernardine passage and its subsequent medieval interpretation. Did the idea that the sacraments are the *sine qua non* causes of grace originate with Bernard?[2] How should the often cited quotation from Bernard be understood in its original context and in later applications?

Carefully argued theories concerning sacramental causality were not developed before the thirteenth century, although analogies describing the nature and efficacy of the sacraments can be found as early as the second quarter of the twelfth century. The eucharist and, more especially, baptism had received considerable attention in patristic theology, but it was only in the twelfth century that theologians attempted to formulate an integrated, internally consistent, and complete examination of the sacraments. Thus Bernard stands within the first generation of theologians who addressed themselves to the issue of

---

2. To my knowledge this problem has not received direct treatment, although it is obliquely referred to by Joseph Lortz when he considers the *Asakramentalität* of Bernard in *Bernhard von Clairvaux. Mönch und Mystiker.* Internationaler Bernhardkongress, Mainz, 1953 (Wiesbaden, 1955), pp. xlvi-xlvii. For background and related issues see: F. Heiler, *Das Gebet* (München, 1920); G. Frischmuth, *Die paulinische Konzeption in der Frömmigkeit Bernhards von Clairvaux* (Beiträge zur Forderung christl. Theologie, 37/4; Gütersloh, 1933); R. Linhardt, *Bernard von Clairvaux* (Regensburg, 1937); D. R. Hesbert, "Saint Bernard et l'Eucharistie," *Mélanges Saint Bernard* (Dijon, 1953), pp. 156-176.

the relation of the sacramental elements to their principal effect, the infusion of grace. The analogy he used to describe that relationship alongside the more frequently repeated analogy of Hugh of St Victor formed the foundation for the theological exploration of sacramental causality.[3]

Bernard did not set out to explain sacramental causality in his Maundy Thursday sermon in 1139. Instead, he was explaining to his listeners the various effects that accrued from baptism, the eucharist and the ceremony of the washing of feet. In that context he defined the sacraments (including what are now called sacramentals) as signs or mysteries that bestow a hidden benefit.[4] In a passage that precedes the one referred to above, Bernard suggests that the sacraments are common, ordinary things or actions that have a special value and significance attached to them. If a person gives a ring to another as a present, the ring has no significance beyond being an expression of the affection of the giver for the recipient. If, however, the ring represents a claim to the future inheritance of some property, then the ring has a value and significance far greater than its intrinsic value. The ring itself remains unchanged; an added value is simply ascribed to it by those party to the agreement, an agreement sufficiently public so that there will be no question of rightful succession at the time of inheritance.[5]

It is this passage that forms the background and clarifies the subsequent passage that received so much attention by later theologians. While pursuing the same analogy Bernard

---

3. Hugh of St Victor defined the sacraments as vessels or receptacles of God's grace, as a doctor's vial would contain the medicine for the patient. *De sacramentis,* I, part ix, ch. 4; H. Weisweiler, *Die Wirksamkeit der Sakramente nach Hugo von St Victor* (Freiburg i. B., 1932).

4. V HM 2 (5,68): "*Sacramentum dicitur sacrum signum, sive sacrum secretum.*"

5. Ibid.: "*Multa siquidem fiunt propter se tantum, alia vero propter alia designanda, et ipsa dicuntur signa, et sunt. Ut enim de usualibus sumamus exemplum, datur anulus absolute propter anulum, et nulla est significatio; datur ad investiendum de hereditate aliqua, et signum est, ita ut iam dicere possit qui accipit: 'Anulus non valet quidquam, sed hereditas est quam quaerebam.' In hunc itaque modum, appropinquans passioni Dominus, de gratia sua investire curavit suos, ut invisibilis gratia signo aliquo visibili praestaretur.*" Landgraf is the only one who has commented on the importance of this passage for the development of what he terms intentional causality. A. M. Landgraf, *Dogmengeschichte der Frühscholastik,* III.1 (Regensburg, 1954), pp. 171-172.

argues that a diversity of graces are caused or communicated by different sacraments, just as investiture into particular offices is effected through different signs or symbols, a book in the case of a canon, a crozier for an abbot, and a crozier and ring for a bishop. In this second passage, as it was later pointed out, Bernard is not principally arguing for ascribed virtue or value but is comparing the effects of different sacraments. When viewed against the background of the previous passage, however, it seems to be Bernard's position that the sacraments are, like the signs used to invest in office, common things that receive their new significance by having an additional value applied or ascribed to them by some person (in the case of the sacraments, Christ), by some agreement or covenant, or by their recognized use in a particular ceremony. The implication is that intrinsically the signs remain what they were before; no special virtue is infused into them that alters their nature. The new or additional virtue is applicable only when these signs or symbols are used properly in a particular ceremony. Moreover, grace does not seem to be communicated directly in and through the sacraments but, like the ring that represents a claim to an inheritance, follows as a direct result of the reception of the sacraments. The sacraments, therefore, are legitimate and efficacious claims or titles to grace, given on the occasion of the proper reception of the sacraments.

In order to understand Bernard's view of the efficacious nature of signs in regard to the promise of future reward it is necessary to look first at Bernard's view of the administration of grace within the plan of salvation and, second, at the meaning of sign and symbol for Bernard's generation.

On first glance Bernard's soteriology seems to be dominated by an active, unrestricted, and possibly unpredictable God, a view which, if true, would make all covenants and agreements between God and man, including the efficacious nature of the sacramental signs, meaningless and undependable. Bernard shared with others within the monastic tradition (such as Peter Damian[6] or Anselm of Canterbury[7]) a high assessment of divine

---

6. *De divina omnipotentia*, 4 (PL 145:601 C).
7. Anselm's statements on the omnipotence of God are scattered throughout his

omnipotence and the extent of divine freedom before creation. Because of that belief Bernard criticized Abelard for maintaining that God's power to act was limited to those things that God in fact did do.[8] Even after creation and the establishment of a system of salvation God's freedom is not entirely restricted by the ordained order. For example, God remains free to accept one to eternal life who has not been baptized, and thus God can save apart from the normal channels of grace.[9]

In general, however, the freedom of God to save or to damn is limited by the divine nature, by the system of salvation that has been ordained, and by the human will. Whatever freedom may exist outside the ordained order (and there is little of it), is the freedom to be more beneficent and forgiving than the ordained order permits.[10] For Bernard, it is the nature of God, as a father, to forgive all those who place themselves in the

---

works. His position changed between *Proslogion* (1078) and *Cur Deus Homo* (1098). For a description of Anselm's development on this issue see: W. J. Courtenay, "Necessity and Freedom in Anselm's Conception of God," *Die Wirkungsgeschichte Anselms von Canterbury*. Acts of the International Anselm Congress, Bad Wimpfen, Sept. 1970 (to appear in 1973).

8. *Capitula Haeresum Petri Abaelardi* (PL 182:1049C - 1050A).

9. Bernard had in mind those who lived before the establishment of the sacrament of baptism or those to whom the gospel has not been preached. His position should not be confused with later *de potentia Dei absoluta* speculation, which discussed God's freedom to accept a sinner who rejected Christianity. Bapt (PL 182: 1033D-1034A): *"Sed forte aliquis dicat, eos quidem qui non audierunt, etsi non de contemptu judicari, damnari tamen propter originale peccatum, a quo utique nisi per lavacrum emundari minime potuerunt. At vero quis nesciat et alia praeter Baptismum contra originale peccatum remedia antiquis non defuisse temporibus? Abrahae quidem et semini eius, circumcisionis sacramentum in hoc ipsum divinitus traditum est* (Gen 17:10). *In nationibus vero, quotquot inventi sunt fideles, adultos quidem fide et sacrificiis credimus expiatos, parvulis autem solam profuisse, imo et suffecisse parentum fidem. Porro hoc ita quidem usque ad Baptismi tempora perdurasse: quo uno substituto, vacasse caetera."* Ibid., 1034A-B: *"Quaerimus itaque Baptismi tempus ex quo coeperit. Ex quo, inquit, primum dictum est:* Nisi quis renatus fuerit, *etc. Tene ergo firmiter dictum hoc ad Nicodemum, utique amicum Jesu, occultum tamem propter metum Judaeorum; occultumque illud de nocte requisisse colloquium. Quanta autem putas obisse interim (ut de gentibus taceam) millia circumcisorum, cum necdum in lucem prodierit quod de Baptismo tunc in tenebris dicebatur? Quid ergo? damnatos illos omnes dicimus, quia baptizati non sunt? Fit ergo iniuria antiquo illi Dei aeque mandato, si novo adhuc furtive quodammodo superveniente, non tamen subveniente, illud ita subito evanuisse putetur, ut prodesse deinceps non valeret."* cf. Ibid., 1031C-1033B.

10. This is also the implication of the parable of the laborers in the vineyard, Mt 20:1-16.

position of being sons of God.[11] Sonship results from acknowledging God as father and willing to be saved, a desire on the part of the human will that cannot be coerced by God.[12] For the one who strives after God, who does his best or, in later terminology, does what is in him, God will not deny him grace and final salvation.[13] According to Bernard, God is not free to reject those who have been baptized and who desire salvation.[14] Nor is he free to accept those who have heard about baptism but have refused it.[15] In sum, God cannot, or at least will not and does not, save men against their own wills. It is in all cases necessary that a man will to be saved, and he must cooperate with God to the extent of willing to be saved. When that has happened, God will perfect that desire through grace. In fact, God is obliged to accept those who turn to him and who partake of the sacraments in the form in which they were instituted.

11. SC 66. *Opera*, II, 184: "*Ita ergo clamant haec omnia, sanguis fratris, fides matris, destitutio miseri, et miseria destituti. Et clamatur ad Patrem; porro Pater seipsum negare non potest: Pater est.*" Cf. Epi 3, *Opera*, IV, 309, 5-18; V Nat 1, *Opera*, IV, 201, 20-202, 15.

12. Gra 11, *Opera*, III, 191, 13-24: "*QUOD DEUS NEMINEM IUDICAT SALU-TE DIGNUM, NISI QUEM INVENERIT VOLUNTARIUM.—Nam quod legitur in Evangelio: NEMO VENIT AD ME, NISI PATER MEUS TRAXERIT EUM, item in alio loco: COMPELLE INTRARE, nihil impedit, quia profecto quantoscumque trahere vel compellere videatur ad salutem benignus Pater, qui omnes vult salvos fieri, nullum tamen iudicat salute dignum, quem ante non probaverit voluntarium. Hoc quippe intendit, cum terret aut percutit, ut faciat voluntarios, non salvet invitos, quatenus dum de malo in bonum mutat voluntatem, transferat, non auferat libertatem. Quamquam tamen non semper inviti trahimur: nec enim caecus aut fessus contristatur cum trahitur. Et Paulus ad manus tractus est Damascum, utique non invitus. Trahi denique spiritualiter volebat, quae et hoc ipsum magnopere falgitabat in Canticis: TRAHE ME, ait, POST TE; IN ODOREM UNGUEN-TORUM TUORUM CURRIMUS.*" Cf. V Nat 1, *Opera*, IV, 201-202.

13. For the later development of this view and for the meaning of the phrase "*facere quod in se est*" see: Paul Vignaux, *Justification et prédestination au XIVe siècle* (Paris, 1934); Werner Dettloff, *Die Lehre von der Acceptatio Divina bei Johannes Duns Scotus* (Werl i.W., 1954); Werner Dettloff, *Die Entwicklung der Akzeptations und Verdienstlehre von Duns Scotus bis Luther* (Münster i.W., 1963); Heiko Oberman, "Facientibus quod in se est Deus non denegat gratiam, Robert Holcot, O. P. and the Beginnings of Luther's Theology," *Harvard Theological Review* LV (1962): 317-342; Heiko Oberman, *The Harvest of Medieval Theology* (Cambridge, Mass, 1963); W. J. Courtenay, "Covenant and Causality in Pierre d'Ailly," *Speculum* XLVI (1971): 94-119.

14. Gra 11, *Opera*, III, 191; V Nat 1, *Opera*, IV, 201-202.

15. Bapt (PL 182:1036B-C).

The grace made available to man through the sacraments, therefore, operates according to a pact or covenant. If the sacraments are taken as a sign of the desire of the recipient to be saved, if a bad will or disbelief does not place a barrier in the way of their effectiveness, then grace will be effected in the recipient. The sacraments are thus visible signs that call forth the gift of grace on the basis of a value attributed to them by God.

When viewed against the background of Bernard's soteriology and the covenantal nature of man's relationship with God, the efficacy as well as the importance of the sacraments become apparent. But does this not mean that, for Bernard, the sacraments are only the accidental causes of grace, the signs or symbols that accompany or declare the gift of grace? [16]

To answer this question one must examine the language used by Bernard in the context of the early twelfth century. The investiture controversy, which came to a formal close in 1122, centered in part around the effective power of symbols and material substances of ascribed value. From the conceptual standpoint the reformers within the Hildebrandine party believed that the symbols of office used in the investiture ceremony possessed an efficacious power that should not be sullied by laymen's hands. If the solution to the investiture controversy lay in the ability to distinguish the temporal and spiritual aspects of ecclesiastical office and to attach particular symbols to those separate aspects, it nevertheless remained true that the valid possession of those symbols or the valid application of them automatically and irrevocably granted the recipient the right to the office and the power which that entailed. Although the symbols of office (unlike the relics of the saints) possessed no inherent virtue that caused their effect, they did infallibly cause or effect a particular result. From the standpoint of the world in which Bernard lived, ascribed virtue could be as effective as inherent virtue, and in the sacraments it was considered effective. The view that ascribed virtue was not sufficiently efficacious, a view held by many theologians

---

16. For the origin and development of the idea of accidental causality in the sacraments see: W. J. Courtenay, "The King and the Leaden Coin: The Economic Background of *Sine Qua Non* Causality," *Traditio* XXVIII (1972): 185-209.

in succeeding generations, resulted from an intellectual transformation that removed from the symbols of investiture the power and significance they once had.

There is no direct line of continuity that runs from Bernard to the major theories of sacramental causality developed in the period from 1225 to 1250. The analogy constructed by Bernard in his sermon was forgotten or ignored, even by those who, like Richard Fishacre and Robert Kilwardby, adopted a theory of covenantal, contractual or juridical causality that closely approximated the ideas of Bernard. Bernard was not, therefore, the inspiration for the theory of *sine qua non* causality that developed around 1240 in opposition to the physical-dispositive theory espoused by William of Auxerre, Alexander of Hales, Roland of Cremona, William of Melitona and Albert the Great, and in opposition to the physical-instrumental theory of Stephen Langton and Hugh of St Cher. Even Bonaventure, who extensively examines the various positions and eventually subscribes to covenantal, or *sine qua non,* causality, does not refer to the passage in Bernard.[17]

The earliest appearance of the quotation from Bernard in the context of sacramental causality occurs in the fourth book of the *Sentences* commentary of Thomas Aquinas (a supporter of inherent virtue) and thus seems to be introduced by the opponents of *sine qua non* causality rather than its defenders.[18] The Bernard quotation is given prominence as the first authority and first argument used to support the idea that the sacraments are not causes of grace. After providing his solution to the problem, Thomas responds to the Bernardine quotation by saying that Bernard intended to show the similitude of the sacraments to the symbols of investiture only in regard to signification, for as signs of grace they are also (and Thomas assumes Bernard shares his opinion) causes of grace.[19]

17. The development of theories of sacramental causality in the thirteenth century is traced elsewhere: W. J. Courtenay, "The King and the Leaden Coin."

18. *Sent.* IV, d. 1, q. 1, a. 4, qu. 1 (Parma, 1858), VII.1, 460-463.

19. Ibid., 463: "*Bernardus, ut ex praecedentibus ibidem patet, non intendit ostendere similitudinem sacramentorum ad illa, nisi quantum ad significationem: quia anulus est signum et baculus, et similiter sacramenta; sed sacramenta ulterius sunt causae.*"

It may well be that Thomas was the first to introduce the Bernard quotation and to associate it with a rejection of sacramental causality. The pro and con arguments used at the beginning of a question by a *sententiarius* did not necessarily reflect or accurately present the positions of certain contemporary or earlier theologians. These initial arguments were often of artificial design, a creation of the bachelor and purposely couched in extreme language to make the two sides of the question seem authoritative and mutually exclusive. It is certain that Thomas did not view Bernard as a supporter of either *sine qua non* causality or the view that the sacraments were not causes at all, two theories that were in Thomas' mind identical. But making Bernard initially *seem* to reject sacramental causality altogether, Thomas colored the way in which that quotation was read by succeeding theologians.

Two years after Thomas commented on the *Sentences,* Peter of Tarantasia, a fellow Dominican who later became Pope Innocent V, treated sacramental causality in his *Sentences* commentary and repeated the Bernard quotation.[20] He introduced the passage in a form almost identical with Thomas' presentation. Later in his discussion he stated that those who reject *sine qua non* causality in favor of instrumental causality (the position with which he agrees) would deal with the authority of Bernard by saying that Bernard was speaking about a difference between the various types of sacraments, not in the way they act.[21]

In his *Summa theologiae* Thomas returned to the problem of sacramental causality and again referred to the quotation from Bernard, this time with one important difference: the Bernard passage does not occur among the arguments at the beginning of the question but rather in the body of the solution, where it is directly associated with the theory of covenantal causality.[22] Moreover, Thomas makes no attempt to explain the passage or put Bernard in a better light. Perhaps

20. *Sent.* IV, d. 1, q. 1, a. 6, qu. 1 (Toulouse, 1651), IV, 11.
21. Ibid.: *"Similitudo beati Bernardi attenditur quoad differentiam sacramentorum agentium, non quoad modum agendi."*
22. *Summa theologiae,* P. III, q. 62, a. 1 (Ottawa, 1944), IV: 2821b-2822a.

on rereading the Maundy Thursday sermon Thomas decided that Bernard had supported *sine qua non* causality.

Thomas's association of the Bernard quotation with the complete rejection of sacramental causality influenced subsequent discussion. No one after 1260, regardless of the stand they took on sacramental causality, tried to disassociate Bernard and the *sine qua non* view. Because of the association, *sine qua non* causality seemed like an ancient view, that is, a view maintained in the twelfth century. Moreover, the idea was repeated, from Thomas on, that the signs or symbols of investiture have no serious causal power but are only declarative signs, and thus if the sacraments were similar signs they also would have no causal power.

These views were maintained by those Thomists at the beginning of the fourteenth century who referred to the passage in Bernard and associated it with *sine qua non* causality. Peter Palude, reciting four opinions on sacramental causality, quotes Bernard as an authority who supports the *opinio antiqua* that the sacraments are the *sine qua non* causes of grace because they operate out of a pact or divine ordination.[23] John of Naples follows the same procedure as Peter Palude.[24]

Among the supporters of *sine qua non* causality, however, were those who happily used the authority of the Mellifluous Doctor in support of their theory. These included John of Bassoles[25] (normally considered a Scotist but, on this issue, a more enthusiastic supporter of *sine qua non* causality than was Scotus) and Durand of St Pourçain.[26] Durand was one of the few who did more than simply quote the passage from Bernard. He analyzed the passage and rejected the construction that Thomas had placed upon it in his *Sentences* commentary, arguing that Bernard had meant more than simply signification and had indeed described the whole relationship between the

23. *Sent.* IV, d. 1, q. 1 (Venice, 1493), IV, 2ʳ-3ᵛ.
24. *Quaestiones variae Parisiis disputatae*, q. 33 (Naples, 1618), 284.
25. *Sent.* IV, d. 1, q. 1 (Paris, 1517) IV, 8ᵛ, 11ᵛ.
26. *Sent.* IV, d. 1, q. 4 (Venice, 1571), 290ʳ.

sacraments and grace through his investiture analogy.[27] Peter Aureol used the Bernard quotation in the counterargument at the beginning of his discussion of sacramental causality in his *Sentences* commentary, and it seems to be this counter-argument that most closely resembles the position he eventually favored.[28]

When the Bernard quotation occurs in discussions of sacramental causality from the middle of the fourteenth century on, it is used in ways that would have seemed strange in the thirteenth or early fourteenth centuries. For example, Peter of Aquila (Scotellus), writing around 1334, rejected *sine qua non* causality along with the quotation from Bernard, only to turn around and support a causality that operates *ex pactione virtus divina*.[29] Michael Aiguani, a mid-fourteenth-century Carmelite from Bologna, supported *sine qua non* causality and looked with favor on the passage from Bernard. However, he regarded the signs of sacramental and canonical investiture as signs that had only an exemplary value, a view that would have horrified most supporters of *sine qua non* causality.[30]

The majority of those who defended convenantal causality in the fourteenth and fifteenth centuries did not use the Bernardine passage, possibly because Thomas and others had brought it into disrepute, or possibly because they agreed with Thomas that the signs and symbols of investiture to office did not possess sufficient causal power, even ascribed power, to provide a good analogy for the operation of the sacraments. Among those espousing covenantal causality who did not refer to Bernard were: William of Ockham, Robert Holcot, Thomas of Strasbourg, Conrad of Ebrach, Marsilius of Inghen, Pierre d'Ailly and Gabriel Biel—in short, many of the major figures associated with late medieval Nominalism. Perhaps, had they had

27. Ibid.: "*Nec fit [Bernardus] ibi comparatio solum quantum ad significationem (ut quidam [i.e., Thomas and the Thomists] dicunt) sed quantum ad omnem habitudinem, quam habent sacramenta respectu gratiae, ut patet diligenter intuenti verba beati Bernardi, in illo sermone.*"

28. *Sent.* IV, d. 1, q. 1, a. 1 (Rome, 1605) IV, 9.

29. *Sent.* IV, q. 3 (Speyer, 1480).

30. *Sent.* IV, d. 2, q. un., a. 1 (Venice, 1622), 344.

a more sophisticated understanding of the context in which Bernard was writing and of the world in which he lived, they might have found in his analogy an appropriate expression of the efficacy of *sine qua non* causality in the sacraments.

William J. Courtenay

University of Wisconsin
Madison, Wisconsin

# THE TWO SAINT MALACHY OFFICES
# FROM CLAIRVAUX

SCHOLARS KNOWLEDGEABLE IN THE FIELD of Bernardine research have occasionally noted that none of Bernard's several twelfth-century biographers have so much as mentioned the considerable work of the Abbot of Clairvaux as a reformer of his Order's liturgical books. This silence is not particularly puzzling. Bernard's first biographer, William of St Thierry, died in 1148 without having got much beyond the year 1130 in the *curriculum vitae* of his hero. Arnold, abbot of Bonneval, continued the biography as far as 1147 (Book II of the *Vita Prima*); and Geoffrey, the ever faithful secretary and propagandist, completed the last three books during the years 1154-1156.[1] However, twelfth-century hagiography being what it was, neither Arnold nor Geoffrey nor any of the later biographers could be expected to be interested in Bernard as a chant reformer. Had Bernard managed to bring off a miracle or two as head of the commission which reformed the Order's liturgical books during the period immediately preceding 1147,[2] we might now have a few edifying paragraphs in the *Vita Prima* about Bernard the Peerless Liturgist.

That Bernard *did* play an important role in the reform of his Order's liturgy is clear from the *Prologus* to the reformed

1. For questions of date and authorship of the *Vita Prima*, the acknowledged authority is A. H. Bredero in his *Etudes sur la "Vita Prima" de saint Bernard, Analecta S. O. Cist.* 17 (1961): 3-72, 21-260; 18 (1962): 3-59.

2. For the approximate date for the termination of this chant reform, see Chrysogonus Waddell, "The Origin and Early Evolution of the Cistercian Antiphonary," *The Cistercian Spirit, A Symposium* (Spencer, Massachusetts, 1970), p. 192, Note 5.

Cistercian Antiphonary of ca. 1147, where Bernard promul-
gates the newly revised antiphonary, and tells how the General
Chapter had burdened him with the chief responsibility for
the work of revision.[3] But Bernard also tells us that he had at
his disposal a number of competent collaborators hand-picked
by himself. What was the personal contribution of each of
these collaborators? Impossible to say at this late date; and
equally impossible to be precise about the extent of Bernard's
participation in the work. Still, there is at least one strangely
neglected text which praises Bernard for his endeavors in the
work of liturgical reform; and this text has been familiar to
generations of Cistercians for almost eight centuries. I refer
to the twelfth-century responsory of St Bernard's Night
Office—a text sung for the Saint's feast (August 20) from
1176 onwards.[4]

> R.  He gave thanks to the Holy One, the Most High, with
> ascriptions of glory;
> he sang praise to the Lord with all his heart,
> * And he loved God his Maker.
> V.  He gave beauty to the celebration of the Holy Work
> [=liturgy], and arranged its times throughout the year.
> * And he.[5]

Anyone familiar with the Sapiential Books will recognize Jesus ben Sirach's eulogy of David, the sweet singer of Israel,

3. Critical edition in Leclercq and Rochais, *Sancti Bernardi Opera, III. Tractatus
et Opuscula* (Romae 1963), pp. 509-516; translation with introductory notes by
Chrysogonus Waddell in *The Works of Bernard of Clairvaux, Treatises* I (Spencer,
Massachusetts, 1970), pp. 153-162.

4. The General Chapter of 1175 (held in September) speaks of the introduction
of a *proper* office of St Bernard, who had been canonized by the Bull of Alexander III, dated from Agnani, January 18, 1174: *"De sancto Bernardo proprium
officum et duae missae et fratres laborent."* Cf. J.-M. Canivez, *Statua Capitulorum Generalium Ordinis Cisterciensis . . .* T. I. (Louvain 1933), p. 82 (Anno
1175/2). *The Chronicon Claraevallense*, PL 185:1248, is equally specific: *"Et se-
quenti anno* (i.e., 1175), *in capitulo generali receperunt cantum beati Bernardi, et
cantum de Trinitate."*

5. R. *Dedit confessionem Sancto, et Excelso in verbo gloriae. De omni corde lau-
davit Dominum,* * *Et dilexit Deum, qui fecit illum.* V. *Dedit decus in celebratione
operis sancti, et ornavit tempora sua usque in finem:* *Et Gloria Patri.* * Et. *

who is praised in Ecclesiasticus 47:9-12 for his reform of the worship of Israel. The parallel, then, is between David, reformer of the Jewish liturgy, and Bernard, reformer of the Cistercian liturgy.

The irony of this is that, while we are unable to assess with precision Bernard's conscious, voluntary role in the general work of his Order's liturgical reform, we *are* able to assess with considerable precision his involuntary and unconscious contribution to the shaping up of two particular Offices which became part of the Cistercian heritage: the Office of St Malachy, and—curiously enough—the Office of St Bernard of Clairvaux.

## St Malachy and Clairvaux

Maolmhaodhog Ua Morgair, better known to most non-Gaelic readers as Malachy O'Morgair (or O'More),[6] was born in Ireland in 1094 or 1095; and he died at Clairvaux on the night between All Saints Day and All Souls Day, 1148. In God's providence, it was doubtless due to this particular circumstance of Malachy's death and burial at Clairvaux that he is now numbered among the officially canonized saints. Bernard's love for Malachy expressed itself in a bulky dossier of writings about his friend. Besides four letters addressed to Malachy himself,[7] we have *Letter 374* written to the Irish brethren on the occasion of Malachy's death and burial at Clairvaux.[8] There are

6. The author of this article is hopelessly confused with regard to the proper forms of Gaelic names. Since Irish scholars themselves seem to admit of a variety of usage, I have generally followed H. J. Lawlor, *St Bernard of Clairvaux's Life of St Malachy of Armagh* (London - New York 1920); and the historical notes provided by Fr A. Gwinn SJ, in the critical edition of the *Vita Sancti Malachiae Episcopi* in Leclercq and Rochais, *Opera* III, 297-378.

7. *Letters 341, 356,* and *357* in PL 182:546, 557, and 558 and a "confraternity letter" first edited by G. G. Meersseman OP, in his article, "Two Unknown Confraternity Letters of St Bernard," *Cîteaux in de Nederlanden* 6 (1955): 174. The same letter was re-edited two years later by Fr Jean Leclercq, who transcribed a different and better ms., in his article "Deux épîtres de saint Bernard et de son secrétaire," *Studien und Mitteilungen zur Geschichte des Benediktiner-Ordens* 68 (1957): 228-229.

8. *Letter 374*, PL 182:578-580.

also two sermons, one delivered on the day of burial,[9] the other on some later anniversary.[10] Most important of all, there is a lengthy *Vita Sancti Malachiae Episcopi.*[11] Finally, there is Malachy's epitaph,[12] and the hymn *Nobilis signis.*[13] (As to Bernard's authorship of this hymn, I remain a bit skeptical for reasons to be explained on a later page of this article.)

A hurried inventory of the *summa capita* of Malachy's life will contribute to a better understanding of the Office texts which we shall examine.[14]

For several centuries the Church in Ireland had effectively been cut off from normal relations with the rest of ecclesiastical Europe. The ninth-century Norse invasions and occupation had brought untold misery and disaster. Irish culture, it seemed at times, was edging closer and closer to the brink of total extinction. Massive though the damage was, the set-back was only temporary; and the pendulum began swinging in the reverse direction with the Good Friday victory at Clontarf in 1014, and with the gradual conversion of the once-pagan invaders. Once the nightmare of Danish occupation was at an end, effective means had to be found to ensure that the future of the Irish people would be worthy of the glory of their distant past. But there were problems. Ireland was about to emerge from its enforced isolation of several centuries. Much stood in drastic need of purification and reform. But there was considerable confusion as to what, in some instances, was truly decadent and corrupt, and what was genuinely part of the distinctive Irish heritage and tradition. Take the organization of the Church in Ireland. It was essentially monastic. Ecclesiastical jurisdiction was vested, not in bishops (of which there were multitudes), but in the abbots of the monasteries—the *coarbs* or successors of the founders of the churches. Interesting as

9. *Sermo in Transitu Sancti Malachiae Episcopi,* in Leclercq and Rochais, 417-423.
10. PL 183:486-490.
11. *Opera,* III, 307-378.
12. Ibid., 519-21.
13. Ibid., 522-526.
14. These sketchy notes are based on the historical notes provided in the two studies referred to above, Note 6.

this type of ecclesiastical organization might be to the student of Church history, it had proved disastrous by the middle of the eleventh century. Contrary to the earlier tradition, abbots frequently held office by right of hereditary succession; and, inevitably, the interests of the local church were identified with the interests of the local clan or tribe. It was only to be expected that in an Ireland still plagued by warfare between clans, a new order of things would have to emerge if any degree of stability and fruitful reform was to be achieved. Thus, the eleventh century gave rise to a far-reaching reform movement; but this reform came to full flower only in the twelfth-century, and its purest expression crystallized in the person of St Malachy of Armagh. Malachy was to Ireland what Charles Borromeo would one day be to post-Tridentine Milan.

By birth and formation Malachy was admirably fitted for the role he was to play in the twelfth-century revival. His father, Mugrón Ua Morgair, had been chief lector (*árd fer leigind*) in the school attached to the primatial see of Armagh. More important an influence, however, was the recluse Imar O'Hagan, whose sympathies were energetically with the pro-reform movement which, since the early years of the twelfth century, had been gaining momentum. At the insistence of the reforming Archbishop Cellach (Celsus), *coarb* of Patrick and Primate of Ireland, Malachy was ordained deacon about the year 1117, two years later was advanced to the priesthood, and shortly thereafter was appointed vicar of Armagh. Malachy soon proved himself to be the ideal reformer, and—if we can give credence to even a few of the facts alleged in Bernard's biography of his friend—there seems to have been rather much which needed reforming. In 1124 Malachy was installed as abbot of the famous monastery at Bangor and was consecrated bishop. Since the area in which he exercised his apostolate had yet to be organized along Roman lines with the bishop as head of the diocese, Malachy could be called "Bishop of Connor" only in a rather loose acceptation of the term; but his activity was certainly that of a bishop-apostle of the early Church, and the concrete manifestation he gave of the ancient Irish ideal of

authentic holiness won for him the total devotion of most of
the faithful in his diocese. Cellach of Armagh died in 1129;
but before dying, he designated Malachy as his successor. In
the cultural context of the period, this nomination was revo-
lutionary, and was bound to cause trouble. For Cellach had
belonged to the family which for generation after generation
had supplied the church of Armagh with its ruler. By way
of exception, he himself had been not only *coarb* of Patrick,
but bishop as well; however, episcopal orders were looked on as
something only incidental, since, for the preceding period of
some 150 years, Cellach's predecessors had been laymen. Malachy, however, was a stranger to the clan, and was in no way
connected by blood with the coarbial family. Only in 1137,
after several years of violence and bloodshed, was Malachy
finally accepted as undisputed *coarb* of Patrick and Archbishop of Armagh. Once the principle of hereditary succession had been overcome, Malachy, according to his own pre-
arranged plan, returned to his monastery at Bangor. Not that
this retirement from Armagh meant a cessation of Malachy's
apostolate as bishop. Far from it, for he functioned in effect
as bishop of Down, and continued to engage in activities which
extended far beyond the territory of Down and Bangor. In
1139 Malachy went to Rome in an attempt to secure the ar-
chiepiscopal pall for the two metropolitans of Ireland. This
favor could be granted, he was told, only in answer to a formal
request framed by a council of Ireland's clerical and lay leaders.
But Malachy failed to obtain yet another request. On his way
to Rome, he had spent some time at Clairvaux—just long
enough to fall in love with the place and the brethren. He
now asked the Pope for permission to retire to Clairvaux and
to live for the rest of his days in one of the chief centers of the
Cistercian reforming movement. Malachy received not only a
firm, "No," but investiture with a new office of considerable
importance—that of papal legate to Ireland. Though Malachy
was unable to remain at Clairvaux, he was able to maintain
close contact with the White Monks; for, not long after his
return to Ireland, he had the deep satisfaction of seeing the

Cistercian Order introduced into Ireland. As for Malachy, he exercised his legatine function for less than a decade. In 1148 he once more left Ireland on a mission to Eugenius III. But he got no farther than Clairvaux. He fell seriously ill on St Luke's Day, October 18; and two weeks later, he died happily and peacefully on the night between November 1st and 2nd. All this had happened exactly as he had desired:

> Being asked once, in what place, if a choice were given him, he would prefer to spend his last day . . . he said, "If I take my departure hence (in Ireland) I shall do so nowhere more gladly than whence I may rise together with our Apostle" —he referred to St Patrick; "but if it behoves me to make a pilgrimage, and if God so permits, I have selected Clairvaux. When asked about the time, (he named in reply) the festival of all the dead.[15]

Bernard's biography of his friend Malachy can doubtless be criticized for the same faults characteristic of most hagiographical literature of the period: uncritical enthusiasm, tendentious manipulation of historical details, excessive credulity with regard to the marvelous. . . . It should be noted, too, that, for the vast bulk of his narrative, Bernard depended on sources of information no longer subject to careful control.[16] It would be a bit risky, then, to depend too heavily on this *Vita* as a principal source for the reconstruction of twelfth-century Irish history. At the same time, there is no evidence to suggest that, in painting this portrait of the ideal bishop-reformer, Bernard was over-manipulating his material and falsifying historical fact. Malachy was clearly a wonderful bishop and an enormously holy and at-

---

15. *Vita Sancti Malachiae* VIII, 67; translation adapted from H. J. Lawlor, *op. cit.* (above, Note 6), p. 117.

16. The chief informant seems to have been Congan, abbot of the Cistercian monastery of the Suir (Inishlounaght). Congan was apparently personally known to Bernard, and might have been one of the Irishmen sent by Malachy to Clairvaux in order to be initiated into monastic life according to the Cistercian ideal. The preface of the *Vita Sancti Malachiae* is addressed to Congan in particular; and there is also mention of him in Section XXIX, 64 of the same *Vita.*

tractive person. Bernard quite simply appreciated him and loved him. And it would seem that the monks of Clairvaux shared in something of Bernard's love for Malachy.

The *unofficial* cultus of Malachy began with his funeral, and was inaugurated by no less a personage that the Abbot of Clairvaux. Geoffrey of Auxerre tells us that, during the washing of Malachy's body, Bernard replaced his friend's tunic with his own. Thereafter he used to wear Malachy's tunic when celebrating Mass; and it was in this same tunic that he himself was to be buried five years later.[17] Even more striking was Bernard's liberty with the rubrics at Malachy's funeral Mass. Instead of using the traditional collect for a deceased bishop, Bernard substituted the formula for a bishop saint: *Deus, qui beatum Malachiam pontificem sanctorum tuorum meritis coaequasti, tribue, quaesumus, ut qui pretiosae mortis eius festa agimus, vitae quoque imitemur exempla.* As if he had not made his point clear enough, he thereupon proceeded to kiss the feet of the dead Malachy, as if venerating the relics of a saint.[18] The burial itself took place within the monastery church which Malachy had so loved. Variant readings of the final paragraph of Bernard's *Vita Sancti Malachiae Episcopi* specify the oratory of Our Lady—*"in oratorio sanctae Dei genitricis Mariae."*[19] The text is problematical. Since the high altar of Cistercian churches was generally consecrated in honor of Our Lady, the reference might be simply to the monastery church; or, again, it might refer to a separate chapel corresponding to the traditional "Lady Chapel."[20] Whatever the precise location of Malachy's first resting-place, Bernard joined his friend five years later, their tombs being in close proximity

17. *S. Bernardi Vita Prima* V, 23, PL 185:364D-365A.
18. Ibid., IV, 21, PL 185:333A-B.
19. *Opera*, III, 378, critical apparatus for line 19.
20. Cf. Jean Leclercq, "Documents on the Cult of St Malachy," in *Seanchas Ardmhacha (Journal of the Armagh Diocesan Historical Society)* III (1959):321, with special reference to Note 4. This study will hereafter be referred to by the abbreviated form, Leclercq, *Seanchas.* . . . The corresponding passage occurs on pp. 135-136, with special reference to Note 1, p. 136, in the same article re-printed in Jean Leclercq, *Recueil d'Etudes sur saint Bernard et ses écrits* II (Roma, 1966); hereafter to be referred to as Leclercq, *Recueil* . . . II.

to each other. The bodies remained undisturbed for several decades. Meanwhile major alterations were being made in the church. In October of 1174—the year of Bernard's canonization—the remains of both Bernard and Malachy were solemnly transferred to a different section of the church.[21] But even here, in a chapel in the south transept near the entrance into the cloister, the mortal remains of Bernard and Malachy received no more than a temporary lodging. By 1178 a splendiferous altar-tomb behind the high altar was ready to receive Bernard's relics. There was yet another solemn translation, and Malachy was once again buried next to Bernard, and so close that there was room between them only for the tomb of Cardinal Henry de Marcey, seventh abbot of Clairvaux, who, at his own special request, was buried in 1186 between Bernard and Malachy. On July 6, 1190, Malachy of Armagh was finally canonized by Clement III. The occasion called for a more honorific tomb; so an altar-tomb similar to Bernard's was prepared in front of the high altar. The final solemn translation of Malachy's relics took place in 1191. Thereafter the remains of Bernard and Malachy rested in peace—until the destruction of Clairvaux in the course of the French Revolution.

1190, then, marks the beginning of the *official* cultus of St Malachy. Between 1191 and 1333, a number of statutes touching on the liturgical honors to be rendered Malachy were decreed by the General Chapter. Since collections of the statutes of the General Chapters of this period are lacunose in the extreme, we can be sure that the references to Malachy in the indices to Fr J.-M. Canivez' edition of the *statuta* are insufficient to allow us to trace in detail the evolution of the Malachy-cultus within the Order.[22] Of the 13 pertinent texts, only a

21. For a careful exposé of all the complications relating to the several translations of the relics of St Bernard and St Malachy, see Charles Lalore, *Reliques des trois tombeaux saints de Clairvaux* (Troyes, 1877). The Author seems rather more accurate than the Bollandist, Fr J. de Backer, whose introduction to the *Vita S. Malachiae* remains nevertheless extremely useful; cf. ASS, Nov. II, p. 142 (edition of 1894), "De translatione corporis, de reliquiis S. Malachiae, deque eius cultu in Hibernia."

22. *Statuta Capitulorum Generalium Ordinis Cisterciensis (1116-1786)*, T. VIII (Louvain, 1941) p. 317. Fr Canivez' *opus magnum* will hereafter be referred to by the abbreviated form, Canivez, *Statuta*. . .

few concern the Order at large; a similarly small number involve only the Irish Cistercian houses; the greater number of these statutes, then, were decreed for Clairvaux. Our study of the origin and evolution of the St Malachy Office will be helped if we situate it against the sketchy background supplied by these statutes.

1191   The feast of St Malachy is assigned to November 3; his Mass and Office are from the Common—as for St Gregory the Great (March 12).[23]

1192   At Clairvaux, the feast of St Malachy is transferred to November 5, and is celebrated with texts from the Common—as for St Nicholas (December 6).[24] Though only Clairvaux is here specified, the date, November 5, must have been adopted by the Order at large at an early date. All extant Cistercian liturgical mss. with reference to Malachy assign his feast to November 5.

1250   At Clairvaux, a commemoration of Malachy, consisting of antiphon, versicle, and collect, is made daily at the end of Lauds and Vespers.[25]

1255   The monasteries founded by Malachy (Mellifont, Newry . . .?),[26] as well as three other Irish monasteries not designated by name, may have a Lauds and Vespers commemoration similar to the one introduced at Clairvaux in 1250.[27]

---

23. Canivez, *Statuta* . . . I, p. 143 (Anno 1191/60). Dom Martène edited a version of this same statute which differs for the date—November 2 (All Souls Day! ); see Martène and Durand, *Thesaurus Novus Anecdotorum* T. IV (Lutetia Parisiorum, 1717) col. 1272, n. 21. For further notes, see Bernard Backaert, "L'évolution du calendrier cistercien," *Collectane O. C. R.* 13 (1951): 110, n. 201.

24. Canivez, *Statuta* . . . I, p. 146 (Anno 1192/1).

25. Canivez, *Statuta* . . . II, p. 347 (Anno 1250/3).

26. The question of the origins and foundation-dates of the early Cistercian monasteries is tangled in the extreme, and Janauschek's classic *Originum Cisterciensium* is no help at all in clearing up the confusion. It would be risky to suggest a specific list of momasteries (besides Mellifont) which look to Malachy as to their founding father. It is hoped that Fr Colmcille O'Conbhúidhe, who has published numerous scholarly articles on this and related subjects in *Cîteaux in de Nederlanden (alias Cîteaux, Commentarii Cistercienses)* and *Collectanea O.C.R.*, will some day publish a synthesis of his conclusions about the origins and foundation-dates of all the medieval Irish Cistercian monasteries.

27. Canivez, *Statuta* . . . II, p. 418 (Anno 1255/35).

1257 At Clairvaux, the Office from the Common is replaced by a proper Office of St Malachy.[28]

1268 At Mellifont, the first Irish house of Cistercians, Malachy's feast is celebrated as for a solemnity, with a sermon in chapter and with three lamps burning in church.[29]

1273 At Clairvaux, a lamp is kept burning before the tomb of Malachy.[30]

1274 At Clairvaux, the Night Office readings are no longer from the Common, but are taken from St Bernard's sermon for the anniversary of Malachy's death, *Liquet, dilectissimi.*[31]

1275 At Mellifont and in the Irish houses founded from Mellifont, a commemoration of Malachy is introduced at Lauds and Vespers of the "Little Office" of Our Lady —a devotional Office celebrated over and above the Canonical Office.[32]

1295 In the Order at large, the Office from the Common is replaced by the proper Office celebrated at Clairvaux since 1257.[33] In effect, this statute must have remained a dead letter, or else have been confined to the houses of the line of Clairvaux. At a later date, printed liturgical books of the Order provide two Offices for St Malachy—a proper Office for Clairvaux and her daughters, and an Office from the Common for the other houses.[34]

28. Canivez, *Statuta* . . . II, p. 431 (Anno 1257/33).
29. Canivez, *Statuta* . . . III, p. 63 (Anno 1268/26).
30. Canivez, *Statuta* . . . III, p. 123 (Anno 1273/48).
31. Canivez, *Statuta* . . . III, p. 136 (Anno 1274/50).
32. Canivez, *Statuta* . . . III, p. 149 (Anno 1275/66).
33. Canivez, *Statuta* . . . III, p. 279 (Anno 1295/5).
34. The proper Office used by Clairvaux and her daughters disappeared with the "romanized" Cistercian breviary printed at Paris in 1656, under the authority of the abbot of Cîteaux, Claude Vaussin. Examples of earlier books providing for two Offices, one proper, the other from the Common, are the Paris breviaries of 1560 (ff.cccxiiii$^r$-cccxc$^v$) and of 1630 (pp.1021-1028); the Salamanca breviary of 1595 (Castille Congregation) (pp.685-690); the Paris diurnale of 1580 (pp. 429-431); and the Paris psalter of 1634 (proper hymn for houses which celebrate the proper Office, p. 242). The *editio princeps* of the Cistercian Antiphonary (Troyes 1545) does not print the proper Office, but does provide a note to the effect that such an Office is celebrated at Clairvaux and elsewhere in her filiation. The above editions have been referred to in preference to others simply because these are the editions available in the Gethsemani collection of Cistercian liturgical books.

1317 Malachy's name is inserted in the Litany of Saints.[35]

1323 Malachy is now honored with *two* conventual Masses on his feast day; and, at First Vespers of the Office, a solemn, prolix responsory replaces the short responsory heretofore in use.[36]

1333 The Lauds and Vespers commemoration of St Malachy introduced at Clairvaux in 1250 is extended to all the houses in the Clairvaux filiation.[37]

With the help of this extremely sketchy background, we can now proceed to an examination of the two St Malachy Offices from Clairvaux.

### THE TWO ST MALACHY OFFICES FROM CLAIRVAUX

Two principal questions must now be considered:

1 - In the preceding summary of the General Chapter statutes, we saw that a proper Office for St Malachy was introduced at Clairvaux only in 1257. How is it, then, that the Bibliothèque Municipale at Douai possesses a manuscript from the Benedictine Abbey of Anchin, datable to a period not long before 1165, and already containing the proper St Malachy Office? How can one explain the existence of this Office, complete with chant notation, a full quarter-century *before* Malachy's canonization in 1190?

2 - When editing the St Malachy Office as found in the above mentioned Anchin manuscript—Douai, Bibliothèque Municipale, ms.372—[38] Fr Jean Leclercq noted that the corresponding version found in a number of late manuscripts from Clairvaux was rather different from the earlier version found in the Benedictine manuscript from Anchin: "Certain parts are missing, others out of place, and the meaning is not always that of An-

---

35. Canivez, *Statuta* . . . III, p. 333 (Anno 1317/1).

36. Canivez, *Statuta* . . . III, pp. 362-363 (Anno 1323/1). At Clairvaux and wherever the proper Office was authorized, there was already in use a solemn First Vespers responsory, *R. Sanctus pontifex.*

37. Canivez, *Statuta* . . . III, p. 404 (Anno 1333/11).

38. Leclercq, *Seanchas* . . . , pp. 327-332; *Recueil* . . . II, pp. 142-148.

chin."[39] How, then, are we to explain the significant differences between the early Anchin manuscript, selected and edited by Fr Leclercq as the more authoritative version, and the later version from Clairvaux which was, after all, the center of diffusion for the Malachy-cultus, and which might reasonably be expected to offer the more authoritative version?

### THE EARLIEST VERSION OF THE ST MALACHY OFFICE

The Anchin manuscript has been the object of close scrutiny by numerous scholars. Its importance stems in part from the fact that it represents the earliest attempt in the direction of a manuscript containing the *opera omnia* of St Bernard of Clairvaux. Anchin was noted for the high caliber of the material produced by its *scriptorium*. Productivity reached a high under Abbot Alvisus (1111-1131), only to be surpassed in excellence under his successor, Bl. Goswin (1131-1166).[40] Both abbots were among Bernard's friends and admirers. Goswin surely had little difficulty in obtaining from Clairvaux Bernardine writings suitable for transcription at Anchin. The bulky manuscript under discussion is a three-volume affair; and since the scribe managed to include notes referring to his modest self in all three volumes, we know that the scribe of this handsome manuscript was none other than the prestigious Siger, who has rightly been called "the abbey's most reputable scribe."[41] Dom Martène and Dom Durand examined the manuscript early in the eighteenth century; and Martène wrote enthusiastically that "I have never seen anything more beautiful of this type."[42] Earlier debates about the date of the manuscript have now been settled to the satisfaction of everyone. As early as 1953, Dom Leclercq convincingly demonstrated that the collection cannot be much later than 1165.[43] Less than a decade later,

39. Leclercq, *Seanchas . . .* , p. 328; *Recueil . . .* II, p. 143.

40. See Giles Constable, *The Letters of Peter the Venerable* II (Cambridge, Massachusetts, 1967), pp. 50-53, with special reference to Note 203, p. 50, which provides a copious bibliography of material relating to the *scriptorium* of Anchin.

41. P. Sejourné, "Les inédits bernardins du manuscrit d'Anchin," *Saint Bernard et son temps* II, (Dijon, 1929) p. 247.

42. *Voyage littéraire de deux religieux bénédictins de la Congrégation de Saint Maur* II, (Paris, 1724), p. 79.

43. *Etudes sur saint Bernard et le texte de ses écrits,* ASOC 9 (1953): 130-132.

the accuracy of Fr Leclercq's dating received a further confirmation from A. H. Bredero, who had occasion to study this
important manuscript in preparation for his masterly study of
the manuscript tradition of the *Vita Prima* of St Bernard.[44]

The St Malachy material is assembled in the first volume of
this tripartite collection. The *Vita Sancti Malachiae Episcopi*
(ff. 177r-188v) opens the dossier; next in order of occurence
is Bernard's second Sermon preached on the occasion of the
anniversary of Malachy's death and burial (ff.188v-189r). On
f. 189r we find the *Versus Sancti Malachiae*—a brief formula
authored by Malachy, and quoted in part by Geoffrey of Auxerre in a sermon preached on the anniversary of Malachy's
death.[45] A rubric slightly posterior to the original hand states,
f.189v: "*Alium sermonem cum epistola ad Hybernienses et
cantu* (sic!) *require inferius,*" This reference is to ff. 194r-198r,
where we find Bernard's *Sermo I in Transitu Sancti Malachiae
Episcopi,*[46] his *Letter 374,*[47] and the Saint Malachy Office in
full chant notation (ff.196r-198r).[48]

This Office is enough to bring joy to the heart of any chant
paleographer. Clarity, grace, elegance. . . . Either Siger or the
scribe responsible for the chant notation was truly a great
scribe. Text and music are in double-columns, and at the rate
of 18 4-line staves per folio. The scribe uses a type of notation
derived from the kind dubbed for better or worse "Metz notation." Restrictions of the typographical order prohibit any
discussion of the *music* of this Office; but, hopefully, this particular topic can be treated separately at a later date. Suffice
it to say, in the meantime, that there can be no doubt as to
the basically Cistercian characteristics of this Office. The monastic structure is typically Cistercian (only a single antiphon
at Lauds, and with the Second Vespers antiphons borrowed

44. *Etudes sur la "Vita prima" de Saint Bernard (Troisième partie),* ASOC 18
(1962): 4-5, Note 5. This study will thereafter be referred to by the abbreviated
form Bredero, *Etudes.* . . .
45. Edited by Fr Leclercq, pp. 169-170 of the collection of studies referred to
above, Note 43.
46. *Opera,* V, 417-423.
47. PL 182:578-580.
48. Leclercq, *Seanchas* . . ., pp. 329-332; *Recueil* . . . II, pp. 144-148.

presumably from the first four antiphons of the Night Office series). As in many Offices of this period, antiphons and responsories follow, for their modality, the numerical sequence of the gregorian modes. A good argument against the Cistercian origins of this Office could be based on the fact that the psalm-tones are not the ones used by the Order from at least 1147 onwards—and the Office could hardly have been written before Malachy's death in 1148! Moreover, the quilisma-neum occurs frequently, although this particular neum is utterly foreign to all Cistercian manuscripts of this period. These objections are rather superficial. Any scribe would have been inclined to adjust the psalm-tones and the conventions of notation to local usage. Besides, the music, though rather clumsy, presents elements which are distinctively, if not exclusively, Cistercian. The invitatory antiphon, for instance, is a first mode melody of a type characteristic of the Order's repertory after ca. 1147. The normal series of Venite-tones with corresponding antiphons excluded chants in the first and eighth modes. The Cistercians, however, turned one of the standard fourth mode Venite-tones into a first mode formula.[49] The texts, too, are cribbed straight from writings by St Bernard; and it would seem that the music is not less Clairvallian in origin.

But how, then, are we to explain the presence of this Office in full chant notation in a manuscript written a quarter-century *before* Malachy's canonization? The Cistercian General Chapter was more than a little touchy about liturgical initiatives taken by any house on even a modest scale. That an important community so much in the limelight as Clairvaux should have begun celebrating the proper Office of an uncanonized Irish bishop, be he ever so holy, was simply out of the question.

I can advance no absolutely apodictic proof in favor of the following hypothesis; but I should nonetheless like to suggest that this complete proper St Malachy Office was composed at Clairvaux with a view to Malachy's canonization.

Objection! Malachy was canonized only in 1190; but this Office had already been composed by 1165 at the latest!

49. Cf. Willi Apel, *Gregorian Chant* (Bloomington, Indiana, 1958), pp. 241-244.

The objection is not sustained. It is true that Clairvaux had to wait till July 6, 1190, to see Malachy officially raised to the honors of the altar; but attempts to secure this canonization had been made on several occasions prior to this date. We know, for instance, that Tromund, abbot of Chiaravalle (near Milan) —a notary of the Roman curia, and a principal agent in the canonization process of St Bernard—had been commissioned to obtain not only Bernard's canonization, but Malachy's as well. We have, indeed, Tromund's letter to Gerard, abbot of Clairvaux, in which he breaks the bitter news that Pope Alexander III's policy was one canonization at a time. A double-request, wrote the Cistercian diplomat, would result in the canonization of neither Bernard nor of Malachy.[50]

This, then, was the way things stood in 1174. It was also the way things had stood more than a decade earlier. For, already in 1162, an energetic but unsuccessful attempt had been initiated to obtain from the same Alexander III the canonization of Bernard, hopefully on the occasion of the Council of Tours in 1163. At that time the Pope deferred Bernard's canonization on the remarkable grounds that similar canonization requests had been pouring in, and that it would be indelicate to say "Yes" for Bernard and "No" for the others. Whether Pope Alexander's excuse was particularly cogent is beside the point. What is more to our immediate purpose is the fact that, not only Bernard, but Malachy as well was up for canonization in 1162. This is, at any rate, the conclusion of A. H. Bredero, in his magisterial study of the *Vita Prima* of St Bernard.[51] The evidence this fine scholar adduces is interesting, though not necessarily decisive. He notes first that, in the manuscript tradition of the *Vita Prima*, a number of manuscripts place the *Vita Prima*, which had been written with a view to Bernard's canonization, side by side with Bernard's own *Vita Sancti Malachiae Episcopi*, which we know was also used later on in 1190, in the final and successful attempt to obtain Malachy's canoni-

50. PL 185:626 CD.
51. Bredero, *Etudes . . .*, pp. 44-45.

zation.[52] This juxtaposition of the two *Vitae*, then, would correspond to the double-request for the canonization of the two partners in holiness buried side by side in the abbey church of Clairvaux.[53] Moreover, in the sections of the *Vita Prima* which were authored by Geoffrey of Auxerre, there are a number of passages allegedly slanted in support of a request for the canonization of Malachy—passages in which Bernard equivalently canonizes his friend.[54]

While it seems (to me) that his line of argument is based on rather meagre evidence, the evidence nevertheless becomes (at least for me) more persuasive against the background of the St Malachy Office included in the Anchin manuscript of Bernard's collected writings. This manuscript, let it be remembered, can now be dated securely as no later than 1165; and a somewhat earlier date is by no means out of question for the first volume, which alone here concerns us. Would it be unreasonable to suppose that the eager Clairvallian supporters of Malachy's canonization not only prepared the dossier of pertinent documents in support of their request, but even, in their overly optimistic enthusiasm, went so far as to shape up the proper Office they intended to celebrate, once their holy patron had been raised to the honors of the altar? The suggestion is tentatively offered, then, that the early version of the St Malachy Office in Douai, manuscript 372, was tossed together from various Bernardine sources with a view to Malachy's canonization, which looked so hopefully imminent around 1162.

## The Later Version of the St Malachy Office

When Malachy was at long last enrolled in the catalogue of saints in 1190, it might have been expected that the proper Office composed decades earlier would have been resurrected from the Clairvaux archives and adopted for use throughout the

---

52. Cf. E. W. Kemp, *Canonization and Authority in the Western Church* (Oxford —London, 1948), p. 96.
53. Bredero, *Etudes . . .*, p. 44, with special attention to Note 3, where a list of mss. is given and analyzed.
54. Bredero, *Etudes . . .*, pp. 44-45, with special attention to p. 44, Note 4.

Order. This is not what happened. Instead, the General Chapter of 1191 decreed that the newly canonized saint would be feasted with texts from the *Commune Sanctorum*—in the same way as St Gregory the Great.[55] In 1192, the reference was to St Nicholas;[56] but since these saints had much the same texts, it came to the same difference. As we have already seen from our earlier survey of the General Chapter statutes, it was only in 1257 that Clairvaux, and only Clairvaux, obtained a proper Office with its own characteristic antiphons and responsories; and even then, this Office in the 1257 redaction differed in parts (as Fr Jean Leclercq has already noted) from the earlier redaction in the Anchin manuscript. Why was not the version of ca. 1162 adopted for the Order in 1190? And why was a new redaction called for when this proper Office was finally authorized for use at Clairvaux in 1257?

The answer to these questions can best be understood if the reader has before his eyes a transcription in which he can see for himself what is common to the two versions, and what is proper to each.

We are dealing with what is basically a single Office in two successive redactions.

Redaction I  (= R I) is that found in the Anchin manuscript, Douai, Bibliothèque Municipale, manuscript 372, vol I, ff. 196r-198r. The text has already been edited by Fr Jean Leclercq.[57]

Redaction II  (= R II) is that found in some six liturgical manuscripts from Clairvaux, all of which are now in the Bibliothèque Municipale at Troyes. These six manuscripts provide the texts, but no music.

R II is based on the following Troyes manuscripts:

1- Ms. 574,  ff. 12r-13v. A twelfth-century antiphonary which still bears the Clairvaux catalogue number Z.41.

55. Canivez, *Statuta* . . . I, p. 143 (Anno 1191/60).
56. Canivez, *Statuta* . . . I, p. 146 (Anno 1192/1).
57. See above, Note 48.

Our Office does not belong to the original manuscript, but is written on a thirteenth-century insert.

2- Ms, 1158,  ff. 311r-313v. A breviary written between 1218 and 1224. The two earlier Clairvaux classification numbers are still visible—Z.13 and Etc.73. The Malachy Office is in a second, late thirteenth-century hand. Detailed description in V. Leroquais, *Les bréviaires manuscrits des bibliothèques publiques de France*. T. IV (Paris, 1934), pp. 226-227, n. 829.

3- Ms. 1977,  ff. 265r-268r. A Clairvaux breviary from the middle of the thirteenth century. Here again the Malachy Office occurs in a supplement compiled in stages by successive hands. Complete description in Leroquais, *Bréviaires* . . . IV, pp. 257-258, n. 862.

4- Ms. 1894,  ff. 258v-261v. A breviary from the second half of the thirteenth century, still bearing the Clairvaux catalogue number Etc.6. Detailed description in Leroquais, *Bréviaires* . . . IV, pp. 243-244, n. 846.

5- Ms. 1970,  ff. 108v-112r. A breviary containing only the sanctoral cycle, and written in 1440 as a companion to another Clairvaux manuscript, Troyes 1910; earlier classification number Z.39. Detailed description in Leroquais, *Bréviaires* . . . IV, pp. 248-249, n. 853, which corrects the brief description given in the *Catalogue générale* (série in-4), T. II, p. 789.

6- Ms. 2005,  ff. 210r-216v. A Clairvaux breviary containing only the summer season sanctoral cycle, and written in the last half of the fifteenth century. Detailed description in Leroquais, *Bréviaires* . . . IV, p. 259, n. 864.

These six manuscripts are, as one might expect, in virtually total agreement. They differ from one another chiefly in orthography, phrasing of rubrics, presence or absence of hymns and of various elements taken from the *Commune Sanctorum*. A few variants are obviously no more than the flubs of drowsy scribes.

Since the sole purpose of the following transcription is to clarify the relationship between R I and R II, no attempt has been made to produce a critical edition such as would take account of orthographical differences, accidental variants, and rubrical formulae. The following transcription, then, uses modern spelling and punctuation, and standardizes the unimportant and merely apparent differences between manuscripts. For the moment we shall be concerned only with the antiphons and responsories. The other elements of the Office will be treated briefly in their proper place.

Most (though not all) of the sources have long since been identified by Fr Jean Leclercq.[58] Apart from an occasional biblical allusion, the identifiable direct sources are confined to two of Bernard's Malachian writings:

V Mal   *Vita Sancti Malachiae Episcopi*, in Leclercq and Rochais, *S. Bernardi Opera, Vol. III: Tractatus et Opuscula* (Romae, 1963), pp. 307-378; PL 182:1073-1118.

Mal 2   *Sermo II in Transitu S. Malachiae Episcopi*. in PL 183:486-490. (The critical text will appear in Vol. VI of the *opera omnia* of Bernard—not yet available).

No attempt has been made to distinguish direct citations from re-workings and conflations of the original sources.

So often as R I = R II, the text in common is printed in the center of the page.

Variant versions and texts proper to R I are reproduced toward the left hand; those proper to R II, to the right. In this way the reader can see at a glance what is common to the two redactions, and what marks one off from the other.

58. In the edition referred to above, Note 48.

### ANTIPHONS AND RESPONSORIES OF THE ST MALACHY OFFICE

*Ad Vesperas super Psalmos*

Mal 2, 7      *A.* Festivitas tua, Malachia, quae merito tuis virtutibus votiva impenditur, tuis nobis efficiatur meritis et precibus salutaris.

Mal 2, 7      *A.* Gloria sanctitatis tuae, quae a nobis frequentatur, continuatur ab angelis,
    sic                                       tunc
erit nobis digne iucunda, si fuerit et fructuosa.

Mal 2, 7      *A.* Liceat nobis aliquas, te migrante, retinere reliquas de fructibus.
    Spiritus                             spiritalibus
quibus onustus ascendis, qui in tuo hodie tam delicioso convivio congregamur.

Mal 2, 8      *A.* Esto nobis, quaesumus, alter Moyses vel alter Elias, impertiens de tuo spiritu nobis, quorum in spiritu et virtute venisti.

Mal 2, 7      *Ad Magnificat Antiphona* Magna est super te, O Malachia, divinae dispensatio pietatis, qui te parvum fecit in oculis tuis magnum in suis; qui magna fecit per te, salvans patriam tuam, magna fecit tibi, introducens te in gloriam suam.

---

*Invitatorium* Mirabilis Deus in
virtutibus                              operibus
Malachiae, mirabilis Malachias in humilitate sua: * Venite, adoremus humilitatis Magistrum. Ps. Venite.

### In I⁰ Nocturno

V Mal 1, 1      *A.* Malachias ab infantia spiritum sortitus est bonum, per quem erat puer docilis et amabilis valde.      *A.* Puer Malachias in divinus exercebatur meditari in lege Domini, refici parcius, orare frequentius.      V Mal 1, 1

V Mal 1, 1      *A.* In disciplina morum profectuque virtutum super omnes docentes se in brevi enituit, unctione magistra.      *A.* Levabat puer puras manus in oratione ubi secrete id posset, cautus declinare virus virtutum, inanem, gloriam.      V Mal 1, 1

ANTIPHONS AND RESPONSORIES OF THE ST MALACHY OFFICE—*contd.*

*V Mal 1, 2*

*A.* Crescente aetate, crescebat simul sapientia et gratia apud Deum et homines.

*A.* Sedebat secus pedes Imarii solitarius et tacebat, sciens cultum iustitiae esse silentium.

*V Mal 2, 5*

*V Mal 3, 7*

*A.* Tradebat iura caelestia optimus legislator, leges dabat plenas iustitae, plenas modestiae et honesti.                                                                                       honestatis.

*V Mal 9, 18*

*A.* Legem quam aliis imponebat, prior ipse portabat, episcopus et magister.

*V Mal 10, 21*

*A.* O virtutem viri, o animi puritatem, nec affectantis honorem, nec formidantis mortem pro Christi nomine.

*V Mal 19, 43*

*R.* Prima virtus Malachiae habitus corporis sui, quod ita composite et uno semper modo agebat, * Ut nil appareret in eo quod posset offendere intuentes.
*V.* Totum in eo disciplinatum, totum insigne virtutis, perfectionis forma. * Ut nil.

*R.* Vita tua, O Malachia, lex vitae et disciplinae; mors tua, mortis portus et porta vitae; memoria tua dulcedo suavitatis et gratiae; praesentia tua corona gloriae in manu * Domini Dei tui.
*V.* Non tibi excidat, quaesumus, nostri memoria, beata fruenti praesentia. * Domini Dei tui.

*Mal 2, 8*

*V Mal 11, 23*

*R.* Precibus viri sancti concutientibus elementa, * Solos turbo tenebrosus involvit, qui parabant opera tenebrarum.
*V.* Illos autem, qui cum Malachia erant, omnino procella non tetigit, nec quidquam molestiae intulit. * Solos.

*V Mal 12, 25
eum*

*R.* Condixerant impii ut                                                         sanctum
dolo tenerent et occiderent; sed ut sese in medio intulit, armatorum concidere facies omnium, * Quia pavor irruit super eos.
*V.* Stabat hostia, carnifices undique circumstabant, et non fuit qui immolaret. * Quia.

*V Mal 15, 35*

*R.* Videns Sycharus Malachiam ait: Hic est de quo dicebam: Veniet de Hibernia pontifex sanctus * Qui scit cogitationes hominum.
*V.* Non potuit latere lucerna sub modio, prodente eam per os Sychari Spiritu Sancto. * Qui scit. Gloria Patri.

*In II⁰ Nocturno*

V Mal 13, 29    A. Infelix mulier clamoribus improbis blasphemias evomebat in sanctum, sed morte horren-
da luit peccatum blasphemiae.

V Mal 20, 46    A. Ut attigit aeger lectulum sacerdotis, demo-
num terror et horror quem patiebatur, et
omnis pariter aegritudo recessit.

V Mal 21, 46    A. Stans Malachias          A. Dum sacrificaret    V Mal 29, 65
et orans super puel-        antistes, columba
lam mutam, sputum           visa est ingredi per
misit in os eius, et        fenestram in clari-
loquentem dimisit.          tate magna, *eaque*
                            sacerdos perfusus est,
                            et basilica tota re-
                            splenduit.

V Mal 29, 65    A. Dum sacrificaret         A. Stans Malachias     V Mal 21, 46
antistes, columba           et orans super pue-
visa est ingredi per        llam mutam, sputum
fenestram in clari-         misit in os eius, et lo-
tate magna, et ea           quentem dimisit.
sacerdos perfusus
est, et basilica tota
resplenduit.

V Mal 25, 54    A. Mulier importabilis iracundiae, orante Malachia, incredibili mutatione subito mansuevit.

V Mal 26, 57    A. Percusso divinitus haeretico iuxta verbum
Malachiae, accitur episcopus, agnoscitur veritas; et uno paene momento perfidia ore ab-
dicatur et morte diluitur.

V Mal 22, 45    R. Pulsus femina demon, alteram propter astan-
tem invadit; quam coactus deserere, redit ad
prima; sic alternatim vexabat eas, * Ut manifesta fieret et maligni praesentia et victoria
Malachiae.
V. Indignans sanctus ab utraque demonem fu-
gat non minus vexatum hiis quas vexaverat.
* Ut manifesta.

V Mal 23, 49    R. Claudus quidam manibus humi repens, orante Malachia, surgit; stupte, * Paene somni-
um suspicatus.
V. Repletus est stupore et extasi in eo quod
contigerat illi. * Paene.

ANTIPHONS AND RESPONSORIES OF THE ST MALACHY OFFICE—*contd.*

*V Mal 29, 65*     *R.* Dum sanctorum memorias vir sanctus circuiret, inter orandum unum ex altaribus ardere conspexit; et accedens \* Sacram amplexatus est aram.
               *V.* Intellexit divinum esse quod cernebatur; et mediis sese flammis immergens. \* Sacram.

*V Mal 19, 44*    *R.* O virum apostolicae gratiae et virtutis, qui sine sumptu posuit Evangelium, et nil minus a magnis apostolis faciens, \* Etiam mortuam suscitavit.

*Mk 7, 37*       *V.* Bene omnia fecit;
       et                                                 *om.*
               surdos fecit audire et mutos loqui. \* Etiam. Gloria Patri.

*Mal 2, 8*       *Ad Cantica Antiphona* O oliva fructifera in domo Dei, O oleum laetitiae
     unguens et lucens,                                 *om.*
               fovens beneficiis, coruscans miraculis, fac nos eius qua frueris lucis suavitatisque participes.

*V Mal 31, 70*    *R.* Celebratis Missarum solemiis.
       *om.*                                              vir sanctus
               febre corripitur; sciens se resolvi, dicebat suis: \* Appropinquat dies quam semper optavi, dies laetitiae cordis mei.
               *V.* Qui me perduxit ad locum quem petii, terminum quem aeque volui non negabit. \* Appropinquat.

*V Mal 31, 74*    *R.* Quinquagesiomo quarto aetatis suae, anno, loco, et die quo praeelegit et praedixerat, Malachias \* Obdormivit in Domino.
               *V.* Imponens prius singulis qui aderant manus, et omnibus benedicens. \* Obdormivit.

*Mal 2, 6*       *R.* Sanctus pontifex, qui in spiritu humilitatis hostias
     pacificas caelis                                  caelis pacificas
               frequenter invexit, hodie per semetipsum introivit ad altare Dei, \* Ipse hostia et sacerdos.
*Heb 9, 12*      *V.* Semel introivit in sancta, aeterna redemptione inventa. \* Ipse.

*Mal 2, 8*

*R.* Vita tua, O Mala-
chia, lex vitae et dis-
ciplinae; mors tua,
mortis portus et
porta vitae; memo-
ria tua dulcedo
suavitatis et gra-
tiae; praesentia
tua corona gloriae
in manu * Domini
Dei tui.
*V.* Non tibi excidat,
quaesumus, nostri
memoria, beata fru-
enti praesentia.
* Domini. Gloria.

*R.* Stabat puer cuius    *V Mal 31, 75*
emortuum pendebat
a latere; quo comperto,
manus eius arida appli-
catur manui gloriosi
praesulis iam defuncti;
* Nempe manus Mala-
chiae fuit mortuae manui
quod mortuo homini
Eliseus.
*V.* Puer ille de longe
venerat, et manum
quam pendentem
attulerat sanam in
patriam reportavit.
* Nempe. Gloria
Patri.

### In Laudibus Matutinis

*Mal 2, 7*

*A.* Domum istam
decet sanctitudo,
in qua tantae fre-
quentatur memo-
ria sanctitatus.
Sancte Malachia,
serva eam in sancti-
tate et iustitia!

*A.* Dedit Dominus    *V Mal 27, 60*
sancto calcandi su-
per serpentes et
scorpiones, alligare
reges eorum in com-
pedibus, et nobiles
eorum in manicis
ferreis.

*Mal 2, 6*

*Ad Benedictus A.*
Benedictus Domi-
nus Deus Malachiae,
qui eius pontificio
visitavit plebem suam,
eius exemplo aedificavit
ecclesiam suam, eius
sollemni recordatione
praesentem hodie con-
solatur familiam suam.

*Ad Benedictus A.*    *Mal 2, 5*
Dilectus Deo et homi-
nibus, hodie Malachias
in consortio angelorum
recipitur; nunc felicius
gloriosi interpretatio
nominis adimpletur,
quando pari cum an-
gelis gloria et felicitate
laetatur.

### Ad Primam

*Mal 2, 8*

*A.* O stella matutina, eo ceteris clarior quo
diei similior,                                              *om.*
         vicinior soli, dignare praeire nobis, ut et nos
         in lumine ambulemus.

ANTIPHONS AND RESPONSORIES OF THE ST MALACHY OFFICE—*contd.*

### Ad Tertiam

Mal 2, 8

*A.* O luminare magnum et lux in tenebris lucens, fuga de cordibus nostris virtutum splendoribus tenebras vitiorum.

---

### Ad Sextam

*A.* O lux meridiana ardens et lucens, dignare nos illius consortio luminis, quo accensus taliter effulsisti. recipe nos in consortio luminis, quo accensus suaviter intus et foris mirabiliter effulsisti.

---

### Ad Nonam

Mal 2, 8

*A.* O odoriferum lilium, spargens ubique vivificum suavitatis odorem, cuius apud nos memoria in benedictione est, apud superos praesentia in honore, da canentibus te tantae plenitudinis participio non privari.

---

### Ad Vesperas

Mal 2, 6

*Ad Magnificat A.* Exsultet in Domino spiritus Malachiae, quod mole levatus corporea, nulla iam terrena meteria praegravatur quominus tota alacritate omnem transiens creaturam, pergat totus in Deum, et adhaerens illi, unus fit cum eo spiritus in aeternum.

We are now in a position to understand why the Office as it appears in the Anchin manuscript could not have been used without redactional changes when Malachy was finally canonized in 1190.

St Bernard was canonized in 1174. In 1175 the General Chapter assigned him an Office which was proper, and which is still familiar to most Cistercians of pre-Vatican II generations. This proper St Bernard Office derives from a number of different sources.[59] Now, one of these sources is clearly the first redaction of the St Malachy Office. Thus, when we compare R I and R II as transcribed above, we note the following:

— The first three antiphons of the First Nocturn in R I are replaced by a new series of three antiphons in R II. Why? Because the three antiphons were purloined for use as the first three antiphons of First Vespers of the St Bernard Office of 1175. (The same antiphons also occurred at Prime, Terce, and Sext.)
— The first responsory of Nocturn I passed from R I into the same position in the St Bernard Office. R II made good the resulting lacuna by transferring Responsory 12 to the beginning of the series, and by providing a new text for the last responsory in R II.
— In the Second Nocturn, R II reverses the order of the third and fourth antiphons of R I. The reason? I have no idea. . . .
— At Lauds, the antiphon proper to R I appears (in a textually shorter version) as the Lauds antiphon of the St Bernard Office. A new antiphon therefore had to be provided in R II.
— In the same way, the Benedictus antiphon of R I became St Bernard's Benedictus antiphon, and a new one had to be provided for St Malachy in R II.

(Curiously enough, the Second Vespers Magnificat antiphon is common to R I, R II, and the St Bernard Office. In the light of the preceding changes, one would have expected a new Magnificat antiphon in R II. Consistency, however, is the last thing one ought to expect from medieval liturgists. . . .)

Besides these major differences, there are a number of minor variants for some of the texts common to R I and R II. In general, the version proper to R II usually represents an intentional

59. These have been carefully tabulated by Fr Bruno Griesser, "Das Offizium des hl. Bernhard in Cisterzienserbrevier und seine geschichtliche Entwicklung," *Cistercienser-Chronik* 60 (1953), pp. 57-86. Unfortunately, the proper St Malachy Office was not used as a possible source of material, probably because Dom Leclercq had not yet published his edition of R I as found in the Anchin ms.

modification of R I. The R I variants almost always correspond
to the textual version of the source from which the particular
antiphon or responsory is drawn. Thus, R I usually agrees with
the Leclercq edition of VM and with the Migne edition of Mal
II against R II.

In summary, the evolution of the St Malachy Office seems
to have developed in this manner:

1— ca. 1162: A proper Office is composed at Clairvaux, with
a view to Malachy's canonization. Since Mal-
achy was not canonized according to schedule,
the Office was shelved—though not before it
had been transcribed in the Anchin manuscript.

2— ca. 1174: A proper Office is composed at Clairvaux for
the newly canonized St Bernard. Sections of
the discarded Malachy Office are salvaged for
adaptation and incorporation into the St Bernard Office.

3— 1190: Malachy officially becomes St Malachy, and
needs an Office. But R I cannot by used without making good the gaps left by texts borrowed in 1174 for Bernard's Office. The sim-
plest solution was to take Malachy's Office
from the Common.

4— 1257: At Clairvaux, the St Malachy Offices of ca.
1162 is revised for authorized use at Clairvaux,
with the new material being taken, like the original texts, from VM and Mal II.

Two further remarks:

1— On reflection, it is easy enough to see why the Clairvaux brethren would have thought of the discarded Malachy
Office as a source of material for the St Bernard counterpart.
Fr Ailbe Luddy once noted that "Anyone who takes the trouble to compare the nineteenth chapter of Bernard's *Life of St
Malachy*, and his second sermon on the same, with the instruc-
tions written for Pope Eugenius' guidance by the great Abbot
in his *De consideratione* cannot fail to perceive a very striking
resemblance in thought and expression. In painting his portrait

of the ideal pontiff, Bernard undoubtedly had his Irish friend in view."[60] Possibly. But Geoffrey of Auxerre, who claims to be the secretary who took down the *Vita Sancti Malachiae Episcopi* at Bernard's dictation, noted that, in painting the portrait of Malachy, Bernard was really, though inadvertently, describing himself:

> *Suos vero santissimus Pater noster commendavit mores, in beato Malachia suam expressit imaginem non advertens. Nam ego fateor, dictante eo, in tabulis quae proferebat excipiens, sine dilatione notavi quod domi abiit ut disceret.*[61]

What then would have been more natural than to use Bernard's penportrait of Malachy as a means of painting the portrait of Bernard himself?

2– Though the proper St Malachy Office was not adopted for use in the Order in 1190, it would be forcing the evidence too much to suggest that the only reason for this was the drastic revision to which R I would have to be subjected. A complety new proper Office put considerable demands on the celebrating community. Much of the material had to be committed to memory, since choir-books were reduced to a minimum. Moreover, it is not clear that all the Cistercians houses were as devoted to Malachy as was Clairvaux. True, the Canonization Bull *Ideo sacrosanctum*[62] was addressed to the General Chapter rather than to the Clairvallians in the first instance. But the generality of Cistercians might possibly have considered a proper Office for a non-Cistercian Irish bishop just a bit exuberant.

## Other Elements of the St Malachy Office

Some readers might be curious about the parts of the St Malachy Office other than the antiphons and responsories.

60. *Life of St Malachy* (Dublin, 1930), p. 71.
61. Leclercq, *Etudes sur saint Bernard et le texte de ses écrits,* ASOC 9 (1953): 164. As Fr Leclercq himself noted, Ibid., Note 2, the final part of the last sentence is none too clear. Could it be an attempt to render into Latin a proverb to the effect that the lessons one expects to learn in foreign parts are sometimes best learned at home?
62. PL 204:1466-1467, n. CXLIX of the documents issued by Clement III.

The short biblical paraphrases used for the *short readings* were taken from the Common of a Bishop, and are without particular interest: *Eccli* 44:25 (Vespers I and II, Lauds, Terce); *Eccli* 44:16-17 (Sext); *Eccli* 44:26-27 (None).

Of greater interest are the *Night Office readings*. The General Chapter of 1192 had specified that Malachy's Office was to be celebrated as for the feast of St Nicholas. Since the latter saint's readings were taken from the Common, the same would be true for Malachy. At least two of the extant pre-1190 Office lectionaries have marginal additions indicating the precise references; e.g., Paris, Bibliothèque Nationale, ms. nouv. acq. lat. 20202 —a lectionary from Aquafredda (on Lake Como, Italy), where we read on f. 111v:

> *Malachie episcopi. VIII lectiones. Beati sunt servi illi. Expositionem euangelii. Sint lumbi uestri precincti. Require in unius confessoris.*

The same references occur in the marginal addition on f. 91r of the famous *ne varietur* Cistercian manuscript-type, Dijon, Bibliothèque Municipale, ms. 114 (*olim* 82). All twelve of these readings are sections of St Gregory the Great's Homily 13 from the first series of homilies in his collection *Homiliae in Evangelia.*[63] As is frequent in the Cistercian lectionary, lessons 9-12 make up the first part of the homily, while lessons 1-8 constitute the rest of the homily to its end. It was only in 1274 that Clairvaux, and only Clairvaux, was allowed to use instead St Bernard's sermon *Liquet, dilectissimi.* Of the six Clairvaux manuscripts listed earlier, only the latter five indicate the readings. Since the various scribes provided only snippets of the complete text, a certain divergence of indications is normal and to be expected. The following table sums up the data:

| Troyes, Bibl.Mun. | Lessons I - VIII | | Lessons IX - XII | |
|---|---|---|---|---|
| | Bernard | Gregory | Bernard | Gregory |
| Ms. 1158 | x | | x | |
| Ms. 1977 | x | | | x |
| Ms. 1894 | | x | | x |
| Ms. 1970 | x | | | x |
| Ms. 2005 | | x | | x |

63. PL 76:1123-1127.

Manuscripts 1894 and 2005 retain the Common readings —perhaps to avoid using the extra space required for proper readings. In general, however, Gregory's commentary on Lk 12:35-40 seems to have been kept for the Third Nocturn, even when Bernard's sermon is used for Nocturns I and II (ms. 1158 is the sole exception). This is confirmed by the later printed breviaries published at a time when the Clairvaux readings were printed in the Order's official breviary; e.g., the Paris breviary of 1560, ff. cccxiijᵛ-cccxvʳ; the Salamanca breviary of 1595, pp. 686-689; and the Paris breviary of 1630, pp. 1022-1027.

The *hymns* raise an interesting problem. Of the six Clairvaux manuscripts analyzed above for establishing the text of R II, four specify the hymn *Malachiae sollemnia*—Manuscripts 574, 1970, 1977, and 2005.[64] The same text appears in another Clairvaux breviary in a fourteenth-century insert added to the thirteenth-century breviary manuscript, Troyes ms. 1160, f. 503r. Printed liturgical books with the proper Malachy Office inevitably include *Malachiae sollemnia* as part of the Office. Besides the three breviaries listed in the preceding paragraph, there are the Paris psalter of 1533, f. clxxjᵛ, the Paris diurnale of 1580, p. 255, and the Paris psalter of 1634, p. 242; and other printed books of the same period not accessible to me, doubtless indicate the same hymn for those authorized to use the proper Office, i.e., Clairvaux and her daughters. (Other monasteries used the Common Office with the Common hymn *Iesu corona celsior*.) Only one proper hymn was needed for Vespers I and II, Vigils, and Lauds; for the Cistercian practice was to divide the single proper hymn into two sections, A and B. Only A was sung at the Night Office; only B at Lauds; and at both Vespers, the entire hymn—A + B—was sung. It seems rather clear, then, that from the middle of the thirteenth century onwards, *Malachiae sollemnia* was the accepted proper St Malachy hymn. Unfortunately, the Anchin manuscript, sole representative of R I, provides no Malachy-hymn. Nevertheless,

---

64. Ms 574, f. 11v (14th-15th century supplement); ms 1970, f. 109r (reference to an earlier folio: *Malachie sollemnia.* Quere ante primam dominicam aduentu domini); ms. 1977, f. 265r; ms 2005, f. 210r-v.

we do know that there was a twelfth-century proper Malachy-hymn; and the text, edited several times in the past, has received a critical edition in Volume III of Fr Leclercq's edition of St Bernard's works.[65] Of the seven manuscripts collated by Fr Leclercq, six are from the fifteenth or sixteenth centuries; but there is a single twelfth-century manuscript, Düsseldorf, B.26, from the abbey of Altenberg near Cologne, which gives us the earliest extant text of *Nobilis signis, moribus suavis.*[66] In this manuscript, the hymn (without music) follows the *Vita Sancti Malachiae*, and is preceded by the rubric: *Ymnus domni Bernardi abbatis de sancto Malachya episcopo et confessore.* On the basis of the early date and general excellence of this manuscript, Fr Leclercq joins G. Dreves[67] and C. Blume[68] in recognizing the authenticity of authorship. Since, at the present time I rather tend to hold that the earliest extant version of the Malachy Office was composed with a view to Malachy's canonization in 1162 or thereabouts, I myself would feel obliged to consider the possibility that the hymn was composed, not by Bernard, but by someone in the group which provided the proper Office of St Malachy, and that, as so often happened, the anonymous text was soon ascribed to the literary genius who was Malachy's boon companion, biographer, and panegyrist. When Bernard wrote a proper Office of St Victor, years before,[69] he had indeed included a hymn (and a rather weak one, at that) from his own pen. But Bernard, so far as we know, was not responsible for the actual compilation of the Malachy Office, even though this Office was almost total-

65. *Opera*, III, 522-526.
66. On p. 523 of his introduction to the edition of *Nobilis signis* referred to in the preceding note, Fr Leclercq observes, in Note 2, that G. M. Dreves, *Analecta hymnica medii aevi*, T. 19 (Leipzig, 1895), pp. 190-191, edited the hymn with the help of a ms. of Clairvaux provenance, but that this ms. can no longer be identified. The edition in C. Lalore, *Religues des trois tombeaux saints de Clairvaux* (Troyes, 1877), pp. xxxix-xli, is based on Troyes 763, a 16th-century ms. from Clairvaux, which is also used by Fr Leclercq for his own critical edition.
67. P. 191 of the volume referred to in the preceding Note.
68. *Analecta hymnica medii aevi*, T. 52 (Leipzig, 1909), p. 320.
69. Critical edition with introductory notes in *Opera*, III, 497-508.

ly excerpted from his own Malachian writings. It is perfectly understandable that Bernard should have authored a Life of Malachy, should have preached his funeral and anniversary sermons, should have written letters about him, and should even have written his epitaph. But why should he have written a *hymn?* The problem of authorship, however, is unimportant to the present discussion. The problem, rather, is this: Since there was already a perfectly respectable St Malachy hymn available before the end of the twelfth century, why was a new one introduced to be used with Recension II of the St Malachy Office? Once again, no apodictic demonstration is possible, only tentative suggestion. For *Nobilis signis*, we have no clue as to the melody envisaged for this hymn; all we know is that the meter is sapphic adonic, and that the only other Cistercian hymn with the same meter in the twelfth century was the hymn for the Dedication of a Church, *Christe cunctorum.* [70] In the case of the much later *Malachiae sollemnia*, written in iambic dimeters, we *do* know which melody was used. It is unfortunate that typographical considerations make it impossible to include a copy of the music, which is familiar enough to most gregorianists: the melody associated with the hymn *Iesu corona virginum* in the *Antiphonale Monasticum pro Diurnis Horis* [71] and in the *Liber Usualis.* [72] But in the Cistercian tradition, this hymn-tune was first introduced in a quite different context. It is one of the melodies used for *Bernardus doctor inclytus.* [73] Our documentation is much too sketchy to admit of clear-cut affirmations. But I suggest, tentatively and with extreme caution, that *Bernardus doctor inclytus* might well have

70. Many early mss. provide two melodies for this text. See, for instance, Carl Weinmann. *Hymarium Parisiense, Veröffentlichungen der Gregorianischen Akademie zu Freiburg (Schweiz)* (Regensburg, 1905), pp. 66.

71. P. 677, the melody for use outside Paschaltide.

72. Pp. 1211-1212 of the 1956 edition with English introduction and rubrics.

73. Fr Bruno Griesser has studied this hymn on pp. 72-73 of the article referred to above, Note 59, without, however, being able to come to a definite conclusion as to the precise date for the appearance of this text and melody in the Cistercian repertory.

been the first to be admitted into the Cistercian hymnal;[74] and that, when a proper hymn for Malachy was needed at Clairvaux, some clever Clairvallian thought that a Malachy-hymn using the melody of the Bernard-hymn would be just the thing: two saints linked in life, death, and song. The earlier *Nobilis signis* could scarcely have lent itself to such a use, since the meter was so different. The melody of *Malachiae sollemnia,* then, would have been an effective means of expressing the deep friendship which united the two saints, since it was a tune which, in the Cistercian repertory, had been exclusively identified with Bernard. Whether this explanation gives the real reason for the rejection of *Nobilis signis* and the shaping-up of the new hymn, *Malachiae sollemnia,* I do not know, but it *is* an attractive hypothesis.

The Office *versicles* call for only passing comment. As one might expect, they were taken from the Common. Printed liturgical books and the manuscripts—or, at least, *most* of the manuscripts—are in agreement. Only the last two and the latest of the six Clairvaux manuscripts listed above provide a proper versicle for Vespers I and II and Lauds:

V. Sancte Dei praesul Malachia.
R. Ora pro nobis Deum.

This presence of a proper versicle in Troyes manuscripts 1970 and 2005 is not particularly problematical. In 1333 the General Chapter extended to all the houses of the Clairvaux filiation the privilege of having a St Malachy commemoration at Lauds and Vespers.[75] This entailed a formulary consisting of

74. Of the two melodies found with this text in early mss., the *Iesu, corona virginum* melody is the only one used in the early printed books; see, for instance, the psalter-hymnal printed at Paris in 1533, f. clxxi^v. In his indices to *Monumenta Monodica Medii Aevi I. Hymnen (I)* (Kassel - Basel 1956), p. 673, Bruno Stäblein refers, for *Malachiae sollemnia,* to the same melody.

75. Canivez, *Statuta. . . .* III, p. 404 (Anno 1333/11). The statute is edited with the help of a single ms. of the late 14th century, Paris, Bibliothèque de l'Arsenal, ms 10894). The text of the statute gives the formula for the versicle and the collect. In Fr Canivez' edition, the versicle begins "*Vir sancte, Dei praesul . . .*" Since liturgical mss. and printed editions have the reading "*Sancte Dei praesul . . .,*" I suspect that the scribe or the editor made a minor slip, and mistook the abbreviation "*Versiculum*" for the very similar abbreviation "*vir.*" Thus, the text in Fr Canivez' edition should probably read: "*V. Sancte Dei praesul. . . .*"

antiphon, versicle and collect. The texts specified in the statute of 1333 were probably those already in use at Clairvaux, where such a commemoration had been authorized as early as 1250.[76] Now, the versicle indicated in the 1333 statute is the one given above. The same text appears in the St Malachy commemoration printed in later breviaries, e. g., the Paris diurnale of 1580, p. 24; the Paris breviary of 1560 and the Paris breviary of 1630 (where the common commemorations are given in a section where the pages or folios are not numbered). Evidently, then, the compiler of Troyes manuscripts 1970 and 2005 simply borrowed the proper versicle from the daily commemoration formulary.

Something similar obtains in the case of the Office collect. Until the Cistercian liturgy was "romanized" in the seventeenth century, the liturgical manuscripts and printed books of the Order persist in assigning Malachy the collect *"Deus qui beatum Malachiam pontificem sanctorum tuorum meritis coaequasti . . . imitemur exempla."* The same collect was also used for St William of Bourges, Julian of le Mans, Ambrose, Peter of Tarentaise, Remigius, Edmund of Canterbury, Eloi, and Nicholas. However, a quite different and rather singular collect was also in use—but for the daily commemoration of Malachy at Clairvaux and (from 1333 onwards) in the houses of the Clairvaux filiation:

*Deus, qui beatum Malachiam pontificem, sanctissimo Patri Bernardo verae charitatis foedere dulciter sociasti, concede propitius: ut et pravorum omnium consensus noxios caute vitemus, et caelestis militiae sacras amicitias semper optemus.*

The collect is rooted in the theme of holy friendship such as was exemplified in the love between Malachy and Bernard; and most monks who were up on their Hebrew etymologies as expounded by Jerome or Isidore would have caught the allusion to the angels, since "Malachy" purports to be derived from the Hebrew word for angel. Admittedly, this is not the sort of collect calculated to bring joy to the heart of most contem-

76. Canivez, *Statuta . . .* II, p. 347 (Anno 1250/3).

porary liturgists; but monks of earlier generations must have found it attractive. Inevitably it crept into some manuscripts of St Malachy's Office, replacing the collect from the Common. It also found a place in the Order's official printed missals, but here a distinction was made: the common collect was to be used for Malachy's feast day Mass; but for votive Masses in his honor celebrated on other days, the proper collect was to be used.[77]

By some irony of history, when the Cistercian breviary of the newly reformed (=romanized) Cistercian liturgy finally appeared in 1656, the only proper elements retained from earlier years were the proper collect (which had never officially been used for the Office) and the Night Office readings excerpted from Bernard's sermon, "Liquet, dilectissimi."[78]

### Current Perspectives

Malachy has all but disappeared from the liturgy of the Cistercians of the Strict Observance. No longer appearing in the liturgical calendar of the Cistercians at large, he must look to the particular calendar of our Irish confrères in order to find the place which is his proper due. Having written at length about the origins and evolution (and disappearance) of the proper Malachy Office, I should like to be able to point to these texts from Clairvaux as to a source of material waiting to be exploited in the present period of liturgical creativity. Unfortunately, I could not do so and keep an easy conscience. Certain elements from the old repertory certainly deserve to be retained—some of the readings, and perhaps an occasional antiphon. But what is needed by our Irish brethren is a quite new

77. By way of example, the Paris missals of 1515, pp. clxj-clxii; of 1560, f. 1j[r] of the sanctoral cycle; of 1584, f. clj[r]. The Castille Congregation missal printed at Salamanca in 1590, allows the option of either the common collect or the proper one, even on the feast day (p. 249, which refers to p. 51 in a later section for the proper collect).

78. For the background of this reform, see P. Colomban Bock, *Les codifications du droit cistercien* (Westmalle, s.d.), pp. 103-121. This edition gathers under a single cover articles which appeared in *Collectanea O.C.R.* between 1947 and 1955.

Office in which Malachy's chief claim to glory is no longer dependent on his friendship with Bernard of Clairvaux. Had Malachy died at Armagh instead of at Clairvaux, it is doubtful that his proper Office would ever have been composed; doubtful that Bernard would have written his Life; doubtful even that Malachy would have been canonized. Yet, nothing of his importance for the Church universal and for the Church in Ireland in particular would have been changed. Malachy would still be the great Irish reformer bishop who helped bring his country through a potentially disastrous crisis, who was responsible for normalizing relations with ecclesiastical continental Europe, who introduced the White Monks into Ireland, and who strikingly manifested in his own person the ancient Irish ideal of sainthood. May the day soon come when some Gaelic son of Bernard and Malachy will be moved to write and sing of Malachy in such a way that his texts and music can be used by us to celebrate the life in Christ of Malachy, *coarb* of Patrick and Primate of Ireland.

Chrysogonus Waddell ocso

Gethsemani Abbey
Trappist, Kentucky

# SAINT BERNARD AND ESCHATOLOGY

AS A RELIGION founded upon the imminent expectation of the return of the risen Lord, Christianity could not help but experience difficulties as that event failed to materialize. In this sense eschatology has been a problem to Christians at least since the time of Paul's Thessalonian converts. By the second century, indeed, the problem of delayed eschatology was responsible for major convulsions in the life of the church.

The solutions offered to the delay of the eschaton in the course of two thousand years of Christian history, despite a bewildering variety of surface differences, still generally tend to fall into certain recognizable groups. Whatever classifications may be assayed concerning the middle range of opinions, two extreme tendencies, recognizable at least as early as the second century, have maintained a surprising vitality. On the one hand, unfulfilled eschatological expectation could be reinterpreted in a purely spiritual sense—imagery originally meant to depict the future history of God's kingdom could be seen as telling the story of the destiny of the soul. On the other, the truly historical and imminent character of eschatological expectation could be reinforced, but at the price of challenging the ultimacy of the Scriptural text either by introducing a new revelation or by an historicizing interpretation so radical as to be virtually equivalent to the same thing. Both these tendencies have been seen to be at work in the second century, respectively in the movements of Gnosticism and Montanism.[1]

1. R. M. Grant, *Augustus to Constantine* (New York, 1970), pp. 142-44.

Admitting the ideal character of these extremes in the history of Christian expectation of the end, it is still surprising to see how useful a viewpoint they provide for the investigation of twelfth-century eschatology. Augustine of Hippo, definitely avoiding the extremes as he did, had attempted to confront the problem of delayed eschatology from a higher viewpoint by the creation of a theology of history.[2] Those who could not follow the profundities of his thought could at least learn from him the method of spiritual interpretation of the historical symbolism of the Apocalypse, which was one of the ways he outflanked the cruder aspects of Chiliasm. Succeeding commentators on the Apocalypse, such as Cassiodorus, Bede, Ambrosius Autpertus and Beatus of Liebana, created a tradition of spiritualized interpretation which dominated early medieval thought.[3] While the main line of early medieval exegesis of the Apocalypse thus tended towards the "spiritualized" solution to the eschatological problem, elements were also present—particularly the new scenario of the last events introduced by the Sibylline literature[4]—which renewed the tradition of immediate, historicizing eschatology.

Both tendencies were to some extent present in medieval exegetical theory of the four senses of Scripture. As Henri de Lubac has shown, the anagogic sense, the sense which leads above or beyond, is really double in function—one aspect being objective, doctrinal, and related to the last things, the other subjective and related to the contemplation of the realities of

2. For a good introduction to some of the main lines in Augustine's theology of history, cf. R. A. Markus, *Saeculum: History and Society in the Theology of St Augustine* (Cambridge, 1970).

3. On the Tychonian-Augustinian tradition, as it is called (since Augustine was much influenced by the Donatist exegete Tychonius in this area), cf. W. Bousset, *Die Offenbarung Johannes* (Göttingen, 1906, reprinted 1966), pp. 65-72; and W. Kamlah, *Apokalypse und Geschichtstheologie: Die mittelalterliche Auslegung der Apokalypse von Joachim von Fiore* (Berlin, 1935, reprint 1965), especially pp. 70-74.

4. On the Sibylline literature of the early Middle Ages the texts may be found in E. Sackur, *Sibyllinische Forschungen* (Halle, 1898). For an introduction to the influence of this literature no modern study has superceded F. Kampers, *Kaiserprophetieen und Kaisersagen im Mittelalter* (Munich, 1895). On the Greek origins of the Tiburtine Sibyl, cf. P. J. Alexander, *The Oracle of Baalkeb* (Dumbarton Oaks, 1967).

the heavenly life[5]—horizontal and vertical tendencies, as they might be termed. In Henri de Lubac's picture of the ideal application of the four senses, these two aspects are both necessary and work together; but he notes the dominance of the vertical tendency and the evisceration of horizontal eschatology in some anagogical interpretation, particularly that influenced by the Dionysian tradition.[6] The Augustinian interpretation of the Apocalypse and a tendency towards the purely "vertical" anagogy were two important influences in the strength of spiritualizing eschatology in the Middle Ages. The presence of this tradition in Cistercian theology is undeniable. Arousing the monk to the contemplation of the heavenly realities and seeing the monastic life as the foretaste of the enjoyment of these realities were among the most common themes in Cistercian authors. To call such categories "eschatological," however,[7] is permissible only if an adequate distinction is made between quite different types of eschatology—the kind of distinction that has been suggested here by the terms "spiritualizing" and "historicizing."

It is obvious that there is much spiritualizing eschatology and purely vertical anagogy in the writings of Bernard of Clairvaux —so much indeed that no paper could really do them justice.[8] Yet the century in which Bernard lived also witnessed a major resurgence of historicizing eschatology. Early medieval contributions to this dimension, such as the Sibylline literature, achieved a new popularity at this time; a basic shift in the ex-

---

5. H. de Lubac, *Exégèse Médiévale* I, 2, (Paris, 1959), p. 624.

6. *Op. cit.* I, 2, pp. 640-42.

7. As does A. Hallier in relation to Aelred in *The Monastic Theology of Aelred of Rievaulx* (Spencer, 1969), pp. 149-55. Cf. also the understanding of eschatology expressed in *The Cistercian Spirit: A Symposium* (Spencer, 1970), p. 263: "There was some concern about the introduction of the concept eschatological into the basic statement since the word was not used by our Fathers. However, the concept which it expresses was found in their lives, in their yearning for the heavenly life, their desire for God, their emphasis on a greater detachment and freedom in the Spirit."

8. E.g., the identification of Clairvaux with the true Jerusalem in Ep 64, PL 182: 169B-170B; the combination of the theme of the heavenly Jerusalem with that of the bride of Christ (SC 27, 6, Opera I, 185-86); and, of course, the very common theme that identified the life of the monks with that of the angels.

egesis of the Apocalypse away from the Augustinian tradition was effected.[9] Popular movements rooted in eschatological expectations (difficult as they are to specify because of the ambiguity of the evidence) seem to have been on the upswing.[10] Reaching their culmination in the writings of Joachim of Fiore at the end of the century, these tendencies mark one of the major shifts in the history of Christian eschatology. In the light of this it seems legitimate to ask what relation, if any, can be found between the writings of the Abbot of Clairvaux and these reintensified eschatological currents. The question is a limited one, especially with regard to texts that can serve as either direct or indirect evidence of Bernard's views (and this must always be kept in mind in evaluating the total place of such speculation in his thought); but it is not a negligible concern, for an adequate answer will serve to specify the Abbot of Clairvaux's relation to one of the most important trends of his age.

One initial pitfall must be avoided before such an investigation can be undertaken. All medieval theologians were eschatological in a sense whose character and strength are difficult to recapture today. They were conscious of living "at the end of time" (1 Cor. 10:11) in a way that few outside certain messianic sects in the modern world could understand. Nevertheless, there is still a most important difference between a general *consciousness* of living in the last age and a *conviction* that the last age itself was about to end, between an *admission* of the proximity of the Antichrist and the *certainty* that his coming would take place in one's lifetime, between seeing events of one's own time as *prefigurations* of the events of the end and viewing them as the *last things themselves*. The failure to distinguish between these two mentalities has been the source of considerable confusion in the study of medieval es-

9. Kamlah, *op. cit.*, pp. 124-26.
10. The most provocative study of the movements, N. Cohn's *The Pursuit of the Millenium* (revised edition, Oxford, 1970), chaps. 2 to 5, tends to go beyond the evidence in a number of areas. M.-D. Chenu discusses the connection of eschatology and twelfth-century evangelical movements in *La théologie au douzième siècle* (Paris, 1957), pp. 272-3.

chatology.[11] It tells us little about the specific character of any medieval thinker's eschatological views to convict him of the former set of alternatives—it merely merges him into a general picture from which it would be difficult to exclude anyone; but a determination of the writer's stance with regard to the latter questions should provide at least some sense of whether or not it is possible to characterize his thought as more specifically eschatological within the medieval context.

The best way to approach this question is from a consideration of those texts in Bernard's writings which in some way bear on the narrower questions of "reinforced," overtly historicizing eschatology as they appeared in the Abbot's historical milieu. Such texts may be divided into three general categories: (1) those related to the proximity of the Antichrist and the signs of the end, (2) those which concern the determination of the ages of the world and of the Church, and (3) a special case, texts concerning the Second Crusade which might be said to have a more or less explicit eschatological character.

The dread figure of the Antichrist haunted the dreams of medieval man.[12] Who was the son of perdition to be and what were the signs of his coming? The Scriptural texts referring to the Antichrist by no means give a consistent doctrine, and the First Epistle of John even speaks of a plurality of Antichrists (2:18-22). The picture was confused not only by the tradition of a double Antichrist which the medievals inherited from the Patristic period, but especially by the two kinds of interpretation which the theme of the Antichrist received in exegetical literature—on the one hand in concrete fashion as representing a definite individual, and on the other abstractly signifying the

11. The point is raised here because the only detailed study of Bernard's eschatology, F. Radcke's *Die eschatologische Anschauungen Bernhards von Clairvaux* (Greifswald, 1915), is a notable example of the failure to make these distinctions.
12. The best general survey of the early stages of thought about the Antichrist remains W. Bousset, *Der Antichrist in der Überlieferung des Judentums, des neuen Testament, und der alter Kirche* (Göttingen, 1895; translated as *The Antichrist Legend* (London, 1896). For the medieval context cf. also E. Wadstein, *Die eschatologischen Ideengruppen* (Leipaig, 1896), Part I, B; E. Bernheim, *Mittelalterliche Zeitanschauungen in ihrem Einfluss auf Politik und Geschichtsschreibung.* Teil I. *Die Zeitanschauungen* (Tübingen, 1918), pp. 70-97; and H. de Lubac, *Exégèse Médiévale*, II, 1 (Paris, 1961), pp. 527-55.

summation of all evil.[13] Naturally, medieval authors saw no conflict between these two types of interpretation; the doctrine of the senses of Scripture allowed for such multiple understandings, just as the explicit words of John's Epistle permitted any evil man to be seen as an agent of the Antichrist or as the Antichrist himself. This sliding scale of meaning, however, never cancelled out belief in the advent of a final personal Antichrist whose persecution of the Church would be a central event of the last days. When we read of the conviction of some that the Antichrist had already been born and was therefore alive in their own times, whether manifested or not, it seems fairly certain that we are dealing with such an individualized figure.

This conviction, known in late Patristic and early medieval times,[14] seems to have become more current in the twelfth century. Certainly references to the approaching advent of the Antichrist grow more numerous at this time, even though many of these must be viewed as a form of moral invective.[15] There were those who clearly asserted that the Antichrist had already been born. Rainer, Bishop of Florence, advanced this position in the last decade of the eleventh century. His views were condemned in a synod which Pope Paschal II held at Florence in 1106, but this does not seem to have put an end to the controversy.[16] Bernard of Cluny, towards the middle of the century, had a very strong sense of the imminence of the Antichrist, though he did not use the "already born" formula;[17] the same may be said for Hildegard of Bingen in her *Scivias* (c. 1170).[18] Gerhoh of Reichersberg in the *De Investigatione Antichristi* written in 1162 spoke of the crisis of the last times

---

13. E. Wadstern, *op. cit.*, pp. 128-33; F. Radcke, *op. cit.*, 12-13.

14. Sulpicius Severus reports that such was the thought of Martin of Tours, *Dialogi* II, 14 (c. 400) (*CSEL* I, p. 197). Early medieval references would include Odo of Cluny († 942) in his *Collationes* II, 37; PL 133:585c.

15. De Lubac, *op. cit.*, II, 1, p. 528.

16. The revelant documents are edited and discussed by C. Erdmann, "Endkaiserglaube und Kreuzzugsgedanke im 11. Jahrhundert," *Zeitschrift für Kirchengeschichte* 51 (1932): 386-94. As Erdmann remarks, the action of the Pope and the earlier letter sent by the bishops of the province of Ravenna, indicate that this view was by no means widespread at the turn of the century, *op. cit.*, pp. 402-3.

17. E. g., *De contemptu mundi*, Liber I, 1. 1026.

18. *Scivias*, Liber III, visio XI; PL 197:714BD, 716C.

as having begun with the conflict between Gregory VII and Henry IV,[19] but made it quite clear that although the end was not far, the exact time could not be known.[20] As R. Manselli has pointed out,[21] Gerhoh's attack upon particular details of the Antichrist's career as found in extra-Biblical sources tended to make it easier to accommodate his career to current events. Hence it is perhaps no surprise when, at the end of the century, several accounts report that Joachim of Fiore was convinced that the Antichrist had already been born and was living in Rome.[22]

Bernard's references to the Antichrist are fairly numerous, even for a twelfth-century author. At the very beginning of his literary career, in his *De Gradibus Humilitatis et Superbiae* (c. 1120-24), he shows his acquaintance with traditional speculation concerning the dread figure in the course of a discussion of the lack of knowledge on the part of Jesus of the time of the end.[23] Far more important, however, are the references to the Antichrist contained in the Abbot's letters written during the time of the Papal Schism between Innocent II and Anacletus II (1130-1138). At the beginning of the Schism, as Bernard threw his weight behind the fortunes of Innocent in a spate of letters dating from 1130 and 1131,[24] Anacletus is definitely viewed as the Antichrist and strongly eschatological language is used. "Those who are of God have freely

19. *De investigatione Antichirsti* I, 19; *MGH, Libelli de Lite,* III, pp. 328-29.

20. Praefatio *(MGH. Libelli de Lite* III, pp. 307-8). Gerhoh explicitly refers to the historicizing interpretation of the past history of the Church he is using as something unusual.

21. *La Lectura super Apocalypsim di Pietro di Giovanni Olivi. Richerche sull' eschatologismo Mediovale* (Rome, 1955, pp. 62-64).

22. Joachim's interview with Richard the Lionhearted in Messina in 1190 or 1191 as reported in Roger Howden, *Cronica* (Rolls Series) Vol. III, pp. 75-9; and in "Benedict of Peterborough," *Gesta Henrici II et Ricardi I* (Rolls Series), Vol. II, pp. 151-5; and his interview with Adam of Persigny in Rome, possibly in 1198, as reported in Ralph of Coggeshall, *Chronicon Anglicanum* (Rolls Series), pp. 67-79. On the authenticity of these accounts, cf. M. Reeves, *The Influence of Prophecy in the Later Middle Ages* (Oxford, 1969), pp. 6-15.

23. Hum 3, 10, *Opera,* III, 23-4. Cf. Radcke, *op. cit.,* pp. 4-8.

24. Cf. B. S. James, *The Letters of St Bernard of Clairvaux* (London, 1953), pp. 186-199, for dating and the translations used here. On the letters, cf. J. Leclercq, "Lettres de S. Bernard: histoire ou littérature?" *Studi Medievali,* 3ª Serie, 12 (1971): 1-74; and "Recherches sur la collection des épîtres de saint Bernard," *Cahiers de civilisation médiévale* 14 (1971): 205-19.

chosen him [Innocent], but he who stands over against him is either Antichrist or his follower."[25] "That beast, spoken of in the book of the Apocalypse [Apoc. 13, 5-7], to whom power has been given to blaspheme and make war on the saints, occupies the See of Peter like a lion ready for its prey;"[26] and ". . . by dividing those whom Christ saved by uniting, he [Gerald of Angoulême, a supporter of Anacletus] makes himself not a Christian but Antichrist, guilty of the cross and death of Christ."[27] It cannot be doubted that such references indicate that Bernard was much in sympathy with the renewal of interest in eschatological language related to the Antichrist that de Lubac and others have noted as characteristic of the century; but several factors indicate that this should not be pushed too far. First of all, there was some tradition in the Middle Ages for viewing one's opponents in a Papal Schism as agents of the Antichrist;[28] and second, during the course of the controversy the references to Anacletus and his followers as the Antichrist tend to disappear and even the eschatological character of the language in general is considerably muted.[29] Rather than seeing Bernard's reaction to the Schism as a sign of his belief in the actual presence of the final personal Antichrist in the world,[30] these letters show that he was well aware

25. EP 124, PL 182:268c: "*Nam qui dei sunt, libenter junguntur ei; qui autem ex adverso stat, aut Antichristi est, aut Antichristus.*" (James, p. 188).

26. Ep 125, PL 182:270A: "*Bestia illa de Apocalypsi, cui datum est os loquens blasphemias et bellum gerere cum sanctis, Petri cathedram occupat, tanquam leo paratus ad praedam*" (James, p. 190).

27. Ep 126, 6; PL 182:275A: "*. . . ut quisquis tentaret dividere quos ille colligeret, et inde redimeret; probare sese non christianum, sed antichristum, reus mortis et crucis Christi*" (James, p. 194).

28. E.g., in Paragraph 28 of the proceedings of the Synod of St Basle (991), Arnulf of Orleans referred to Pope Boniface VI as Antichrist (PL 139:314A & *MGH SS.* III, p. 672), as did dissident Cardinals in referring to Gregory VII (cf. Ep. III, 4, *MGH, Libelli de Lite* II, p. 383).

29. The letters to the people of Milan, Ep 131, PL 182:287AB, and to Godfrey, the Prior of Clairvaux, Ep 317, PL 182:523AB seem to contain some eschatological flavor. Radcke, *op. cit.*, pp. 85-90, argues for an eschatological interpretation of Ep 130,144 and 145 concerning the part of the Emperor Lothair II in the Schism. This is not immediately evident from the text and is based upon Radcke's extremely questionable assertion of the dominating influence of the Sibylline literature upon the Abbot of Clairvaux. The same point may be made concerning his interpretation of Bernard's letter of rejoicing over the death of Anacletus, Ep 147, PL 182:305AB; cf. *op. cit.*, p. 38.

30. Radcke, *op. cit.*, pp. 28-35.

of the advantages of using eschatological invective in such a position, convinced as he was that Anacletus was a member of the Antichrist. His own eschatological position, however, was still moderate.

This general interpretation is substantiated by a glance at the most important of the Abbot of Clairvaux's other references to the Antichrist. In *Letter 56* addressed to Geoffrey of Chartres,[31] Bernard writes:

> I do not know whether Norbert is going to Jerusalem or not. When I last saw him a few days ago and was deemed worthy to drink in his heavenly wisdom, he never mentioned the matter to me. When I asked him what he thought about the Antichrist, he declared himself quite certain that it would be during this present generation that he would be revealed. But upon my asking, when he wished to explain to me the source of this same certainty, I did not think, having heard his response, that I ought to take it for certain. He concluded by saying that he would live to see a general persecution of the Church.[32]

While it is clear that Norbert, the founder of the Premonstratensians, is to be numbered among those who thought that the Antichrist was already born (one wishes that the letter told us more about his reasons!); Bernard obviously took a more guarded view.[33] This letter reinforces the interpretation that

31. PL 182:162A-165A. There is some doubt about the date of the letter. Radcke, *op. cit.*, p. 21, note 4, and E. Vacandard, *Vie de St Bernard* (Paris, 1910, 4th ed), I:261, date it to 1128 after the Council of Troyes. Other authorities prefer a date around 1124, cf. F. Petit, "Bernard et l'Ordre de Prémontré," *Bernard de Clairvaux* (Paris, 1953), p. 292.

32. "*Quod a me de domino Norberto sciscitamini, si videlicet iturus sit Jerosolymam, ego nescio. Nam, cum ante hos paucos dies ejus faciem videre, et de coelesti fistula, ore videlicet ipsius, plurima haurire meruerim; hoc tamen ab ipso non audivi. Verum de Antichristo cum inquirerem quid sentiret, durante adhuc ea, quae nunc est, generatione revelandum illum esse se certissime scire potestatus* [read *protestatus*] *est. At, cum eamdem certitudinem unde haberet, sciscitanti mihi exponere vellet; audito quod respondit, non me illud pro certo credere debere putavi. Ad summam* [Radcke reads *summum* according to a Venice ms.] *tamen hoc asseruit, non visurum se mortem, nisi prius videat generalem in Ecclesia persecutionem.*" Translation of B. S. James, *op. cit.*, p. 86, with some changes.

33. Radcke, *op. cit.*, pp. 21-24, claims that the encounter with Norbert did at least convince the Abbot that a general persecution of the Church was at hand and that this outlook colored his reaction to the Schism of 1130. This is possible, but the mere absence of any response on Bernard's part to Norbert's conviction of a general persecution is not definite proof of his agreement.

the Abbot of Clairvaux took a strong interest in the eschatological tendencies of his time and was quite willing to see the enemies of the Church in an eschatological light, but that in the early part of his career he never asserted that the final Antichrist was already present in the world.

Most of Bernard's other statements concerning the Antichrist and the signs of the end conform to this interpretation. In two sermons for the first Sunday in November he uses eschatological language in describing his age as one dominated by Satan but clearly thinks of the final Antichrist as still to come.[34] In a sermon for the feast of the conversion of St Paul, the Abbot reminds his listeners that persecution never ceases, but that the evil of the present persecution is that it comes from within the Church, indeed from those in the highest offices.[35] "Others too have acted wickedly and there are many Antichrists in our time."[36]

Similar language is also used in the controversy with Peter Abelard, but again in a very diffuse fashion. Abelard's words and works are "mysteries of iniquity,"[37] and he himself goes "before the face of the Antichrist to prepare his way;"[38] but this is surely no more than the metonymy by which he can refer to Abelard and his follower Arnold of Brescia as "Satan."[39]

The only passage in which Bernard may go beyond this caution comes at the end of his life in the Prologue that he wrote to his *Vita sancti Malachiae* (1152). Here the language is much stronger and Bernard comes closer to predicting the imminent arrival of the last Antichirst than he ever did in his earlier career:

And, as I suspect, he concerning whom it is written "Want

34. I Nov 1,11; and I Nov 3, 1; *Opera*, IV, 307, 311-12. On the difficulties of dating the *Sermones per Annum*, cf. *Opera*, III, 127-28. F. Radcke, *op. cit.*, p. 9, seems to think that these sermons are pre-Schism.

35. PL 1, 3; *Opera*, IV, 328-30. Radcke, *op. cit.*, pp. 24-6, also sees this as pre-Schism.

36. *"Inique agunt et ceteri contra Christum, multique sunt nostris temporibus antichristi."* (p. 329).

37. Ep 338, PL 182:543A.

38. Ep 336, PL 182:539CD: *"Praecedit jam Petrus Abaelardus ante faciem Antichristi parare vias ejus."*

39. Ep 189, 3; PL 182:355B.

will go before his face" (Job 41: 13), is either at hand or near. Unless I am mistaken, Antichrist is the man whom hunger and a lack of all goodness both precedes and accompanies. Therefore, whether these are messages of his presence or messages already sent ahead of his coming, want is evident.[40]

Has the Abbot of Clairvaux really changed his attitude? Again the moralistic intent of the work is important. Malachy's sanctity is enhanced by painting the age in the blackest possible colors, but it is also possible that Bernard's increasing disillusionment with the Church of his time, coupled with the disaster of the Second Crusade, had moved his pessimism in the direction of a more directly historicizing eschatology.

The mention of hunger and dearth of goodness as signs of the approach of the Antichrist in this passage raises the question of the Abbot's attitude towards the question of eschatological signs in general. Here, again, one must beware of reading too much into the text. Radcke seizes upon every passage in which Bernard condemns the evils of his time as evidence that he was strongly influencied by the Sibylline concept of the *ferreum regnum* as the immediate antecedent to the time of the Antichrist.[41] It is not at all impossible that Bernard was familiar with the Sibylline literature, but there is no direct and incontrovertible evidence for this in any of the texts that Radcke cites. Moral evils being pretty much the same from century to century, a distressing sameness can also be found in the attacks directed against them. What the Tiburtine Sibyl had to

40. "*Et, ut suspicor ego, aut praesto, aut prope est, de quo scriptum est: Faciem eius praecedet egestas. Ni fallor, Antichristus est iste, quem fames ac sterilitas totius boni et praeit, et comitatur. Sive igitur nuntia iam praesentis, sive iamiamque adfuturi praenuntia, egestas in evidenti est.*" *Opera* III, 307. Cf. Radcke, *op. cit.*, p. 52-3, discusses this passage and compares it with the roughly contemporary SC 72, 5-6. *Opera*, II, 228-29. The latter passage, however, is really a doctrinal treatment with no sense of connection with present troubles—a perfect example of traditional "historical" anagogic interpretation.

41. He sees three periods of major emphasis here: (1) before the Schism when Bernard is convinced he is living in the *ferreum regnum* and that Louis VI is the evil king mentioned in the Tiburtine Sibyl (pp. 69-83); (2) from roughly 1140 down to 1146, the time of the preaching of the Crusade (pp. 102-8); and (3) after the crusade when he seems to return to a strong emphasis on the *ferreum regnum* (p. 128-30).

say about the last age is generally similar to what any medieval preacher who, like Bernard, was convinced that the evils of his age were the work of Antichrist (taken in the broad sense) was bound to say. If there is anything specific about Bernard's doctrine of eschatological signs (for even the stress on famine is quite traditional), it must be sought after in that series of texts in which he engaged in the typically twelfth-century pursuit of delineating the ages of the world and of the Church.

The doctrine of the ages of the world displayed a remarkable development in the Patristic period.[42] Patterns of seven, four, and three were the most popular. Thus the seven days of creation became the cosmic exemplar for a division of history into six ages (the seventh age being that of eternity) whose divergent forms can be traced back to Origen and Hippolytus. Divisions into three ages, either Trinitarian or based on the Pauline doctrine of salvation (before the law, under the law, under grace) were also popular. This Pauline distinction, by the addition of heavenly age in glory, could found a fourfold division; other four-age theories were based on the visions of the second and seventh chapters of Daniel or on the four rivers of paradise.

Twelfth-century authors took up the problem of the divisions of the history of the world with gusto. The material with which they worked was Patristic, but the widespread interest they showed in it and the advances they effected beyond the Patristic treatment were a sign of their creative handling of the tradition. The roots of this interest were undoubtedly connected with the resurgence of historicizing eschatology, though also influenced by other factors, such as the tensions over the nature of the Church and the forms of the religious life. It is obvious the twelfth-century thinkers were much more concerned with the narrower question of the time of the Church than with that of the ages of the world in general. Knowing that they were living in the last age, that of the Church, they exercised their wit over the subdivisions predicted for this final age. Un-

42. For a general introduction, cf. R. Schmidt, "Aetates mundi. Die Weltalter als Gliederungsprinzip der Geschichte," *Zeitschrift für Kirchengeschichte* 67 (1955-56): 288-317. The best introduction to the Patristic period is A. Luneau, *L'Histoire du Salut chez les Pères de L'Eglise. La doctrine des âges du monde* (Paris, 1964).

derneath it all brooded the question: how close were the awesome events which would usher in the final judgment and the day of eternity?

This is not the place to attempt to outline the variety of theories put forward among Bernard's contemporaries regarding such questions.[43] It is important, however, to see how the Abbot of Clairvaux shared in this mentality. Bernard is a proponent of a four-age theory of the history of the Church. The form which this takes in his writings is distinctive, for it is usually expressed through an exegesis of the four temptations mentioned in Psalm 90:5-6: "Like a shield his truth will surround you, so that you shall not fear from the peril of the night, nor from the arrow flying in the day, nor from the terror walking in darkness, nor from the attack of the noonday devil."[44] The most extended treatment of the theory is found in the thirty-third of the *Sermones in Cantica* (composed shortly before 1139). A salvation history theme is built into this sermon from the very beginning—the action of the Word in the history of mankind considered as a single day; but the early development is in terms of the individual soul, a good illustration of the "vertical" eschatology referred to earlier.[45] The discussion in section six of the four varieties of temptation the monk encounters leads on to an expansion in the seventh section of how these four temptations are to be assigned to the Body of Christ, that is, to the Church.[46] The temptations ground a distinction of the history of the Church into four ages. The *timor nocturnus* is the age of the primitive Church when those who killed the saints thought they were offering a service to God. This temptation, overcome by the patience of the martyrs, was succeeded by the age of the *sagitta volans in die,* the time of here-

43. For twelfth-century thought concerning the divisions of ages, cf. M.-D. Chenu, *op. cit.,* pp. 72-84; H. de Lubac, *op. cit.,* II, 1, pp. 504-27; and H. Grundmann, *Studien über Joachim von Fiore* (Leipzig, 1927; photographic reprint, 1966), chap. II, *passim.*

44. *"Scuto circumdabit te veritas eius, non timebis a timore nocturno, a sagitta volante in die, a negotio perambulante in tenebris, ab incursu et daemonio meridiano."* (Vulgate text).

45. SC 33, 1-6; *Opera,* I, 233-243.

46. *Op. cit.,* 243-245.

tics who afflicted the Church with false dogma and who were overcome by the wisdom of the saints. The second age was followed by that of the *negotium perambulans in tenebris,* the age which Bernard sees as his own and one whose primary characteristic, that of hypocrisy, is even more dangerous than the previous temptations.

> Today the stinking corruption slowly spreads throughout the whole body of the Church, both more desperate insofar as it is more widespread, and more dangerous insofar as it is more internal. Were an open heretic to rise up, he would be cast outside and wither away; were a violent enemy to come, the Church might hide herself from him. But now whom will she cast out or from whom hide herself? All are friends, all are enemies; all are supporters, all adversaries; all of the household, but none peaceful. All are neighbors, but each one seeks his own advantage. They are ministers of Christ and serve the Antichrist.[47]

The last, and worst age, is still to come: the time of the Antichrist, the *daemonium meridianum.* Bernard says nothing about either its proximity or distance in this passage. The text does, however, give us some information about the Abbot's view of the characteristics of the various ages. The contrast between the time of the Church and that of eternity is primarily in terms of *pax*—peace is lacking in the history of the Church because of attacks within or without, but the *eschaton* will be an age of true eternal peace. Hypocrisy, as seen especially in the avarice and wealth of those pledged to follow the poverty of Christ, is the specific mark of the third age, as the lying deception of the Antichrist will be of the fourth.

How prevalent is this theory in Bernard's other writings? The

---

47. *Serpit hodie putida tabes per omne corpus Ecclesiae, et quo latius, eo desperatius, eoque periculosius quo interius. Nam si insurgeret apertus haereticus, mitteretur foras et aresceret; si violentus inimicus, absconderet se forsitan ab eo. Nunc vero quem eiciet, aut a quo abscondet se? Omnes amici, et omnes inimici; omnes necessarii, et omnes adversarii; omnes domestici, et nulli pacifici; omnes proximi, et omnes quae sua sunt quaerunt. Ministri Christi sunt, et serviunt Antichristo."* op. cit., p. 244.

evidence is that it is rather widespread, as well as being subject to a number of interesting variations. These other examples, however, involve complex textual questions which have only been clarified in recent times by the exacting and monumental labors of Jean Leclercq on the textual tradition of the writings of the Abbot of Clairvaux. The order adopted in surveying these texts will not be chronological, but rather will attempt to indicate how closely the text as we have it stands to the exercise of Bernard's actual responsibility as author. The complexities of questions of authorship in the Middle Ages in the case of the famous masters of the Schools have long been known; it has been one of the important merits of Fr Leclercq's work to show us how involved are the analogous problems that exist in the case of monastic authors.

Bernard's seventeen sermons on Psalm 90, a liturgical text for the first Sunday of Lent, must be numbered among his authenticated works.[48] Probably written in 1139,[49] they come down to us in three redactions—one short (B), one longer (L), and a perfected one (Pf). The sixth of these sermons, in commenting on the four temptations of verses five and six of the Psalm, begins from a moral interpretation of the temptations as related to the life of the monk;[50] but end in a consideration of the four temptations of the Church which is explicitly referred back to the similar treatment in the *Super Cantica* text. The discussion here is so similar that the parallels are frequently word-for-word; the only significant difference comes in the sixth paragraph where the *daemonium meridianum,* still the spirit of deception (but here taken in the moral and not the eschatological sense as the Antichrist) is related to the temptation that the Apostles experienced when they saw Christ walking upon the waters in the fourth watch of the night.[51] This reference may give a clue to the antecedents of Bernard's four-

48. On these sermons, cf. J. Leclercq, "Les sermons sur le psalme 'Qui habitat'," *Bernard de Clairvaux* (Paris, 1953), pp. 435-6; and the same author's introduction to his edition in *Opera,* IV, 119-25.

49. *Opera,* IV, 119.

50. QH S 6, 1-6; *Opera,* IV, 404-9. It should be noted that B and L contain a variant text for nn. 2-4.

51. Mt 14:25-6.

age theory, as will be discussed below.[52] The picture becomes more complex in turning to the variations on the theme of the four ages as they appear in other texts more or less related to Bernard, but not usually connected with his authentic corpus. Nevertheless, all these texts may be called Bernardine in a real sense, as Leclercq has demonstrated.[53] Among them the *Sententia* which he edited from Engelberg ms. 34 does not differ appreciably from the texts already discussed;[54] the same may be said for two sermons supposedly given at the Council of Reims in 1148 which, although not by Bernard, are obviously culled from his writtings.[55] The other appearances of the four-age theory, however, introduce a significant new dimension into Bernard's eschatological views.

A sermon of Geoffrey of Auxerre, Bernard's one-time secretary, connects the four temptations of the Church with the four beasts mentioned in the seventh chapter of Daniel and explicitly refers to Bernard's exegesis of Psalm 90, 5-6.[56] One might view this as Geoffrey's expansion of Bernard's originally more cautious views, but two other texts indicate that if Bernard did not utilize the four beasts of Daniel, he was certainly not adverse to the introduction of apocalyptic animal symbolism into his interpretation of the ages of the Church.

In an extremely interesting *Sententia,* called "Quatuor sunt tentationes," found in a number of early manuscripts, not only are the four temptations of the individual soul linked to the four cardinal virtues, but the four temptations of the Church

52. The possibility is heightened by the way in which the four temptations are applied to the Church in the shorter text given in L. Here the fourth temptation of the Church is explained in terms of the fourth watch of Mt 14:25 and Mk 6:48: "*In hac quarta tentatione veniet Jesus ad laborantes electos, qui venit in quarta vigilia noctis, ambulans super mare, ad discipulos suos.*" (*ed. cit.,* p. 412).

53. Cf. J. Leclercq, *Études sur Saint Bernard et le texte de ses écrits, ASOC 9* (1953), "Une parabole restituée à Saint Bernard," pp. 133-36.

54. J. Leclercq, "Inédits bernardins dans un ms. d'Engelberg," *Revue Mabillon* 37 (1947): 11-12.

55. PL 184:1083B-84B, an almost direct version of SC 33,6; *Opera,* I, 243-45; and 1092C-93A which is obviously based on the Bernardine schema, but does not discuss the fourth age of the Church. Instead the latter contains an unusual analysis of the three temptations in terms of three powers of the soul—*ratio, voluntas* and *sensualitas.*

56. Fragment edited in Leclercq, *Études . . .,* p. 133, from ms Troyes 503, f. 137.

are compared with the four horses of Rev 6:2-8:

> The attack of the noonday devil is the nearby time of the
> Antichrist.
> And so there are four horses in the Apocalypse: the first
> white, that is calm and peaceful, and its rider went out to
> conquer and conquer. . . . The second was red, the color of
> blood, bearing a rider with a great sword to take away peace
> from the earth. . . ; the third black, that is dusky, having hy-
> pocrisy for a rider. . . . The fourth was pale, nigh to the mo-
> ment of death; its rider death and hell hard behind. The order
> has to be changed a bit, for the first age was that of persecu-
> tion. The white horse is the age of peace in the Church, the
> red of persecution, the black of hypocrisy, the pale of the
> Antichrist. The following parable will better disclose these
> four ages.[57]

The parable to which this text alludes introduces us to a bi-
zarre piece, but one which only preconceived notions and later
hagiographic idealization would deny to the Abbot of Clairvaux.[58] The *Parabola de Aethiopissa*, while probably not edited
by Bernard himself, must be seen as expressing a genuine Bernardine tradition.[59] This highly allegorical rendering of salvation history (the *littera* concerns the marriage of the king's son
to an Ethiopian rescued from the king of Babylon), may not
appeal to some modern tastes, but it does present another viewpoint on Bernard's ideas of the time of the Church. The four
horses of the Apocalypse do not appear explicitly in this text,
contrary to what might have been expected from the reference

57. Edited by Leclercq from three mss. in *op. cit.*, p. 134. "*. . . Incursus daemo-
nii uicinum iam tempus est Antichristi.*

"*Inde quatuor equi in Apocalypsi: primus albus, id est lenis et placidus, et qui
sedet exit ut uincens uincat . . .; secundus rufus, id est sanguineus, habens sessorem
cum gladio magno ad tollendam pacem de terra . . .; tertius niger, id est obscurus,
sessorem habens hypocrisim . . .; quartus pallidus, id est extremae morti proximus,
qui sessorem habet mortem et infernum sequentem. Mutato paululum ordine,
primum enim tempus fuit persecutionis; equus albus in ecclesia tempus est pacis,
rufus persecutionis, niger hypocrisis, pallidus Antichristi.*

"*Haec autem quatuor tempora sequens parabola indicabit.*"

H. M. Rochais lists 9 mss containing this *Sententia* in his "Enqûete sur les
sermons divers et les sentences de S. Bernard," *Analecta Cisterciensia* 18 (1962):
48-9.

58. Leclercq, *op. cit.*, p. 78, on the authenticity of the *parabola* in general.

59. *Op. cit.*, p. 135.

in the *Sententia*; but there is a point of connection. When the Apostles after Pentecost wish to find an animal upon which the spouse of Christ, the Church, may ride through history, they do not choose the horse because of its proud and quarrelsome spirit (and presumably also because of its association with the various temptations of the Church), nor the unclean and foolish ass, but the mule whose mixed parentage indicates the Church's origin from both Jew and gentile.[60] As the Church rides off on her mule we are treated to an allegorical rendering of a three-age theory of history (the age of open persecution, the age of heresy, and the age of the temptation of avarice) which probably represents an early stage of Bernard's more evolved theories.[61]

The Abbot of Clairvaux's undoubted interest in finding the Scriptural sources which would enable him to penetrate to the meaning of the history of the Church and to specify its ages is evident. Even more strongly than his speculation on the Antichrist it ties him in with some of the newer currents in the historicizing eschatology of the twelfth century. The debate over the nature of the Church and its relation to the society in which it found itself, initiated by the Gregorian Reform movement, could not help but turn the attention of many to the question of where the Church now stood in relation to its eschatological goal. The failure to achieve right order in the world and the attendant heightening of moral consciousness which this involved could and did lead many reformers to the pessimistic conclusion that the evils of their time were particularly fraught with eschatological danger. It is true that some Patristic and early medieval authors had felt the same way. What is distinctive about the twelfth-century eschatologists is not only their expression of these views in an age that was obviously not one of decline or decay but of organization and progress, but also that, in typically twelfth-century fashion, they

60. PL 190:964CD. The parable is, oddly enough, edited under the letters of Gilbert Foliot.

61. PL 190:965-66B. Leclercq, *op. cit.*, p. 135, notes that a passage from this *Parabola* is inserted in the longer version of the *Brevis commentatio in cantica canticorum*, which he holds to be authentic (*op. cit.*, pp. 105-121). The *Brevis commentatio* has a brief passage outlining a three-fold theory of the history of the world (PL 184:431D-32A).

were not satisfied with generic expressions of pessimism and eschatological pronouncements, but wanted a clearly-organized logical schema in which to fit these feelings. Hence the concern for schemas of the ages of the Church.

Theories connecting the ages of history with the watches of the night (either three according to Lk 12:35-40 or four according to Mt 14:25-26) did have some Patristic roots. One of the elements in Bernard's picture, the use of the four cardinal virtues to describe four ages in the *"Quatuor sunt tentationes"* has a vague parallel in a passage in St Ambrose.[62] Augustine, of course, was the Father who had popularized the four-age Pauline theory, but he does not seem to have made use of either the three or four watches as a figure.[63] Gregory the Great connected the three watches of Luke with the ages of man.[64] At the beginning of the twelfth century we find several authors who use the figure of the three or four watches to describe the whole course of history from creation to the Last Judgment.[65] Bernard and his contemporary, the eschatological author Gerhoh of Reichersberg (1093-1169), are the first to apply the four watches to the age of the Church and to make them central to a theology of history.

The four watches are the theme of Gerhoh's *De quarta vigilia noctis* written in 1167.[66] Like Bernard, the first age is that of the persecutors, the second that of the heretics, but the third age, stretching from Gregory I to Gregory VII, is that of the corruption of morals. The fourth and most dangerous age, in which Gerhoh finds himself, is characterized by avarice.[67] Despite certain similarities, then, Bernard and Gerhoh's uses of

62. Ambrose was speaking of the four ages of the world under the figure of the four rivers of Paradise, cf. *De Paradiso 3,* 19-22; CSEL 32, 1, pp. 277-79.

63. A. Luneau, *op. cit.,* pp. 357-83.

64. *Homiliarum in Evang.,* I, 13; PL 76:1125BD.

65. Bruno of Segni († 1123). *Comm. in Lucam* II, 27; PL 165:398B: *"Tres enim vigiliae, tria tempora sunt, ante legem, sub lege et sub gratia."* Honorius Augustodunensus (†c. 1137) uses the four watches and the four virtues in his *Spec. Ecc.* PL 172:1080BD-1082B.

66. On this work, cf. D. von den Eynde, *L'Oeuvre littéraire de Geroch de Reichersberg* (Rome, 1957), pp. 169-73. On Gerhoh in general, E. Meuthen, *Kirche und Heilsgeschichte bei Gerhoh von Reichersberg* (Leiden-Köln, 1959); and Manselli, *op. cit.,* pp. 63-67.

67. *De quarta vigilia noctis* 11, ed E. Sackur, *Libelli de Lite* III, pp. 509-10.

the four watches are probably independent, since in Gerhoh the fourth watch is the present time of the Church, whereas for Bernard it is still to come, and Gerhoh is willing to give a chronological and historical content to his theories which the Abbot of Clairvaux is not.

Bernard's real originality is shown in his use of Psalm 90:5-6, as the basic exegetical touchstone of his theory of history. This was his own creation; that it was always a mark of his influence is demonstrated by its other appearances in twelfth-century theology.[68] Bernard's use of the four horses of the Apocalypse is not quite so original, but is another indication of the Abbot's temperamental affinity with the noted eschatological writers of his time. Bede, in his influential *Explanatio in Apocalypsim,* had already begun to apply the seven seals of Revelations 6-8 to the age of the Church. He also initiated historicizing explanations of the four horses—the white is the primitive Church, the red the bloody persecutor, the black false brethren, and the pale heretics.[69] Historicizing interpretation of the seven seals and four horses was developed at length by Anselm of Havelberg in the first book of his *Dialogi* (written in 1149), but the horses and riders here are used in very different senses from what has been seen in Bernard.[70] Both Anselm and Bernard were probably aware of the text in Bede, and both made use of the symbol of the four horses in their own way—two independent witnesses to the fascination of eschatology in the twelfth century.

One final question and set of texts remain to be investigated to complete a picture of Bernard's attitude towards the histo-

---

68. E.g., Geoffrey of Auxerre, *Sermo in Ps. 90* see J. Leclercq, *Études,* p. 133; Gebouin of Troyes, see J. Leclercq, "Gebouin de Troyes et S. Bernard," *Revue des sciences philosophiques et théologiques,* 41 (1957), pp. 636-37; Otto of Freising, *De duabus civitatibus* VII, 1; and Garnier of Rochefort, *Sermo 4,* PL 205:598D.

69. PL 93:146D-147C. The four horses are given more spiritualized interpretations in other early medieval commentaries on the Apocalypse. Eg., Alcuin (?), *Comment, in Apoc.* IV, 6; PL 100:1123C-1125D; Haymo of Auxerre, *Expos. in Apoc.* II, 6; PL 117:1024A-1027D.

70. *Dialogi* I, chap. 7 (the white horse is the beautiful state of the origin of the Church; its rider is Christ): chap. 8 (the red horse signifies the time of persecution beginning with Stephen); chap. 9 (the black horse is heresy); and chap. 10 (the pale horse is false brethren in the fourth age of the Church). Cf. edition of G. Salet in *Sources Chrétiennes* (Paris, 1966), pp. 68-70; 72; 76; and 84.

ricizing eschatology of his time. F. Radcke has postulated a strong influence of Sibylline literature on the Abbot of Clairvaux and seen that influence to be particularly evident in the crisis connected with the Second Crusade.[71] The question of a Sibylline background to Bernard's invective against the evils of the age has already been considered and rejected; but is it possible that the myth of the last world Emperor colored his attitude towards the Crusade?

The question of the eschatological element in the Crusading movement is one that has continued to divide modern research. Some authors, like N. Cohn in dependence on the mass of material gathered by F. Alphandéry, view the Crusades as one of the great examples of popular eschatology in the Middle Ages;[72] others, such as C. Erdmann are far more cautious.[73] The paucity and ambiguity of the evidence inclines one towards the more cautious viewpoint, but it cannot be denied that there were important eschatological overtones to the Crusades both in the broad and narrow senses mentioned earlier. In terms of the narrower, "hard" eschatology which thought of the last events as definitely at hand, the diffusion of the Sibylline material with its accounts of savage people from the East who would attack Christianity (easily interpreted as the Moslems) and a last world Emperor who would conquer all the enemies of the Church, restore peace and hand his crown over to Christ in Jerusalem obviously had an effect upon the attitude of some towards the Crusades.[74]

The most convincing evidence for a Sibylline interpretation of the Crusades comes from the time of the preaching of the Second Crusade. At the beginning of his *Gesta Frederici I*, Otto of Freising preserves for us the text of a letter which he says was read widely in France at the time of the Crusade. The

71. *Op. cit.*, pp. 109-30.
72. N. Cohn, *op. cit.*, pp. 53-107. P. Alphandéry and A. Dupront, *La Chrétienté et l'idée de Croisade* (Paris, 1954-59), 2 vols.
73. "Endkaiserglaube und Kreuzzugsgedanke," *Zeitschrift für Kirchengeschichte* 51 (1932): 384-414.
74. *Sibylla Tiburtina*, ed. Sackur, pp. 186-87. The imperial bishop Benzo of Alba in his *Panegyrikus* (1086) appears to have been the first to connect Sibylline eschatology and the crusading movement, cf. Erdman, *op. cit.*, pp. 403-7.

letter is addressed to Louis and promises him victory over the whole Orient. It closes with the significant remark: "Therefore your L will be changed into C, who diverted the waters of the river, until those who toil to procure sons have crossed the stream,"[75] quite possibly a reference to the last world Emperor Constans of the Sibylline tradition.[76] Otto remarks that: "This document was then considered by the most excellent and pious personages of Gaul to be of so great authority that it was declared by some to have been found in the Sibylline books, by others to have been divinely revealed to a certain Armenius."[77] Radcke argues that since Bernard's first reaction to Pope Eugene's proclamation of the Crusade was definitely lukewarm, his strong support for the Crusade in 1146 was the result of his acquaintance with this letter and the decision of Louis VII to go on Crusade.[78] The argument is based in part upon the unlikely supposition that Bernard's dealings with European monarchs since the 1120's had always been the result of his ideas concerning the good and bad kings of the penultimate age of history.[79] Nevertheless, since Otto specifically notes that it was considered authentic by the "most excellent and pious personages of Gaul," it is not unlikely that it was known to Bernard in his position as the chief promulgator of the Crusade. However, it, is much less likely that it was responsible for a major shift in his views.

Several other passages in Bernard's works may suggest that there was an eschatological dimension to his attitude towards the Crusades. Two of the letters connected with the Crusading appeal may fit this category. *Letter 363*, a Crusading Encyclical

75. "*Tuum ergo L vertetur in C, qui dispersit aquas fluminis, donec pertransirent illud qui student in procuratione filiorum.*" *Gesta*, ed. alt. G. Waitz (Hannover, 1884), p. 8 (trans. C. C. Mierow).

76. A shorter version of the letter is found in the *Annales Corbeienses* under 1146 (*MGH. SS.* XVI, p. 14), and is referred to in the *Annales Sancti Jacobi Leodienses (MGH. SS.*, XVI, p. 641). For further information, cf. F. Kampers, *op. cit.*, pp. 53-4; F. Radcke, *op. cit.*, pp. 112-13 and N. Cohn, *op. cit.*, pp. 73-4.

77. "*Quod scriptum tantae auctoritatis a probatissimis et religiosissimis Galliarum personis tunc putabatur, ut a quibusdam in Sibillinis libris repertum, ab aliis, cuidam Armenio divinitus revelatum affirmaretur.*" loc. cit. (trans C. C. Mierow).

78. *Op. cit.*, pp. 109-13.

79. *Op. cit.*, pp. 76-108.

addressed to the people of England in one of the texts that comes down to us and to those of eastern France and Bavaria in others, speaks of the danger present from the enemies of the cross in most dramatic terms.[80] This may be typically Bernadine rhetoric, but *Letter 467* connected with the campaign against the Wends goes further:

> But the evil one feared far more the damage he would incur from the conversion of the pagans, when he heard that their tale was to be completed and that the whole of Israel was to achieve salvation. This is what he believes to be threatening him now at this very time, and with all his evil cunning he is endeavoring to see how he can oppose such a great good.[81]

Bernard's bloodthirsty insistence on conversion or death in this particular letter may well spring from an eschatological perspective. Finally, in book two of his *De Consideratione* (1149), Bernard reflects back upon the failure of the Crusade. The Abbot blames the disaster on the lack of *pax* among the princes.[82] *Pax*, the mark of the *eschaton*, can only be the gift of God; its lack among the leaders of the Crusade was a sign that the Church was still plunged in the miseries of history *somewhere* on the road to the final day.

The extent of the eschatological influence on Bernard's attitude towards the Crusade is obviously difficult to determine. Since any evil, internal (like the quarrels of the Christian princes) or external (like the attacks of the Moslems), formed one body with the work of the Antichrist, the Crusade could be viewed from an eschatological perspective, both in its original intention and in its subsequent failure. Bernard may have been aided in seeing this perspective by the Sibylline prophecies current at the time, but there is no conclusive evidence.

---

80. Ep 363, 1; PL 182:564C-565B.
81. Ep 467; PL 182:651B-52B: "*Sed aliud damnum veretur longe amplius de conversione gentium, cum audivit plenitudinem eorum introituram, et omnen quoque Israel fore salvandum. Hoc ei nunc tempus imminere videtur, et tota fraude satagit versuta malitia, quamadmodum obviet tanto bono.*" (James, p. 467).
82. Csi 2, 1; *Opera*, III, 411.

How far can the Abbot of Clairvaux be said to have taken part in the re-emphasized, historicizing eschatological movement of the twelfth century? While there is much in his writings that bespeaks a more traditional approach, the texts that have been examined here indicate that lines of connection that tie him to this movement are not lacking. Guarded as he usually was in his pronouncements about the end, it must be remembered that such cautions were also typical of writers for whom eschatology played a much greater role, such as Gerhoh of Reichersberg.

Like Gerhoh and so many of the twelfth-century eschatologists, Bernard seems to have made the transition from the generalized eschatology common to all Medieval authors to a more intense eschatology at least partly as the result of his involvement in and reflection upon major contemporary crises in the life of the Church. The texts seem to point in this direction. Two of the major passages which discuss the four-age theory of the Church, *Super Cantica 33, 7,* and *In Psalmum Qui inhabitat* 6, 7, date from the latter part of 1138 and early 1139. An exact dating of the other texts, particularly the important *Sententia, "Quatuor sunt tentationes,"* with its invocation of the four horsemen of the Apocalypse, is not possible. Nevertheless, is it not at least plausible that the events of the Papal Schism, the first crisis in which Bernard had played a truly decisive role on an international scale, relived in the meditative tranquillity of Clairvaux after his return there in the second half of 1138, provided the stimulus for his reflections upon the stages of the history of the Church? Something similar may well have happened with regard to the Second Crusade. The evidence here is much more fragmentary, and therefore no general statement can be made with security. It is worthwhile, however, to note that Bernard's most emphatic statement on the proximity of the Antichrist, that contained in the Preface to the *Vita sancti Malachiae,* occurs after the terrible disillusionment of the failure of the Crusade and may in part be conditioned by it.

Bernard was a man plunged into the history of his time. His contemporaries and heirs in the Cistercian Order rarely had the opportunity, let alone the personality, to enter into the public life of the Church in the way in which he did. Interestingly enough, one of the few who to some degree at least approached Bernard in this, Henry, monk of Clairvaux and later Cardinal Bishop of Albano (†1189), also left provocative reflections on the eschatological structure of the history of the Church.[83] While Bernard's eschatological views may not be central to his thought, and are certainly not among the major bequests which he left to the Cistercians, they are not insignificant in showing him to be not only a man of his own times, but also a man ever alive to the mystery of the Church.

Bernard McGinn

University of Chicago

---

83. Y. Congar, "Église et Cité de Dieu chez quelques auteurs cisterciens a l'epoque des croisades, en particulier, dans le *De peregrinante civitate Dei* d'Henri d'Albano," *Mélanges Gilson* (Toronto-Paris, 1959), pp. 173-202.

# ST BERNARD AND THE ANGLICAN DIVINES

REFLECTIONS ON MARK FRANK'S SERMON FOR THE CIRCUMCISION

*The text is plain enough, that "at the Name of Jesus every knee should bow"*. . . *and was there ever more need to do it than in an age where it is doubted whether he be our God or Saviour,—where it is questioned so often whether there were ever such a name to be saved by, and we not rather saved every one in his own?*[1]

THESE WORDS FORM PART OF A SERMON for the Feast of the Circumcision, "On the Name of Jesus," preached by Mark Frank, one of the less well-known Anglican divines, in the chapel of Pembroke College, Cambridge, at the beginning of the seventeenth century. He was speaking to a university assembly, consisting mainly of candidates for holy orders in the newly reformed Church of England, in Cambridge, one of the centers of Puritanism. And yet he speaks within the tradition of the Fathers of the Church, and here specifically in the tradition of medieval preaching typified by St Bernard. This sermon is in fact based on the fifteenth of St Bernard's *Sermons on the Song of Songs: Qualiter nomen Jesus est medicina salubris fidelibus Christianis in omnibus adversis,* with some reference also to St Bernard's first sermon on the Circumcision, *In Circumcisione Domine,* and to the Cistercian sequence, *Dulcis Jesu Memoria.* Mark Frank's

1. Frank, Mark, *Collected Sermons,* Library of Anglo-Catholic Theology (Oxford, 1849), 1:258-272: *Second Sermon on the Circumcision.*

187

use of St Bernard seems to illustrate some important aspects of Anglican theology and devotion, both in the seventeenth century and today.

Mark Frank was born in 1613, and became a fellow of Pembroke College in 1634; during the Puritan commonwealth, he remained loyal to the king and the established church and therefore left his post; he was restored by Charles II as Master of Pembroke, where he died in 1664. By his time, the Church of England had been in existence for more than a century and had in many ways defined its theology and ethos. Hooker and Jewel had laid the foundations of a specifically Anglican tradition, and at the turn of the century Lancelot Andrewes, in particular, further defined Anglican theology. The idea of being part of the undivided church which looks to the first four Councils and the teaching of the Fathers led these men to make a zealous study of the writings of the Patristic age, especially Chrysostom and Basil, Augustine and Gregory. Andrewes, that "oracle to grave divines," wrote with ease in both Latin and Greek, and turned to the Fathers as readily as to Scripture. This sober patristic and biblical scholarship was combined with a deep concern for the right ordering of liturgy and sacrament; a care for sober and right conduct of life, whether in the family or at court; and a reliance upon Scripture as "the very pure word of God." The seventeenth century divines never explicitly reject the medieval tradition, and in fact some, like Donne, were influenced by Ignatian methods of meditation, but political circumstances in the "new" church tended to turn their attention rather to the Scriptures and the earlier Fathers. Thus there was an unrecognized parallel between their situation and that of a twelfth-century monk like St Bernard—a similar care for right conduct, for simplicity in devotion, and especially a love of the Scriptures and a warm devotion toward them. In Donne and Andrewes there is a constant return to the letter of Scripture, a natural use of the text without direct quotation, which is the method of Anselm, Jean of Fécamp and Bernard.

The seventeenth century in England was the age par excellence of the sermon. The Sunday sermon at St Paul's Cross drew the whole citizenry of London. There were sermons by popular preachers at Whitehall. And, a marked feature of the age, there were sermons in the great households; colleges and schools had their own measure of preaching, as did the parish churches. The sermon was a dynamic force, holding an important position in social and religious life; the great preachers had power to influence devotion and shape religion in an unprecedented way.

These preachers were influenced by the sermons of the Fathers of the Church, not by accident but by their deliberate choice. Donne, for instance, refered to Bernard as the "Father of Meditation," and frequently used the term meditation to describe his own preaching. The Augustinian relationship between knowing and loving God is the basis of both Bernard's preaching and Donne's. Their sermons are meditations because their aim is spiritual development and growth. In his fourth Prebend Sermon, Donne uses the same sermon of St Bernard on the Name of Jesus that Mark Frank used later for his Circumcision sermon:

> . . . from the sole name of Christ thousands of thousands of believers are called Christians, . . . Hidden as in a vase, in this Name of Jesus, you my soul, possess a salutary remedy against which no spiritual illness will be proof. Carry it always to your heart, always in your hand and so insure that all your affections, all your actions, are directed to Jesus.[2]

Donne speaks of this "hiding in the name" but it is interesting to see the differences as well as the similarities between the two:

> We consist in the humility of the ancients; we are Christians, Jesus is merely a Savior, a name of mystery, Christ is Anointed, a name of communication, of accommodation, of imitation; and so this name, the name of Christ, is *Oleum effusum* (as

---

2. Bernard of Clairvaux, *Sermons on the Song of Songs*, 15, 3-7, *Opera*, I, 84-87. Trans. K. Walsh, *The Works of Bernard of Clairvaux*, Vol, 2, Cistercian Fathers Series 4 (Hereafter CF 4) (Spencer, Mass. 1971) p. 108-111.

the Spouse speaks);an oyntment, a perfume poured out upon us and we are Christians. In the name of Jesus St Paul abounded, but in the name of Christ more. . . . If we will call ourselves or endanger or give occasion to others to call us from the names of men, Papists or Lutherans or Calvinists, we depart from the true glory and serenity, from the lustre and splendour of the Sunne; this is *Tabernaculum Solis:* here in the Christian church God hath set a tabernacle for the sunne; and as in nature man hath light enough to discern the principles of reason; so in the Christian church (considered without subdivisions of names and sects) a Christian hath light enough of all things necessary to salvation.[3]

Here Donne is presenting the ideal of the Anglican Church as the true and undefiled church, the *tabernaculum solis*, which abhors the "errors both of Rome and Geneva." There is also the world view of the renaissance man, his belief in the "right reason" which is ready to receive the light of Christ in the Church. But there is the same concern and understanding that St Bernard evinces for the relationship of men with Christ Jesus.

Not only the use of the Scriptures, the approach to preaching, the theology and the devotion to the Fathers appealed to the Anglican divines; they were also strongly influenced by the Patristic prose style and use of language. Andrewes based his style on the Fathers just as much as his theology. In St Ambrose he saw a "witty" preacher, in St Bernard a master of antithesis and balanced prose whom he was delighted to follow. The early theology of *kenosis*, the concern with the contrast between the greatness of Christ and the mean conditions to which he descended, found expression in the carefully wrought sentences of these metaphysicians, with their understanding of tension and contrast in ideas and words. The great contrasts of Augustine and Bernard awake again when Donne writes:

> God clothed himself in vile man's flesh that so
> He might be weak enough to suffer woe.[4]

3. Donne, John, *Sonnet XI, Poems of John Donne.* Ed. Herbert J. C. Grierson, (Oxford, 1912), 1:XX.
4. Ibid.

Or when Andrewes exclaims that Christ "that thundereth in heaven cry in a cradle; he that so great and so high should become so little as a child"[5]; and in Mark Frank's introduction to his *Second Sermon of the Nativity*:

Seeing the infinite greatness of this day become so little, Eternity a child, the rays of glory wrapt in rags, heaven crowded into the corner of a stable, and he that is everywhere want a room.[6]

Their meditations on the Passion followed the same pattern, but with a more clearly medieval devotional tone, as in Donne's phrase about the Cross:

And thou lookst towards me
O savior as thou hangest on the tree.[7]

The strange medieval use of the image of a book for the crucified Christ, with the wounds seen as red capital letters finds expression several times in these Anglicans, including Mark Frank.[8]

Andrewes and Taylor especially wrote in the tradition of the Fathers, but they were strongly influenced, though perhaps more by unconscious inheritance than by choice, by the medieval tradition. And here they found in Bernard a writer who combined the theology of the undivided Church with the *affectus* of the *devotio moderna*, and wrote in a prose admirably suited to their way of expression. In theory, of course, St Bernard rejected a careful prose style: "Peter and Andrew and the sons of Zebedes, and all the other disciples, were not chosen from a school of rhetoric or philosophy; and yet through them the Savior made his salvation effective throughout the world."[9]

5. Andrewes, Lancelot, *Second Sermon on the Nativity, Ninety-six Sermons.* (Oxford, 1841), 1:29.
6. Frank, Mark, *Second Sermon on the Nativity, op. cit.,* 1:69.
7. Donne, John, *Good Friday 1613 Riding Westward, op. cit.,* p. 336.
8. See Andrewes, *Sermons on the Passion. Ninety-six Sermons,* 2:XX.
9. Bernard of Clairvaux, *On the Song of Songs,* 36, 1, *Opera,* II, 4; CF 7:213.

But in the very words he uses he belies his theory. The seventeenth-century Anglicans looked to style as well as to meaning; this was in accord with their understanding of the role of words in the expression of right reason and order. "The Holy Ghost," wrote Donne, "in penning the Scriptures delights himself, not only with a propriety, but a delicacy and harmony and melody of language . . . and they mistake it much that think that the Holy Ghost hath rather chosen a low and barbarous and homely style, than an eloquent and powerful manner of expressing himself." Of St Bernard he wrote, "*Pax non promissa sed missa*, says St Bernard in his musical and harmonious cadences . . . St Bernard who evermore embraced all occasions of exciting devotion from the melodious fall of words."[10]

In Mark Frank this appreciation of words finds a less complex expression than in Donne or Andrewes; his prose is often as fine, but less strained, less fanciful, simpler. In his Sermon on the *Circumcision*, Frank relies closely on St Bernard and that in much more than the direct borrowings. The first paragraph introducing the theme of "the Name" is a sequence of prose devices, put together with the simplicity of complete mastery: "A Name that has all things in it; that brings all good things with it; that speaks more in five letters than we can do in five thousand words; speaks more in it than we can speak today; and yet today we intend to speak of nothing else, nothing but Jesus, nothing but Jesus."[11] This combination of warm devotion and good prose is found constantly in St Bernard. Apart from one passage from St Ambrose's *De Virginibus (Omnia Christus est nobis. Si vulnis curate desiderans, medicus est . . .)*,[12] the Bible and St Bernard are the sources for Frank's sermon.

Like St Bernard, he uses several adjectives to describe the Name and deals with them in turn, in the orderly manner of a teacher. They are not precisely the same terms as those used by Bernard, but they fall into the same two basic categories of *majestas* and *pietas*. Frank deals first with the titles of majesty:

10. Donne, John, *LXXX Sermons* (Oxford, 1920) 5:556-557.
11. Frank, *op. cit.*, p. 258.
12. Ambrose, *De Virginibus* (Paris, 1549), 3:110.

"truth and fidelity, might and power, majesty and glory," just as St Bernard does with "admirable, the mighty God, and the Father of the age to come." These titles of the Name "cover heaven and earth with the majesty of its glory. And yet," Frank continues, "so it might and we never the better, but that, fourthly, it is a name of grace and mercy as well as majesty and glory." The remaining titles therefore are, like St Bernard's "Counselor and Prince of Peace," names of mercy—"grace and mercy, sweetness and comfort, wonder and admiration, blessing and adoration." "He wants nothing that has Jesus," Frank continues, "and he has nothing that wants him."[13]

Frank then takes from St Bernard the comparison of the Name to oil: *"Est autem, dico, in triplici quadam qualitate olei, quod lucit, pascit et ungit,"*[14] says St Bernard; and Frank begins: "Thy name, says the spouse, is ointment poured forth, now oil has three special uses: for light, for meat and for medicine."[15] He then asks St Bernard's questions, "Dost thou want health? He is the great physician. Art thou fired in the flames of a burning fever? he is the well-spring to cool thy heat. . . ." The next passage, about "the name of sweetness and comfort too," is based on the parallel passage in the *Sermon on the Song of Songs: "Mel in ore, in aure melos, in corde jubilus,"* says St Bernard, "It is honey in the mouth, it is music in the ear, it is melody in the heart." Frank then refers to a passage, "as says the devout Bernard," which I am unable to trace: *Gyra et regyra, versa et reversa, et non inverties pacem vel requiem nisi in solo Jesu. Quapropter si quiescere vis, pone Jesum ut signulum super cor tuum, quia tranquillus ipse tranquillat omnia*: "Turn you and turn you again, which way you will, which way you can, you can never find such peace and quite as there is in Jesus; you will find none anywhere but in him. If you would fain therefore lay you down to rest in peace and comfort, set the seal of Jesus upon your heart and all will be quiet."[16]

13. Frank, *op. cit.*, p. 262.
14. Bernard of Clairvaux, *On the Song of Songs,* 15, 5; *Opera,* I, 85; Cf 4:109.
15. Frank, *op. cit.*, p. 262.
16. Frank, *op. cit.*, p. 262-263.

"I and this point" he continues, "though so sweet I part with it unwillingly, with a stave or two of devout Bernard's jubilee or hymn upon it."[17] He quotes in Latin two sections of the *Dulcis Jesu Memoria*[18]: "*Nil canitur suavius . . . quid sit Jesum diligere.*" Dom Wilmart has established that this hymn on the Holy Name was produced in the twelfth century, probably by an English Cistercian, but it is so imbued with the thought of St Bernard that earlier ages had no doubt in attributing it to him.[19] Frank translates and comments on it thus:

> There is nothing sweeter to be sung of, nothing more pleasant to be thought of, than this Jesus. Jesus, the delight of hearts, the light of minds, above all joy, above all we can desire; the tongue cannot tell, words cannot express, only he that feels it can believe what sweetness is in Jesus. A long song he makes of it; it would not be amiss that we also made some short ones, some ejaculations, and raptures now and then upon it. Give us but a taste and relish of thy blessed name, O Jesus, and we shall sing of it all the day long, and praise thy name for ever and ever and sing with the same Father *Jesu decus angelicum . . . coelicum:* "O Jesu, thou joy and glory of men and angels, thy name is music in our ears, honey in our mouths, heavenly nectar to our hearts," all sweetness, all pleasure to us throughout, wonderful sweet.[20]

The conclusion of the sermon applies the "sweetness" of devotion in a very practical and Anglican way:

> Bless we ourselves in this name, when we lie down and when we rise up, when we go out and when we come in. . . . The text is plain enough, that "at the name of Jesus every knee should bow," when we hear the name of Jesus I suppose there is none so little Christian but that he will confess that I may lift up my heart and praise him for the mercy and the benefits that I remember and am put in mind of by it; and where I bow my soul, may I not bow my body? Say good of it and

17. Ibid.
18. The whole of this beautiful hymn can be found in PL 184:1317-1320.
19. See "Remarques et Conclusions" in A. Wilmart, *Le "Jubilus" dit de St Bernard: Etudes avec textes* (Rome, 1944) pp. 219-222.
20. Frank, *op. cit.*, p. 266.

make others say good of it . . . carry ourselves we will, I hope, as men that have a portion in Jesus, a share in salvation . . . . Be we not afraid then of the tongues of foolish men, but open we the morning and shut in the evening with it, begin and end our days with it in our mouths.[21]

This plain concern with conduct, with applying *theoria*, vision, devotion, in practical daily life is something basic to monastic life especially as understood by St Bernard. In the *Sermons on the Song of Songs*, he interprets the text constantly in terms of the humanity of Christ and his relationship to himself and to the monks who were listening. The famous passage on the Name of Jesus has this note of evangelistic piety very clearly:

For when I name Jesus I set before me a man who is meek and humble of heart, kind, prudent, chaste, merciful, flawlessly upright and holy in the eyes of all; and this same man is the all-powerful God whose way of life heals me, whose support is my strength.[22]

This is a recurring theme in Anglicanism; "Let us," says Jeremy Taylor, "press after Jesus, which is truest religion and most solemn adoration."[23] And it is this unity of warm affection with theology and conduct that Frank expresses in his conclusion, together with that essential monastic dimension of the Parousia:

Jesus runs through all with us. So then remember we to begin and end all in Jesus; the New Testament, the covenant of our salvation, begins and ends so, "The generation of Jesus," so it ends. May we all end so too; and when we are going hence, commend our spirits with Stephen into his hands; and when he comes, may he receive them to sing praises and alleluias to his blessed name, amidst saints and angels in his glorious kingdom for ever. Amen.[24]

Benedicta Ward SLG

Convent of the Incarnation
Oxford, England

21. Frank, *op. cit.*, p. 272.
22. Bernard of Clairvaux, *On the Song of Songs*, 15,6; *Opera*, 1, 87; CF4:111.
23. Taylor, Jeremy, *The Great Exemplar of Sanctity and Holy Life* (Oxford, 1887), p. 34.
24. Frank, *op. cit.*, p. 272.

# ST BERNARD AND THE BARUNDI ON
# THE NAME OF GOD

AFRICAN CHRISTIANS are in the process of developing an indigenous African theology. During the past ten
years African theologians have been coming together
in study weeks, investigating new ways of bringing the gospel
of Christ into contact with African cultural patterns.[1]

This Africanization of theology must ultimately be realized
"by the African clergy itself."[2] But since African theology is
just beginning to find its own way, and also because the whole
Church will eventually be enriched by this "new theology," it
seems that it will develop best in a spirit of dialogue with other
traditions in the Church, rather than in some sort of "theological 'isolation.' "[3]

Monks and nuns of today, heirs to a living monastic theology
and encouraged by the current development of monastic life in
Africa, should be particularly interested in this new African
theology. Comparing monastic tradition with African religious
traditions is one way of contributing to its growth and sharing

---

1. For example, see Kwesi A. Dickson and Paul Ellingworth, editors, *Biblical
Revelation and African Beliefs* (Maryknoll, N.Y.: Orbis Books, 1969), for the
principal papers presented at the January, 1966, consultation of African theologians at Immanuel College, Ibadan, Nigeria; and Pol J. Vonck WF, "The Problems
of African Theology," *African Ecclesiastical Review* 11 (1969), pp. 73-87, for a
description of the July, 1968, seminar on African theology at the University of
Kinshasa (formerly Lovanium University), Kinshasa, Zaire.

2. J. Voorn CSSp, "Africanisation of Theology," *African Ecclesiastical Review*
8 (1966), p. 315.

3. Ibid., p. 313.

in its fruits. But in recent years both monastic studies and African studies have developed to such a point that general studies now retain only a limited value. It is becoming more necessary to examine specific areas of these traditions.

In this article I would like to compare one monastic author, St Bernard, and one group of Africans, the Barundi; and to limit the comparison to their theology of God, especially the name of God. In doing so I am doubly inspired by the example of Dom Jean Leclercq, who has done so much to increase our knowledge of St Bernard, and to foster the growth of Christian monasticism in Africa.

## The Barundi

Although St Bernard needs no introduction, it is necessary to give some background information on the Barundi.

The Barundi are composed of the three ethnic groups, the Tutsi (Batutsi, Tusi, Watusi), the Hutu (Bahuta, Bahutu, Rundi), and the Twa (Batwa, Baganwa), who presently inhabit the country of Burundi in east central Africa.

The country itself "was formerly the southern half of the Belgian trust territory of Ruanda-Urundi, and . . . became an independent country on July 1, 1962."[4] Located on the northeast shore of Lake Tanganyika, Burundi is a land of hills and lakes, grasslands and forests. The people live mostly in rural areas and maintain a meager existence by farming.[5] Kirundi, a Bantu language, is spoken, but French also has official status.[6]

With over three million people living in an area of less than eleven thousand square miles, Burundi is one of the most densely populated countries in Africa.[7] Moreover, the history of the area gives the present population a unique character:

There are three ethnic groups: the Tutsi (13 percent), the Hutu (86 percent) and the Twa (1 percent). The Tutsi, tall,

4. Leonard J. Desmond Jr, "Burundi," *The Catholic Encyclopedia For School And Home* (New York: McGraw-Hill, 1965), 2:141.
5. "Tanzania, Rwanda and Burundi," *The World of Man* (Chicago: Creative World Publications, 1969), 16:55-57.
6. J. Perraudin, "Burundi," *New Catholic Encyclopedia* (Washington: Catholic University of America, 1967), 2:907.
7. "Tanzania, Rwanda and Burundi," *op. cit.*, pp. 55-57.

slim people of Hamitic origin, came into Burundi about four hundred years ago from Ethiopia and became the rulers of the Hutu, who were shorter in height. The Hutu were farmers of Bantu origin who had long been living there. The easygoing Twa are pygmies who are probably the last survivors of an aboriginal people driven into the forest by the Hutu.[8]

Throughout the history of Burundi there have been tensions between these three groups. The civil war between the Tutsi and the Hutu, which drew the attention of the world to Burundi in 1972, was the latest, and most terrible, chapter in this history of tribal strife.

## *Catholicism in Burundi*[9]

Although the Catholic Church has been present only since the end of the nineteenth century, Burundi, along with Rwanda to the north, had become by the mid-1960's "the most flourishing Catholic mission area in the world."[10] The mission, under the direction of the White Fathers, got off to a slow start. But the missionaries gradually made friends,[11] and for fifty years the Church grew so rapidly in Burundi that by 1970 two-thirds of its more than three million inhabitants had become Catholics.[12]

The sight of Catholics killing each other during the massacres of 1972, however, forces us to question the quality of these conversions. And even before the war, a Barundi nun could claim that "belief in God is mixed with other false beliefs," and that many "have undertaken the Christian life, but without being fully detached from their very tenacious pagan men-

8. Leonard J. Desmond, Jr, *op. cit.*, p. 141.

9. The present article was originally completed in April, 1971, a full year before the war in Burundi. Thus at the proofreading stage it has been necessary to re-write this section in the light of a more critical judgment on the degree of evangelization. But I am primarily concerned with the pre-Christian Barundi tradition; here I simply wish to provide some general information on the contemporary scene, so fluid and difficult to appraise.

10. J. Perraudin, *op. cit.*, p. 907.

11. Gerard Rathe WF, *Mud And Mosaics* (Westminster, Md.: Newman, 1960), pp. 161-76.

12. "Flourishing Christian Community in Africa," *L'Osservatore Romano* (Weekly Edition in English), N. 40 (131), October 1, 1970, p. 11.

tality."[13] Yet we must also keep in mind that there has been no feeling of enforcement in the process of conversion, and adults, not children, have taken the lead in entering the Church.[14] Catechumens have been baptized only after passing through a well-organized catechumenate lasting at least four years,[15] and in 1970 it could be reported that about eighty percent of Barundi Catholics practice their faith.[16]

The bloody conflict of 1972 has intensified the shortage of priests which already existed,[17] and rendered precarious the situation of the religious orders. Before the catastrophe religious life had been showing favorable progress; in the mid-1960's it was noted that alongside several European orders, "two Burundi congregations of sisters have developed and, at a slower rate, one congregation of brothers."[18] There is, or at least was until the war, a convent of Dominican contemplative nuns at Mureke, Burundi; and there are several other contemplative and monastic communities, Benedictines, Cistercians and others, in nearby countries.[19]

## Situating Barundi Theology

Before we can compare St Bernard and the Barundi, we must clarify certain aspects of the Barundi religious tradition and the theology it embodies.[20]

First, although the Barundi are the group I am primarily

13. Sr Thérèse-Marie, Sisters of Bene-Maria, Ngozi, "Practical Training in Prayer Starting from the Old Testament: Adaptation fot the Women of Burundi," *Lumen Vitae* 18 (1963): 272. But in order to understand the context of this quotation, it must be noted that Sr Thérèse-Marie also says that these attitudes are "found everywhere, especially in young countries," and that "the souls of our women are deeply religious." Ibid.

14. Adrian Hastings, *Church and Mission in Modern Africa* (New York: Fordham University Press, 1967), p. 121.

15. J. Perraudin, *op. cit.*, p. 907.

16. "Flourishing Christian Community in Africa," *op. cit.*, p. 11.

17. Ibid.

18. J. Perraudin, *op. cit.*, p. 907.

19. For a description of African monastic communities, see *Monastic Growth*, Special Issue of the A.I.M. Bulletin (1970), pp. 8-35.

20. Throughout this paper I am using the term *theology* in a rather loose sense to mean any objectification of a response to God, which can serve as a frame of reference and source of nourishment for further relations with God.

interested in, it is not possible to study them in isolation from other Bantu peoples. Along with the Bashi, Bakongo, Baluba and Babira in Zaire, and the Rwanda, the Barundi share a common Bantu heritage in which "participation in a common life is the main if not the only basis of all . . . family, social, political and religious institutions and customs."[21] This means that it is difficult to locate a specifically Barundi religious tradition. This is especially true with regard to the Rwanda, for both groups are made up of Tutsi, Hutu and Twa,[22] and are monotheists who refer to God as Imâna.[23] Actually, there is room for some distinction of traditions. Bernard Zuure has written a lengthy article entirely devoted to a study of Immâna as God of the Barundi;[24] and the Rwanda and Barundi themselves make a distinction in the way they refer to Immâna: the Rwanda refer to *"Immana y'i Rwanda* (the God called Immana in Rwanda),"[25] and the Barundi refer to "Mâna of the Barundi."[26] But the Rwanda and Barundi traditions are still very similar.

Also, it would be nice if we could identify elements of the Barundi tradition as coming from one or another of the three ethnic groups which make up the people—but this is very difficult. The three groups have been living together for so long

21. Vincent Mulago, "Vital Participation: The Cohesive Principle of the Bantu Community," *Biblical Revelation And African Beliefs, op. cit.,* in note 1, p. 137.

22. "Tanzania, Rwanda and Burundi," *op. cit.,* in note 5, pp. 54-59.

23. For the Rwanda, see Dominic Nothomb PB, "Man and God: Values and Stepping-Stones in an African Humanism," *Lumen Vitae* 20 (1965):265; for the Barundi and the Rwanda, see Jean Bucumi SJ, "Imâna: Some Names of God in the Kirundi Language," *International Philosophical Quarterly* 4 (1964): 394-418. Throughout the present article the name Imâna and all Kirundi words will be spelled as in the sources. The spelling of words in Kirundi is fluid, and varying forms occur. Here it must also be noted that the Barundi tradition is an oral tradition without any written sources. But Fr Bucumi (himself a Barundi) and Fr Zuure (whose article is cited in note 24), my two main sources for Barundi tradition, based their articles on personal contact with the Barundi and detailed investigation throughout the country. Other articles cited, i.e. those of Frs Mulago, Nothomb, Loupias and Classe, are also based on direct personal studies of the peoples involved.

24. Bernard Zuure PB, "Immâna le Dieu des Barundi," *Anthropos* 21 (1926): 733-76.

25. Dominic Nothomb PB, *op. cit.,* p. 265.

26. Jean Bucumi SJ, *op. cit.,* p. 402.

that a certain cultural convergence has occurred,[27] and to attribute a part of the Barundi tradition to one or another of them it is necessary to rely heavily on whatever external evidence may be available.[28]

Then again, it is mainly the pre-Christian Barundi tradition that I would like to compare with St Bernard. But Christianity has been in the country for over seventy years and a certain absorption of Christian notions into the original Barundi tradition is by now quite possible.[29]

One final difficulty in interpreting Barundi tradition will be treated in the context in which it arises.

## St Bernard and the Barundi on the Name of God

Since Barundi theology appears most clearly in the rich abundance of names which the Barundi use in referring to the one God, Immâna, the best way to compare it with the theology of St Bernard is to select some Barundi names for God, study them and the theological themes they open up, and then study similar names and themes in St Bernard's writings.

It should be evident that it is not easy to make such a comparison. St Bernard's theology is the work of an individual Christian, which has come down to us in a relatively complete and unified form in his writings, and bears the imprint of his monastic vocation. Pre-Christian Barundi theology, the heritage of an entire nation, is more diffuse, passed on from generation to generation in "traditional cradle songs, proverbs and folk tales;"[30] and it has a decidedly domestic flavor.[31]

But the effort to bring African theology into dialogue with

27. For a description of a similar development among the Rwanda, see P. Loupias PB, "Tradition et Légende des Batutsi sur la Création du Monde et leur Établissement au Ruanda," *Anthropos* 3 (1908): 1.

28. An example of this is Vincent Mulago's relating the Barundi to other Bantu peoples through the common emphasis on participation in a common life, or *bumwe*, as the Barundi refer to it (*op. cit.*, in note 21, p. 137). This would suggest that this aspect of Barundi tradition comes from the Hutu, the only Bantu people among the Barundi.

29. P. Loupias PB already noted this difficulty, with reference to the Rwanda, in 1908 (*op. cit.*, in note 27. p. 1).

30. Jean Bucumi SJ, *op. cit.*, in note 23, p. 394.

31. Ibid., *passim.*

other traditions in the Church must begin somewhere, and I feel that in the present case there really is a sufficient basis for a fruitful dialogue.

St Bernard's theology is rooted in his own concrete experience of the monastic life of personal and liturgical prayer, and expressed mostly in sermons to his fellow monks. Similarly, Barundi theology is contained in popular tales and fables, in which "universal ideas are rooted in the soil of . . . earthly existence."[32] St Bernard's theology is not systematic or exhaustive, but intuitive, and expressed in poetic language. Barundi theology is also expressed in "rich concrete imagery," in a "mythic language" which "supplies something that is often sacrificed in technical expressions."[33] And St Bernard's theology, though the expression of a celibate monk, is deeply influenced by the bridal imagery of *The Song of Songs*—this suggests the possibility of relating it to a theology full of images of family life, in which "names that refer directly to Ímâna . . . are also given to children, and they constitute a kind of *journal intime* of a family's relations with God throughout the course of its existence."[34]

So now we can proceed to a comparison of St Bernard and the Barundi, based on Barundi names for God.

## I. Immâna

"The name *par excellence* by which the Barundi refer to the Being above all things, master of all, all-powerful, benefactor, etc. . . . is *Immâna*."[35] In his etymological analysis of this name Zuure notes its similarity to the *Mana* of the Polynesians and Melanesians, the *dii Manes* of the Roman pantheon, the *Mena* of the first Egyptian dynasty, and the Kiswahili expression *Usiku wa manane* (night of the friendly gods).[36] But he admits that he is unable to judge these similarities, and prefers to find

32. Ibid., p. 395.
33. Ibid., p. 418.
34. Ibid., pp. 394f.
35. Bernard Zuure PB, *op. cit.*, in note 24, p. 736.
36. Ibid.

an explanation in the Kirundi language itself. After examining the linguistic components of the name, he concludes that in Kirundi it means: "the Being, He who is *par excellence (l'Etre, Celui qui est par excellence)*;" or: "He who is with everything *(Celui qui est avec les choses)*."[37] The meaning intended is not metaphysical, but more simple: *Immâna* is the supreme, invisible Being who is everywhere and in whose presence one finds happiness and peace.[38]

The similarity of the meaning of this name to the meaning of the divine name Yahweh, as it is currently interpreted by biblical scholars,[39] should be clear. But its similarity to another divine name is even more striking.

Some of St Bernard's most beautiful passages on the love of God occur in his *Christmas Sermons*. In *Sermon Five* he explains that the Father manifests his love for us by sending us his Son, in whom we have peace—by sending us his Son as an infant.[40] And what is the name of this infant sent by God? It is "Emmanuel, God with us."[41]

Moreover, this infant is not silent; he is the Word, and he speaks to us. The stable, the crib, the tears and the swaddling clothes all join together in a cry to men to come to this little child.[42] And when St Bernard invites us to come and adore him in his crib,[43] we can find inspiration for a fitting chant of praise among the songs Barundi women sing to their little ones. For it is in such cradle songs that the Barundi also sing most beautifully of their God, of Immâna, of the God who is with them, who gives them peace, who shows his love by giving a child. A Barundi mother will sing:

---

37. Ibid., pp. 736f.
38. Ibid., pp. 737f. Vincent Mulago says the name Imâna means "source of all good and all happiness," but he gives no explanation (*op. cit.*, in note 21, p. 138).
39. For example, see B. W. Anderson, "God, Names of," *The Interpreter's Dictionary of the Bible* (New York and Nashville: Abingdon Press, 1962), 2:407-17, esp. pp. 409-11.
40. *Sermones in Nativitate Domini,* 5, *S. Bernardi: Opera* (Rome: Editiones Cistercienses, 1957-1968), vol. 4, p. 266.
41. Ibid., p. 267.
42. Ibid., pp. 266f.
43. Ibid., p. 267.

The moon was shining and you came to me.
Imâna made fire and you came to me.
He had His arms open to give.
Imâna who gave you to me.
If I could but meet Him
I would bend the knee and adore Him.
I would pay Him homage.
I would make Him fire to warm Himself.
I would serve Him good wine the night long.
Soft, now, my child, that I have received in sharing,
In sharing with Imâna.[44]

God is Imâna—he who is with everything. He is Emmanuel—
God with us.

## 2. *Hangimâna*

The name *Hangimâna* means "Have your eyes fixed on Imâna."[45] It is compounded of the verb *guhanga,* to regard with attention or to fix one's eyes on a spectacle without wishing to
look away, and Imâna.[46] The verb *guhanga* may be used to
describe one's response to a natural phenomenon such as a
beautiful sunset or a newborn baby, but it also elicits the sense
of something beyond—behind the immediate object of contemplation is Imâna, whom no one has ever seen but who is
represented by these natural symbols.[47]

But it is difficult to judge the nature of this contemplation
of Imâna. I have had access to Barundi tradition only through
the few authors who have written about it. And while these
authors agree about the loftiness of the concept of Imâna in
Barundi tradition,[48] their emphasis is different when it comes

44. Jean Bucumi SJ, *op. cit.,* p. 401.
45. Ibid., p. 414. In using Fr Bucumi as a source, we must keep in mind that he
says of his article: "The area of study is Rwanda as well as Burundi, but since I am
a native of Burundi . . . I treat the latter country and its traditions in greater detail.
. . . After all, in these matters we differ very little; the names are almost the same,
although they occur with greater frequency among the Barundi," Ibid., p. 396.
46. Ibid., p. 411.
47. Ibid., pp. 411-13.
48. Zuure, *op. cit.,* pp. 766-68; and Bucumi, *op. cit., passim.*

to the response of the people to Imâna. Bernard Zuure claims that the Barundi think and speak of the perfections of God but do not draw practical conclusions about worshipping him —so that it is more a question of a monotheistic thought pattern than a religion. He also mentions certain superstitious practices.[50] Jean Bucumi places more emphasis on the profound religious sentiments of the Barundi and a real intimacy with Imâna.[51]

Other authors, who have written about the Imâna concept among the Rwanda, write in a vein much closer to Zuure.[52] This might lead one to suppose that Bucumi has either overemphasized the intimacy of the Barundi with Imâna, or even unwittingly introduced some of his own Christian sentiments. But since he refers to many proverbs and customs to substantiate his views,[53] it is not possible to conclude one way or the other. We must simply keep this difference of emphasis in mind as we see how Bucumi goes on to describe the nature of the contemplation which the name *Hangimâna* evokes:

> *Guhanga* in the divine name suggests the idea of a loving contemplation nourished on hope. God is not directly seen, but one hopes to see Him and to find Him in His home, because He awaits us: *Nindolêra* (It is He [Imâna] who awaits me). . . . This movement of hope will be fixed on God like the dart of contemplation where one's glance will not be quickly dulled because it is sustained by the upsurge of a love that is always renewed by God, the God who awaits me: *Nindolêra.* [54]

And when Bucumi speaks of the "longing for the supreme and decisive meeting with Imâna,"[55] we must note that Dominic Nothomb says that "God . . . is never thought of in Rwanda

49. Zuure, *op. cit.*, pp. 767f.
50. Ibid., pp. 773f.
51. Bucumi, *op. cit.*, pp. 401-03, 413f., 417f.
52. See Dominic Nothomb PB, *op. cit.*, in note 23; and Léon Classe PB, "The Supreme Being Among the Banyarwanda of Ruanda," *Primitive Man 2* (July-October, 1929): 56-57.
53. Bucumi, *op. cit.*, *passim.*
54. Ibid., pp. 413f.
55. Ibid., p. 414.

as the 'last end' of man."[56] And though Bucumi claims that "God reveals Himself as a Father who loves us,"[57] Nothomb holds that "The only One able to speak truly . . . has not spoken our language to give us a message."[58]

Thus it is hard to determine how much loving intimacy the Barundi notion of contemplation entails; but this is not the case with regard to St Bernard. In his *Sermons on the Song of Songs* Bernard treats many of the themes suggested by the Barundi name *Hangimâna*, but all in the context of the "marriage" of the soul to the Word of God as bride to bridegroom.

Thus if the Barundi wish to look beyond the phenomena of nature to Imâna, St Bernard portrays the soul seeking intimate union with the Word to be "not at all content that the bridegroom should manifest himself through the things that are made," but to desire "the special prerogative of receiving him into the depths of her heart with the most intimate affection."[59] If among the Barundi there is a "disproportion between the sentiment, the inner idea and exterior acts,"[60] St Bernard takes care to point out that the practice of the virtues must precede the holy rest of contemplation.[61] If there is some question as to whether the Barundi really aspire to eternal union with Imâna, St Bernard describes the soul which "sighs for the presence of Christ, is disappointed that the kingdom has not yet arrived, and calls out to the desired homeland from afar with tears and sighs."[62] And if we cannot be sure that the Barundi actually feel that Imâna is to be loved, there is no question for St Bernard, who explains that the relationship proper to a bride is love, and this love reaches its full fruition when rendered back to him who gives it in the first place—God.[63]

---

56. Dominic Nothomb PB, *op. cit.*, p. 275.
57. Bucumi, *op. cit.*, p. 414.
58. Nothomb, *op. cit.*, p. 270.
59. *Sermones Super Cantica Canticorum,* 31, *Opera* I, 223. All translations from St Bernard in this article are the author's own.
60. Zuure, *op. cit.*, p. 768.
61. *Sermon 46, Opera*, II, 58.
62. Ibid., *Sermon 59*, p. 137.
63. Ibid., *Sermon 7*, I, 31.

Throughout all these sermons St Bernard sings the delights of the bride's loving contemplation of the Word and reaches a climax in *Sermon Eighty-five* when he exclaims: "When you see a soul who has left all things to cleave to the Word with all her might, to live for the Word, to rule herself by the Word . . . who is able to say: 'for me to live is Christ and to die is gain' —know that she is the bride of the Word and wed to him."[64]

## 3. Mushinzimâna

When given to a child, the name *Mushinzimâna* means: I confide you to the solid protection of Imâna.[65] The root word is *gushinga,* to fix, drive in or imbed vigorously.[66] This word is used in such expressions as: *gushinga igiti*—to hammer a post into the ground; *gushinga urugo*—to take up quarters in some new land, or to consolidate one's position in human relations or business matters; and *gushinga ikintu uwundi*—to confide a thing or person to the care of another.[67]

If a mother bears a child after having lost several others, she will pray:

> The first ones that came before are dead in spite of my mother's love, in spite of my arms that were uplifted to keep them alive. . . . But this one, O Lord, I confide to your strong hands, to your Father's heart. . . . And I know, Lord, that you are vigilant, that you do not sleep: *Ntisinzira.* Whoever is in your hands is safe from every danger. I confide him to you. Bring him up for me.[68]

St Bernard also speaks movingly of the solid protection of God. In a series of *Sermons on Psalm Ninety-One,* preached at Clairvaux one Lent, he encourages his monks to dwell in the shelter of the Most High, since whoever does this has nothing to fear;[69] for "night and day he watches over us with the love

---

64. Ibid., II, 315.
65. Bucumi, *op. cit.,* p. 416.
66. Ibid., p. 414.
67. Ibid., pp. 414f.
68. Ibid., p. 416.
69. *Sermones De Psalmo "Qui Habitat,"* 1, Opera IV, 388.

which is his alone; he who guards Israel neither slumbers nor sleeps."[70] He shields us from temptations,[71] and gives us refuge from "outward battles and inner fears."[72] And even when we fall, he is ready to help us as if he had abandoned all the rest and come to help us alone,[73] for his attention is so loving that "like a mother, he fosters us with his own warmth."[74]

St Bernard urges us to respond to this divine lover by making him our hope, and having that "perfect love which seeks only that which is highest, and cries out with all the ardor of true desire: 'Whom else have I in heaven? And when I am with you, the earth delights me not.' "[75] And he assures us that God will hear us when we call upon "the only name by which we are to be saved . . . the name which we bear," in true prayer, saying: "hallowed be thy name."[76] God will lead us through all our tribulations and give us the greatest happiness of taking us to himself, filling us with the good things of his house, and making us like himself in glory,[77] the glory of the final day, "the day of Resurrection, when what is now sown in dishonor will rise in glory."[78] This will be the full realization of our union with Jesus. For "this glory lies hidden in the present tribulation,"[79] and when we have died with Christ we will rise with him.[80] He is with us in tribulation and his name is: "Emmanuel, God with us. . . . He is with us in the fullness of grace, and we will be with him in the fullness of glory."[81]

In the final verse of the psalm the Father declares: "I will show him my salvation;"[82] and Bernard, applying this verse to Jesus, whose name means "Yahweh is salvation,"[83] explains:

70. *Ibid.*, *Sermon 11*, p. 448.
71. Ibid., *Sermons 5-6*, pp. 401-11.
72. Ibid., *Sermon 9*, p. 440.
73. Ibid., *Sermon 2*, p. 391.
74. Ibid., *Sermon 4*, p. 401.
75. Ibid., *Sermon 9*, p. 441.
76. Ibid., *Sermon 15*, p. 480.
77. Ibid., *Sermon 16*, p. 483.
78. Ibid.
79. Ibid., *Sermon 17*, p. 488.
80. Ibid., *Sermon 16*, p. 482.
81. Ibid., *Sermon 17*, p. 489.
82. Ps 91:16.
83. John L. McKenzie, "Jesus Christ," *Dictionary of the Bible* (Milwaukee: Bruce, 1965), p. 432.

"I will show him my salvation: I will show him my Jesus, that he may behold for all eternity him in whom he has believed, whom he has loved, whom he has always desired."[84]

Yes, as the Barundi believe, whoever is in God's hands is safe from every danger; and as St Bernard explains, God will eventually bring him up, through all the tribulations of the present life, to full union with himself in the glory of heaven.

### 4. Nduwimâna

The name *Nduwimâna* is a combination of *nduwayo*, a word which "expresses the desire for an intimate union of life, of family, and of common interests shared within a single community,"[85] and Imâna. It means: "I belong to God, I am 'His thing,' one of His children."[86] A more detailed explanation shows that for a Barundi this name means that:

> I am not only 'had' by God, as is the case with all things, but God has raised me to a higher level in His house, where I am no longer a stranger but bound by deep ties of intimacy. I might even say that I am of His stock and family, His very own. This is my secret ambition and it is what His conduct towards me reveals.[87]

But here again we run into the problem of interpretation, for Bucumi himself admits that "one might object that it is going too far to find a prayer of such depth in the faithful soul of a non-Christian,"[88] and other authors voice this very objection. Léon Classe, writing of the Banyarwanda of Rwanda, notes that "they ask favors of Him (i.e. God), but nothing more. . . . Worship is confined to the sole prayer of petition;"[89] and Dominic Nothomb, also writing of the Rwanda, claims that "The relations between man and God are not . . . marked with an

84. *Sermon 17, Opera* IV, 491f.
85. Bucumi, *op. cit.*, p. 417.
86. Ibid.
87. Ibid.
88. Ibid.
89. Léon Classe PB, *op. cit.*, in note 52, p. 57.

intimate and filial character,"[90] because God "does not transmit his own life."[91] But Bucumi claims that God does transmit his own life: "Not only does He enjoy the fullness of life, but He imparts this same life without fear of exhausting Himself;"[92] and Vincent Mulago, writing about several Bantu peoples, including the Rwanda and the Barundi, also holds that God does will "to transmit his life to other beings."[93]

So it is difficult to judge how pervasive in Barundi religious life is the spiritual attitude which Bucumi portrays in this description of the Barundi relation to God:

> God reveals Himself as a Father who loves us, and we in turn are touched. Little by little the soul opens to Him and is enamored of His beauty and bounty, until it comes to love Him for Himself.[94]

But with St Bernard we see the theme of divine sonship treated unequivocally in the light of Christian revelation. In his treatise *On the Love of God* Bernard speaks of the law by which God lives—the law of love.[95] He goes on to show that, although servants and hirelings are led by the law of self-love,[96] those who have received the adoption of sons live by the same law as God, and are led by the spirit of liberty.[97]

While granting that "those who do not know Christ are sufficiently admonished by the natural law, through the gifts of body and soul they receive, that they too should love God for his own sake,"[98] he emphasizes that Christians have a greater incentive to love God because of our knowledge of "Christ dying for our sins, rising for our justification, ascending for our

90. Dominic Nothomb PB, *op. cit.*, in note 23, p. 274.

91. Ibid. Here we must recall the great similarity of the Rwanda and Barundi traditions, and that Bucumi himself does not completely distinguish the two.

92. Bucumi, *op. cit.*, p. 407.

93. Mulago, *op. cit.*, in note 21, p. 140.

94. Bucumi, *op. cit.*, p. 414.

95. *De Diligendo Deo,* Chapter 12, *Opera*, III, p. 149.

96. Ibid., pp. 150f.

97. Ibid., p. 151.

98. Ibid., Chapter 2, p. 123.

protection, sending the Spirit for our consolation and coming again for our glorification.''[99]

And he encourages the Christian to go even beyond loving God for God's own sake to the point of loving himself only for the sake of God—something he thinks can be attained only in the glory of heaven.[100] Only then can one attain the perfection of that filial love in which, "inebriated with divine love, and forgetful of self . . . he proceeds completely into God and, clinging to God, becomes one spirit with him."[101]

### 5. Other Names

There are several other names which the Barundi use in referring to Imâna. Bernard Zuure gives a list of about thirty such names, and several proverbs, stories and names given to children involving the use of variations of the name Imâna.[102] And Jean Bucumi gives lengthy explanations of these names: "*Incanyi*—(Imâna) who makes fire for men; . . . *Rutungane*—He whose proportions are perfectly balanced; . . . *Iyakare*—the One who is at the origin of time; . . . *Habiyambere*—the Principle . . . the one who alone fully *is* without limits in all the exuberance of life; and . . . *Rurema*—Creator."[103]

St Bernard speaks of some of the themes evoked by these Barundi names for God.[104] But at this point it might be good to go beyond comparisons to a name which the Barundi could not use, but which is central in St Bernard's approach to the name of God—the name Jesus.

With Isaiah, Bernard calls Jesus "Wonder-Counselor, God-Hero, Father-Forever, Prince of Peace;"[105] and for Bernard, the name Jesus is "light. . . . food. . . . medicine. . . . the name

---

99. Ibid., Chapter 3, p. 126.
100. Ibid., Chapter 15, p. 153.
101. Ibid., Chapter 10, p. 142.
102. Zuure, *op. cit.*, pp. 740-58.
103. Bucumi, *op. cit.*, pp. 397-411.
104. For example, see *Sermones Super Cantica Canticorum*, 31, *Opera* I, 219-26, for thoughts on God's eternity (p. 219), and the fire which precedes his coming to the soul (pp. 221f.).
105. Ibid., *Sermon 15*, pp. 82f. See Is 9:6.

of life,"[106] in which we find "life. . . . assurance. . . . certainty. . . . strength."[107] The name of Jesus, like oil poured forth, is poured out on all men, offering the salvation of God to all who call upon it.[108]

And perhaps the name of Jesus would be the most fitting theme with which to draw this study of St Bernard and the Barundi on the name of God to a conclusion.

## Conclusion

At a time when a new African theology and Christian monasticism in Africa are both developing rapidly, I have tried to bring African tradition and Christian monastic tradition into dialogue by comparing one representative of each tradition. In spite of difficulties in interpreting the Barundi religious tradition, we have seen similarities between St Bernard and the Barundi on themes connected with the name of God.

Of course, the results of this study are applicable primarily to St Bernard on the one hand, and the Barundi (and the Rwanda and other Bantu peoples) on the other. But a knowledge of St Bernard may serve African Christians as a gateway to the whole monastic tradition, and a knowledge of the Barundi may open up the whole area of African tradition for Christian monks.

When it comes to the specific theme of this article, I would like to conclude thus:

The lofty concept of one transcendent God in the Barundi tradition, expressed in a rich variety of names for the one God, Imâna, has proved fertile soil for the seed of the gospel, and Burundi has become a Christian nation. But there is one name the Barundi had not been able to formulate, "the name above every other name,"[109] the name of which it is said that "there is no other name in the whole world given to men by

---

106. Ibid., p. 86.
107. Ibid., pp. 86f.
108. Ibid., p. 83.
109. Phil 2:9.

which we are to be saved,"[110] the name which means Yahweh is salvation—the name Jesus. This name has now been poured out on the Barundi, and perhaps Christian theology in Burundi will make rapid headway when a people who have continually had the name of God, Imâna, on their lips,[111] listen attentively to a monk who could speak thus of the God who became man to save us: " 'Jesus' is honey in the mouth, a melody in the ear, a song of gladness in the heart. . . . Let 'Jesus' come into your heart, and then leap onto your lips."[112] For:

> When I utter the name "Jesus" I place before myself both a man, meek and humble of heart, kind, sober, chaste, loving and singularly virtuous and holy; and almighty God himself, who heals me by his example and strengthens me by his aid. All these things resound in me when "Jesus" is pronounced.[113]

Patrick Ryan ocso

Abbey of the Genesee
Piffard, New York

110. Acts 4:12.
111. Zuure, *op. cit.*, p. 742.
112. *Sermones Super Cantica Canticorum*, 15, *Opera*, I, 86.
113. Ibid., p. 87.

# A BIBLIOGRAPHY OF JOHN LECLERQ

THE PREPARATION OF A BIBLIOGRAPHY of the works of John Leclercq has been undertaken several times before. It is a difficult task because his writings are both many and very dispersed. Father Leclercq has not made the task any easier by his inability to say "no" to the many editors of reviews who, aware of his competence, make demands upon him.

In his "Bibliographie de Dom Jean Leclercq"[1] Reginald Grégoire OSB corrected and completed, up to 1968, the work of three predecessors; the "Bibliografia di Jean Leclercq" published by L. di Fonso in *Miscellanea Francescana*[2] and later presented separately, and the two American editions of *The Love of Learning and the Desire of God*[3] which amended the work of di Fonso and continued it up to 1960. In the present bibliography which has been compiled at Clervaux, the work of Father Grégoire is brought up to the end of 1971. It has also been corrected, thanks especially to the addition and precision offered by Father N. Huyghebaert OSB, a professor of Louvain. The limits here are the same as those adopted by Father Grégoire: ". . . all the reviews published since 1940 in the *Revue d'histoire ecclésiastique*, the *Revue d'histoire de l'Eglise de France*, the *Revue belge de philogie et d'histoire*, the *Revue du moyen âge latin*, the *Revue bénédictine*, *Scriptorium*, *Studia monastica*, *La Maison-Dieu*, *La vie spirituelle*, etc., are not included . . . only those which were of some length, the ones for which Father Leclercq received a reprint. Also not included are the brief articles which have appeared in the bulletins of the Benedictine oblates in the different countries, and other like periodicals; nor have we included brief entries published in encyclopedias such as *Catholicisme, Lexicon für Theologie*

1. *Studia Monastica* 10 (1968): 331-359.
2. Vol 58 (1958).
3. Bbg 13.

215

*und Kirche*[4], *Enciclopedia Dantesca,* etc. . . ."[5] Works which have appeared in languages other than that of the title of the study or of the publication in which it appears are indicated by the abbreviations: E = English, F = French, I = Italian, S = Spanish. Articles which have been reprinted in a later volume are indicated by the letter R (= Reprinted).

4. Second ed. (Freiburg, 1967). See the Register, p. 549.
5. R. Grégoire, *Studia Monastica* 10 (1968): 333-334.

# BIBLIOGRAPHY

## I. Books

1. *Jean de Paris et l'Ecclésiologie du XIII<sup>e</sup> siècle* (Paris, Vrin, 1942), pp. 268.

2. *La spiritualité de Pierre de Celle (1115-1183)* (Paris, Vrin, 1946), pp. 246.

3. *Pierre le Vénérable* (Saint-Wandrille, Ed. de Fontenelle, 1946), pp. XIX, 407.

4. In collab. with J. P. Bonnes: *Un maître de la vie spirituelle au XI<sup>e</sup> siècle: Jean de Fécamp* (Paris, Vrin, 1946), pp. 236.

5. *Analecta Monastica.* Première série. *Studia Anselmiana,* 20 (Rome, Pont. Institutum S. Anselmi, 1948), pp. VIII, 240.

6. *Saint Bernard mystique* (Bruges et Paris, Desclée de Brouwer, 1948), pp. 494.

7. *La vie parfaite. Points de vue sur l'essence de l'état religieux* (Turnhout et Paris, Brepols, 1948), pp. 170. *The Life of Perfection* (Collegeville, Minn., 1961); *La vita perfetta* (Milan, Ancora, 1961); *La vida perfecta,* (Barcelona, Herder, 1965).

8. *Lettres d'Yves de Chartres.* Edition critique et traduction précédées d'une introduction (Paris, Les Belles-Lettres, 1949), pp. XLII, 313.

9. *Un humaniste ermite. Le B<sup>x</sup> Paul Giustiniani (1476-1528)* (Rome, Ed. Camaldoli, 1951), pp. 182.

10. *Analecta Monastica.* Deuxième série. *Studia Anselmiana,* 31 (Rome, Pont. Institutum S. Anselmi, 1953), pp. VIII-206.

11. *Etudes sur S. Bernard et le texte de ses écrits (Analecta S. Ordinis Cisterciensis* IX, Rome, 1953), pp. 247.

12. *Seul avec Dieu. La vie érémitique d'après la doctrine du Bˣ Paul Giustiniani.* Préface by Thomas Merton (Paris, Plon, 1955), pp. 175. *La dottrina del B. Paolo Giustiniani* (Frascati, 1953); *Alone with God* (New York, Farrar, Strauss and Cudahy, 1961; Londres, The Catholic Book Church, s.d.).

13 *L'amour des lettres et le désir de Dieu. Initiation aux auteurs monastiques du moyen âge (*Paris, Ed. du Cerf, 1957), pp. 269; 2ᵉ éd. (Paris, 1963). *The Love of Learning and the Desire for God* (New York, Fordham Univ. Press., 1961, and Mentor Omega Book, New York, 1962); *Wissenschaft und Gottverlangen* (Düsseldorf, Patmos-Verlag, 1963); *Cultura umanistica e desiderio di Dio* (Florence, Ed. Sansoni, 1965); *Cultura y vida cristiana* (Salamanca, Ed. Sigueme, 1965).

14. In collab. with C. H. Talbot et H. Rochais: *S. Bernardi Opera.* Vol. I (Rome, Editiones Cistercienses, 1957), pp. LXVIII, 264; vol. II (ibid., 1958), pp. XXXV, 328. In collab. with H. Rochais, vol. III (ibid., 1963), pp. XXXIV, 532; vol. IV (ibid., 1966), pp. XVI, 496; vol. V (ibid., 1968), pp. XVIII, 452; vol. VI, 1 (ibid., 1970), pp. 416.

15. *L'idée de la royauté de Christ au moyen âge.* Coll. Unam Sanctam (Paris, Ed. du Cerf, 1959), pp. 235.

16. *S. Pierre Damien ermite et homme d'Eglise* (Rome, Ed. Storia e Letteratura, 1960), pp. 284. S. Pietro Damiano eremita e uomo di Chiesa (Brescia, Morcélliana, 1972)

17 In collaboration with F. Vandenbroucke et L. Bouyer: *La spiritualité du moyen âge* (Paris, Aubier, 1961). *The Spirituality of the Middle Ages,* (London, Burns & Oates, 1968); *Spiritualità del medivevo* (Bologna, Ed. Dehoniane, 1969).

18. *Etudes sur le vocabulaire monastique du moyen âge, Studia Anselmiana,* 48 (Rome, 1961), pp. VIII-186.

19 *Recueil d'études sur S. Bernard et ses écrits,* I (Rome, Ed. Storia e Letteratura, 1962), pp. VIII, 370; II (ibid., 1966), pp. IV, 405; III (ibid., 1969), pp. 436.

20 *La liturgie et les paradoxes chrétiens* (Paris, Ed. du Cerf, 1963), pp. 306. *La liturgia y las paradojas cristianas* (Bilbao, Ed. Mensa-

jero, 1967); *La liturgia e i paradossi cristiani* (Rome, Ed. Paoline, 1967).

21. *Otia monastica. Etudes sur le vocabulaire de la contemplation au moyen âge, Studia Anselmiana,* 51 (Rome, 1963), pp. 186.

22. *Aux sources de la spiritualité occidentale* (Paris, Ed. du Cerf, 1964) pp. 318. *Espiritualidad occidental. Fuentes* (Salamanca, Ed. Sigueme, 1967).

23. *Témoins de la spiritualité occidentale* (Paris, Ed. du Cerf, 1965), pp. 410. *Espiritualidad occidental. Testigos* (Salamanca, Ed. Sigueme, 1967).

24. *Chances de la spiritualité occidentale* (Paris, Ed. du Cerf, 1966), pp. 382.

25. *S. Bernard et l'esprit cistercien* (Paris, Ed. du Seuil, 1966), pp. 190.

26. *Aspects du monachisme hier et aujourd'hui* (Paris, Ed. de la Source, 1968).

27. *Vie religieuse et vie contemplative* (Gembloux-Paris, Ed. Duculot, 1969); *Vida religiosa y vida contemplativa,* (Bilbao, Ed. Mensajéro, 1970); *Vita religiosa e vita contemplativa* (Assisi, Cittadella editrice, 1972).

28. *Le défi de la vie contemplative* (Gembloux-Paris, Ed. Duculot, 1970); *El desafio de la vida contemplativa* (Bilbao, Ed. Mensajèro, 1971).

29. *Moines et moniales ont-ils un avenir?* (Bruxelles-Paris, Ed. Lumen vitae, 1971).

II. Articles

30. "Jean de Paris. Le Christ médicin," in *La vie spirituelle,* 59 (1938-1939), p. 293-300.

1939

31. "La théologie comme science d'après la littérature quodlibétique,"

in *Recherches de théologie ancienne et médiévale* 11 (1939) 351-374.

32. "La renonciation de Célestin V ėt l'opinion théologique en France du vivant de Boniface VIII," in *Revue d'histoire de l'Eglise de France* 25 (1939) 1-12; in *Philip the Fair and Boniface VIII,* edited by Charles T. Wood (New York, 1967) 42-46; in *Felipe el Hermoso y Bonifacio VIII* (Uteha, Mexico, 1967).

33. "Des stations romaines au missel jociste," in *La vie sprituelle* 59 (1939) 307-309.

### 1940

34. "La realeza de Jesucristo en las obras de Santo Tomás," in *Ciencìa Tomista* 59 (1940) 144-156. R in *L'idée de la royauté* . . . (n. 15).

### 1941

35. "Les bénédictins en France au temps de Philippe le Bel et de Boniface VIII," in *Revue Mabillon* 31 (1941) 85-100; 32 (1942) 1-14.

### 1942

36. "Un témoignage du XIIIᵉ siècle sur la nature de la théologie," in *Archives d'histoire doctrinale et littéraire du moyen âge* 13 (1940-1942) 301-321.

37. "La royauté du Christ dans les lettres des papes du XIIIᵉ siècle," in *Revue historique du droit français et étranger* (1942) 112-120. R in *L'idée de la royauté* . . . (n. 15).

38. "Une Lamentation inédite de Jean de Fécamp," in *Revue bénédictine* 54 (1942) 41-60.

39. "Un ancien recueil de leçons pour les vigiles des défunts," in *Revue bénédictine* 54 (1942) 16-40.

40. "Cluny et le Concile de Bâle," in *Revue d'histoire de l'Eglise de France* 28 (1942) 1-15.

41. "Cluny pendant le Grand Schisme d'Occident," in *Revue Mabillon* 32 (1942) 1-14.

### 1943

42. "Prédicateurs bénédictins aux XI^e et XII^e siècles," in *Revue Mabillon* 33 (1943) 48-73.

43. "La consécration légendaire de la basilique de Saint-Denis et la question des indulgences," in *Revue Mabillon* 33 (1943) 74-84.

### 1944

44. "L'idée de la royauté du Christ au XIII^e siècle," in *L'Année théologique* 5 (1944) 217-242; R in *L'idée de la royauté* . . . (n. 15).

45. "Les méditations d'un moine du XII^e siècle," in *Revue Mabillon* 34 (1944) 1-19.

46. "L'interdit et l'excommunication d'après les lettres de Fulbert de Chartres," in *Revue historique de droit français et etranger* (1944) 67-77.

47. "Dévotion privée, piété populaire et liturgie au moyen âge," in *Etudes de pastorale liturgique* (Rome, 1944) 149-183.

48. "Lecture et oraison," in *La vie spirituelle* 70 (1944) 392-402.

### 1945

49. "L'exégèse médiévale," in *Bulletin Thomiste* 7 (1942-1945) 59-67.

50. "Le sermon sur la royauté du Christ au moyen âge," in *Archives d'histoire doctrinale et littéraire du moyen âge* 14 (1943-1945) 143-180, R in *L'idée de la royauté* . . . (n. 15).

51. "Fleury au moyen âge, Introduction à Saint-Benoît-sur-Loire" (Paris, Ed. du Cerf, Coll. "Eglises et monastères de France," 1945) 10-12.

52. "Le De Grammatica de Hugues de Saint-Victor," in *Archives*

*d'histoire doctrinale et littéraire du moyen âge* 14 (1943-1945)
263-322.

53. "L'Ascension, triomphe du Christ," in *La vie spirituelle* 72 (1945)
289-300, R in *La liturgie* ... (n. 20).

54. "Un traité De fallaciis in theologia," in *Revue du moyen âge latin*
1 (1945) 43-46.

55. "Un sermon prononcé pendant la guerre de Flandre sous Philippe
le Bel," in *Revue du moyen âge latin* 1 (1945) 165-172.

56. "Un nouveau fragment du Traité, De unitate divinae essentiae et
pluralitate creaturarum?," in *Revue du moyen âge latin* 1 (1945)
173-177.

57. "L'amitié dans les lettres au moyen âge," in *Revue du moyen âge
latin* 1 (1945) 391-410.

58. "Un art liturgique populaire," in *Cahiers de l'art sacré* 2 (1945)
17-23.

59. "Les paradoxes de l'économie monastique," in *Economie et humanisme* 4 (1945) 15-35.

60. "Une série de bénédictions pour les lectures de l'Office," in
*Ephemerides liturgicae* 60 (1945) 318-321.

61. "Comment fut construit Saint-Denis," (Paris, Ed. du Cerf, Coll.
"La Clarté-Dieu" 1945) 1-56.

62. "Les Anges au Baptême," in *Bible et Missel* (1945) 1-16. R in *La
Liturgie* ... (n. 20).

63. Review of P. Salmon, Le lectionnaire de Luxeuil, in La Maison-
Dieu 3 (1945) 119-124.

### 1946

64. "Deux sermons inédits de S. Fulgence," in *Revue bénédictine* 56
(1945-1946) 93-107.

65. "La Collection des Lettres d'Yves de Chartres," in *Revue bénédictine* 56 (1945-1946) 108-125.

66. "Les décrets de Bernard de Saintes," in *Revue du moyen âge latin*
2 (1946) 167-170.

67. "Technique et rédemption. La mystique du vol," in *Revue nouvelle* 3 (1946) 161-170.

68. "Victor Leroquais," in *Revue du moyen âge* 2 (1946) 126-128.

69. "La Chaise-Dieu au moyen âge, Introduction à La Chaise-Dieu" (Paris, Ed. du Cerf, Coll. "Eglises et monastères de France", 1946) 3-7.

70. "Plaidoyer pour le temps présent," in *Revue nouvelle* 4 (1946) 3-7.

71. "Pour l'iconographie des Apôtres," in *Revue bénédictine* 56 (1945-1946) 216-217.

72. "Les méditations eucharistiques d'Arnauld de Bonneval," in *Recherches de théologie ancienne et médiévale* 13 (1946) 40-56.

73. "Médiévisme et unionisme," in *Irénikon* 19 (1946) 6-23.

74. "L'idée de la royauté du Christ dans l'oeuvre de Saint Justin," in *L'Année théologique* 7 (1946) 83-95. R in *L'idée de la royauté* ... (n. 15).

75. "Katolsk Blomstring i Frankrig," in *Catholica* 3 (1946) 121-130.

76. "Le genre épistolaire au moyen âge," in *Revue du moyen âge latin* 2 (1946) 63-70.

77. "Recherches sur d'anciens sermons monastiques," in *Revue Mabillon* 36 (1946) 1-14.

78. "Aux origines du cycle de Noël," in *Ephemerides liturgicae* 60 (1946) 7-26.

79. "Le sermon, acte liturgique," in *La Maison-Dieu* 8 (1946) 27-46. R in *La liturgie* ... (n. 20).

80. "Deux anciennes versions de la Légende de l'Abbé Macaire," in *Revue Mabillon* 36 (1946) 65-79.

81. "Le magistère du prédicateur au XIIIe siècle," in *Archives d'histoire doctrinale et littéraire du moyen âge* 15 (1946) 105-147.

82. "Bénédictions pour les lectures de l'Office de Noël," in *Miscellanea Giovanni Mercati*, II (Rome 1946) 1-7.

83. "Pierre le Vénérable et l'invitation au salut," in *Bulletin des missions* 20 (1946) (145)-(156). R in *Témoins* . . . (n. 23).

84. "L'Epiphanie, fête du sacre," in *La vie spirituelle* 75 (1946) 6-17. R. in *La liturgie* . . . (n.20).

85. "Aspects de la dévotion mariale au moyen âge," in *Cahiers de la vie spirituelle*, "La Sainte Vierge, Figure de l'Eglise" (Paris, 1946) 241-261. R in *La liturgie* . . . (n. 20).

86. "Catholica Unitas," in *Cahiers de la vie spirituelle*, "La Communion des Saints" (Paris, 1946) 37-53. E in *Worship* 8 (1961) 470-485.

87. "La lecture divine," in *La Maison-Dieu* 5 (1946) 21-33. R in *La liturgie* . . . (n. 20).

88. "Points de vue sur l'histoire de l'état religieux," in *La vie spirituelle* 74 (1946) 816-833; 75 (1946) 127-137.

89. Review of I. Herwegen, *Sinn und Geist der Benediktinerregel*, in *La Maison-Dieu* 6 (1946) 135-139.

90. "Un sermon inédit de S. Thomas sur la royauté du Christ," in *Revue thomiste* 46 (1946) 152-166; cf. ibid., 572. R in *L'idée de la royauté du Christ* (n. 15).

91. "Dom Germain Morin," in *La Maison-Dieu* 6 (1946) 160-162.


### 1947

92. "Le latin chrétien, langue d'Eglise," in *La Maison-Dieu* 11 (1947) 55-75.

93. "Le florilège d'Abbon de Saint-Germain," in *Revue du moyen âge latin* 3 (1947) 113-140.

94. "Inédits bernardins dans un manuscrit d'Engelberg," in *Revue Mabillon* 37 (1947) 1-16. R in *Recueil* . . . II (n. 19).

95. "Les études universitarires dans l'Ordre de Cluny," in *Mélanges bénédictins* (1947) 351-371.

96. "Passage authentique inédit de Guitmond d'Aversa," in *Revue bénédictine* 57 (1947) 213-214.

97. "Prédication et rhétorique au temps de Saint Augustin," in *Revue bénédictine* 57 (1947) 117-131.

98. "Une prière des moines de Saint-Airy," in *Revue bénédictine* 57 (1947) 224-226.

99. "Autour d'un manuscrit de la Règle du Maître," in *Revue bénédictine* 57 (1947) 210-212.

100. "Simoniaca heresis," in *Studi Gregoriani* I (Rome 1947) 523-530.

101. "Symbolique chrétienne de la lune," in *Lunaires, Cahiers de Puésie,* 4 (1947) 133-148.

102. "Fragmenta Reginensia," in *Ephemerides liturgicae* 61 (1947) 289-296.

103 "Une lettre inédite de Saint Pierre Damien sur la vie érémitique," in *Studia Anselmiana* 18-19 (Rome, 1947) 283-293.

104. "Le III$^e$ livre des homélies de Bède le Vénérable," in *Recherches de théologie ancienne et médiévale* 14 (1947) 211-218. R in *Corpus Christianorum,* Series latina, 122 (1955) 381-384.

105. "Un miracle de Notre-Dame à Avesnes au XI$^e$ siècle," in *Société archéologique et historique d'Avesnes, "Mémoires,"* 18 (1947) 79-85.

106. "L'idéal du théologien au moyen âge. Textes inédits," in *Revue des sciences religieuses* 21 (1947) 121-148.

107 "Les prières inédites de Nicolas de Clamanges," in *Revue d'ascétique et de mystique* 23 (1947) 170-183.

108. "La vie évangélique selon la Règle de saint Benoît," in *La vie spirituelle* 76 (1947) 848-855.

109 "La royauté du Christ dans la spiritualité française du XVII$^e$ siècle," in *La vie spirituelle, Supplément* 1 (1947) 216-229, 291-307.

110. "Un opuscule inédit de Jean de Limoges sur l'exemption," in *Analecta Sacri Ordinis Cisterciensis* 3 (1947) 147-154.

111. "Un recueil espagnol d'opuscules ecclésiologiques au XIV$^e$ siècle," in *Analecta Sacra Tarraconensia* 20 (1947) 2-6.

112. "Introduction aux sermons de S. Léon le Grand," in *Sources chrétiennes* (Paris, 1947) 7-62; 2ᵉ éd. (1965) 7-55.

113. "Jours d'ivresse *(Sobria ebrietas),*" in *La vie spirituelle, "Le huitième jour,"* 76 (1947) 574-691. R in *La liturgie* ... (n. 20).

114. Review of J. Travers, OP, *Valeur sociale de la liturgie d'après S. Thomas d'Aquin,* (Paris, 1946), in *La Maison-Dieu* 12 (1947) 145-152.

1948

115. "La Sainte Eglise et la rémission des péchés," in *Cahiers de la vie spirituelle, "L'Eglise et le pécheur"* (Paris, 1948) 12-28. R in *La liturgie* ... (n. 20).

116. "L'Eglise pénitente," in *Cahiers de la vie spirituelle, "L'Eglise et le pécheur"* (Paris, 1948) 226-235.

117. "La voie royale," in *La vie spirituelle, Supplément* 2 (1948) 338-352.

118. "Le doigt de Dieu," in *La vie spirituelle* 78 (1948) 492-507; *Worship* 7 (1962) 426-437. R in *La liturgie* ... (n. 20).

119. "Une homélie-prière sur le Saint-Esprit," in *Revue d'ascétique et de mystique* 24 (1948) 80-86.

120. "Smaragde et la grammaire chrétienne," in *Revue du moyen âge latin* 4 (1948) 15-22.

121. "Pour l'histoire de deux processions," in *Ephemerides liturgicae* 62 (1948) 53-72.

122. "Les inédits africains de l'homéliaire de Fleury," in *Revue bénédictine* 58 (1948) 53-72. Partly R in *Patrologiae latinae, Supplementum* 3, 1412-1424.

123. "Nouveau témoin du Conflit des Filles de Dieu," in *Revue bénédictine* 58 (1948) 110-124.

124. "La vie économique des monastères au moyen âge," in *Inspiration religieuse et structures temporelles* (Paris 1948) 211-259.

125. "L'idée de la royauté du Christ au XIVᵉ siècle," in *Miscellanea Pio Paschini, Lateranum,* 14 (Rome, 1948) 405-425. *Revista española de teologia* IV (1950) 249-265. R in *L'idée de la royauté* ... (n. 15).

126. "Les deux compilations de Thomas de Perseigne," in *Mediaeval Studies* 10 (1948) 204-209.

127. "Tables pour l'inventaire des homéliaires manuscrits," in *Scriptorium* 2 (1948) 195-214. Partly R by C. L Smetana, in *Traditio* 15 (1959) 165-180.

128. "La discrétion bénédictine," in *Prudence chrétienne* (Paris, 1948) 100-107.

129. "Les manuscrits des bibliothèques d'Espagne," in *Scriptorium* 3 (1948) 140-144.

130. "Les études médiolatines en Espagne," in *Revue du moyen âge latin* 4 (1948) 440-447.

131. "Un florilège attribué à un moine de Poblet," in *Analecta Sacra Tarraconensia* 21 (1948), 153-156.


1949

132. "Le centenaire de la liberté religieuse au Danemark," in *La vie intellectuelle* (1949) 112-125.

133. "Documents pour l'histoire des chanoines réguliers," in *Revue d'histoire ecclésiastique* 44 (1949) 556-569.

134. "Une nouvelle édition des oeuvres de S. Bernard," in *Revue d'histoire écclésiastique* 44 (1949) 194-197.

135. "Le commentaire du Cantique des cantiques attribué à Anselme de Laon," in *Recherches de théologie ancienne et médiévale* 16 (1949) 29-39.

136. "Textes et manuscrits de quelques bibliothèques d'Espagne," in *Hispania sacra* 2 (1949) 91-118.

137. "Smaragde et son oeuvre. Introduction à la traduction de I a Voie Royale," *La Pierre-qui-vire* (1949) 3-23. R in *Témoins* ... (n.23).

138. "L'idée de la royauté du Christ pendant le grand Schisme et la crise conciliaire," in *Archives d'histoire doctrinale et littéraire du moyen âge* 24 (1949) 249-265. R in *L'idée de la royauté* . . . (n. 15).

139. "Un tratado sobre los nombres divinos en un manuscrito de Cordoba," in *Hispania Sacra* 2 (1949) 327-338.

140. "Sermons de l'école de S. Augustin," in *Revue bénédictine* 59 (1949) 100-113.

141. "Bref discours pastoral attribuable à Paulin d'Aquilée," in *Revue bénédictine* 59 (1949) 157-160.

142. "Saint Bernard et Origène d'après un manuscrit de Madrid," in *Revue bénédictine* 59 (1949) 183-195. R in *Recueil*... *II* (n. 19).

143. "Sermon ancien sur les danses déshonnêtes," in *Revue bénédictine* 59 (1949) 196-201.

144. "Saint Jerôme docteur de l'ascèse d'après un centon monastique," in *Revue d'ascétique et de mystique, "Mélanges Marcel Viller,"* 25 (1949) 140-145.

145. "Recherches dans les manuscrits cisterciens d'Espagne, I. Textes relatifs aux institutions et à la liturgie," in *Analecta Sacri Ordinis Cisterciensis* 5 (1949) 109-112.

146. "Recherches dans les manuscrits cisterciens d'Espagne, II. Textes hagiographiques; III. Textes doctrinaux," ibid., p. 114-119.

147. "Manuscrits cisterciens dans des bibliothèques d'Italie," in *Analecta Sacri Ordinis Cisterciensis* 5 (1949) 94-108.

148. "Les manuscrits des bibliothèques d'Espagne. Notes de voyage," in *Scriptorium* 3 (1949) 140-144.


1950


149. "L'idéal monastique de Saint Odon d'après ses oeuvres," in *A Cluny. Congrès scientifique, 9-11 juillet 1949* (Dijon, 1950) 227-232. R in *Témoins*... (n. 23).

150 "Vienne (Concile de), XVe concile oecuménique (1311-1312)," in *Dictionnaire de Théologie Catholique*, XV/2 (Paris, 1950) coll. 2973-2979.

151. "L'édition de Saint Bernard," in *Revue d'histoire ecclésiastique* 45 (1950) 715-727.

152. "Vivre à Dieu seul," in *Rythmes du monde* 2 (1950) 28-31.

153. "Les manuscrits cisterciens du Portugal," in *Analecta Sacri Ordinis Cisterciensis* 5 (1950) 131-139.

154. "Textes et manuscrits cisterciens en Suède," in *Analecta Sacri Ordinis Cisterciensis* 6 (1950) 125-130.

155. "L'office divin et la lecture divine," in *La Maison-Dieu* 21 (1950) 60-70.

### 1951

156. "Origène au XII^e siècle," in *Irénikon* 24 (1951) 425-439.

157. "L'exégèse médiévale de l'Ancien Testament," in *L'Ancien Testament et les chrétiens* (Paris, 1951) 168-182.

158. "Le traité de Guillaume de Saint-Jacques sur la Trinité," in *Archives d'histoire doctrinale et littéraire du moyen âge* 25-26 (1951) 89-102.

159. "Lettres du temps de Saint Bernard," in *Studien und Mitteilungen zur Geschichte des Benediktiner-Ordens* 63 (1951) 1-7. R in *Recueil* ... II (n. 19).

160. "Une épître d'Innocent II à l'évêque Henri de Bologne," in *Rivista di storia della Chiesa in Italia* 5 (1951) 263-265.

161. "Saint Bernard et ses secrétaires," in *Revue bénédictine* 61 (1951) 208-229. R in *Recueil* ... I (n. 19).

162. "Manuscrits cisterciens dans les bibliothèques d'Italie," in *Analecta Sacri Ordinis Cisterciensis* 7 (1951) 71-77.

163. "L'ancienne version latine des sentences d'Evagre pour les moines," in *Scriptorium* 5 (1951) 195-213.

164. "Textes cisterciens dans des bibliothèques d'Allemagne," in *Analecta Sacri Ordinis Cisterciensis* 7 (1951) 46-70.

### 1952

165. "Une élévation sur les Gloires de Jérusalem," in *Mélanges Lebreton* (Paris, 1951-52) 326-334.

166. "Le mystère de l'autel," in *La Maison-Dieu* 39 (1952) 60-70. R. in *La liturgie* . . . (n. 20).

167. "Anciennes sentences monastiques," in *Collectanea Ordinis Cisterciensium Reformatorum* 14 (1952) 117-124.

168. "Passage supprimé dans une épître d'Alexandre III," in *Revue bénédictine* 62 (1952) 149-151.

169. "Contemplation et vie contemplative du VI^e au XII^e siècle," in *Dictionnaire de spiritualité* II (Paris, 1952) coll. 1929-1948.

170. "Une ancienne rédaction des coutumes cisterciennes," in *Revue d'histoire ecclésiastique* 47 (1952) 172-176.

171. "Les manuscrits de l'abbaye de Liessies," in *Scriptorium* 6 (1952) 51-62, with 7 plates; R in *Mémoires de la Société historique et archéologique de l'arrondissement d'Avesnes* 19 (1948-1953).

172. "Les écrits de Geoffroy d'Auxerre," in *Revue bénédictine* 62 (1952) 274-291. R in *Recueil* . . . I (n. 19).

173. "Textes sur S. Bernard et Gilbert de la Porrée," in *Mediaeval Studies* 14 (1952) 107-128. R in *Recueil*. . . II (n. 19).

174. "Bénédictions épiscopales dans un manuscrit de Huesca," in *Hispania Sacra* 5 (1952) 79-101 (in collab. with J. Laporte).

175. "L'éloge funèbre de Gilbert de la Porrée," in *Archives d'histoire doctrinale et littéraire du moyen âge* 19 (1952) 183-185.

176. "Le commentaire de Teuzon sur la Règle bénédictine," in *Studien und Mitteilungen zur Geschichte des Benediktiner-Ordens* 64 (1952) 5-12.

177. "Pour l'histoire de l'expression philosophie chrétienne," in *Mélanges de science religieuse* 9 (1952) 221-226.

178. "Dévotion et théologie mariales dans le monachisme bénédictin," in H. du Manoir, *Etudes sur la Sainte Vierge*, t. II (Paris, 1952) 547-578.

179. "Carême et pénitence," in *La Maison-Dieu* 31 (1952) 44-59; R in *La liturgie* . . . 114-132.

## 1953

180. "Le texte complet de la vie de Christian de l'Aumône," in *Analecta Bollandiana* 71 (1953) 21-52.

181. "Le premier traité authentique de Saint Bernard," in *Revue d'histoire écclésiastique* 48 (1953) 196-210. R in *Recueil* . . . II (n. 19).

182. "Le mystère de l'Ascension dans les sermons de Saint Bernard" in *Collectanea Ordinis Cisterciensium Reformatorum* 15 (1953) 81-88.

183. "Drogon et Saint Bernard," in *Revue bénédictine* 63 (1953) 116-131. R in *Recueil* . . . I (n. 19).

184. "Sermon pour l'Assomption restitué à Saint Bernard," in *Recherches de théologie ancienne et médiévale* 20 (1953) 5-12, R in *Recueil* . . . II (n. 19).

185. "Un document sur Saint Bernard et la seconde croisade," in *Revue Mabillon* 43 (1953) 1-4. R in *Recueil* . . . II (n.19).

186. "Les sermons de Bernard sur le psaume *Qui habitat,*" in *Bernard de Clairvaux* (Paris, 1953) 435-446. R in *Recueil* . . . II (n. 19).

187. "Der Heiliger Bernhard und wir," in *Einführung zu Bernhard von Clairvaux. Die Botschaft der Freude* (Einsiedeln, 1953; 2e éd. 1954) 9-37; *Ora et labora* 14 (Milan, 1959) 1-12.

188. "S. Bernardo maestro di carità," in *Camaldoli* (1953) 151-155.

189. "Une vie qui donne le change," in *S. Bernard homme d'Eglise* (Desclée de Brouwer, 1953) 195-201.

190. "S. Bernard et la dévotion joyeuse," ibid., 237-247.

191. "L'image de Saint Bernard dans les manuscrits," in *Saint Bernard et l'art des Cisterciens* (Dijon, 1953) 22-24.

192. "Les sermons synodaux attribués à Saint Bernard," in *Revue bénédictine* 63 (1953) 292-309. R in *Recueil* . . . I (n. 19).

193. "Saint Bernard et la théologie monastique du XII^e siècle," in *Analecta Sacris Ordinis Cisterciensis* 9, (1953) 7-23.

194. "Ecrits monastiques sur la Bible aux XI^e-XIII^e siècles," in *Mediaeval Studies* 15 (1953) 95-106.

195. "Die Verbreitung der bernhardinischen Schriften im deutschen Sprachraum," in *Bernhard von Clairvaux Mönch und Mystiker* (Mainz, 1953) 176-191. R in French in *Recueil*... II (n. 19).

196. "Les manuscrits de l'abbaye d'Hautmont," in *Scriptorium* 7 (1953) 59-67, with 1 plate.

197. "Vivre à Dieu seul," in *Moines. Témoignages. Cahiers de la Pierre-qui-vire* (Bruges-Paris, 1953), 189-194.

198. "Nouveaux témoins sur Origène au XII^e siècle," in *Mediaeval Studies* 15 (1953) 104-106.

199. "Notre Dame abbesse," in *"Priez sans cesse." Trois cents ans de prière* (Paris, 1953) 175-177.

200. "Un nouveau manuscrit d'Echternach à Luxembourg," in *Scriptorium* 7 (1953) 219-225 with 7 plates.

201. "Un témoignage sur l'entretien des manuscrits," in *Scriptorium* 7 (1953) 260.

### 1954

202. "Grandeur et misère de la dévotion mariale au moyen âge," in *La Maison-Dieu* 38 (1954) 122-135.

203. "Poèmes sur la bataille de Courtrai conservés à Tolède," in *Handelingen van het Genootschap "Société d'Emulation" te Brugge* 91 (1954) 155-160.

204. "Saint Bernard docteur," in *Collectanea Ordinis Cisterciensium Reformatorum* 16 (1954) 284-286. R in *Recueil*... II (n. 19).

205. "Saint Bernard et la dévotion médiévale envers Marie," in *Revue d'ascetique et de mystique* 30 (1954) 361-375. R partly in *Témoins* ... (n. 23).

206. "Epîtres d'Alexandre III sur les Cisterciens," in *Revue bénédictine* 64 (1954) 68-42.

207. "Saint Bernard théologien," in *San Bernardo* (Milan, 1954) 30-41. R in *Témoins* ... (n. 23).

208. "Un coutumier de Saint-Martial," in *Revue Mabillon* 44 (1954) 37-42.

209. "Pour l'histoire de l'enluminure cistercienne," in *Scriptorium* 8 (1954) 142-143.

210. "Gratien, Pierre de Troyes et la seconde croisade," in *Studia Gratiana* II (Bologna, 1954) 585-593.

211. "Recherches sur les sermons sur les Cantiques de Saint Bernard," in *Revue bénédictine* 64 (1954) 208-223; 65 (1955) 71-89, 228-258; 66 (1956) 63-91; 69 (1959) 237-257; 70 (1960) 562-590. R in *Recueil* ... I (n. 19).

212. "S. Bernard et la tradition mariale de l'Eglise," in *Marie* (Nicolet, Québec 1954) 33-36.


1955

213. "Points de vue sur le grand schisme d'Occident," in *1054-1954. L'Eglise et les Eglises* (Chevetogne, 1955) 223-240.

214. "Manuscrits cisterciens dans diverses bibliothèques," in *Analecta Sacri Ordinis Cisterciensis* 11 (1955) 139-148.

215. "La poste des moines," *Cahiers de Saint-André* 12 (1955) 74-77.

216. "Lettres de Mabillon et de Rancé sur Saint Bernard," in *Revue Mabillon* 45 (1955) 29-35. R in *Recueil* ... II (n. 19).

217. "Un recueil d'hagiographie colombanienne," in *Analecta Bollandiana* 73 (1955) 193-196.

218. "Messes pour la profession et l'oblation monastiques," in *Archiv für Liturgiewissenschaft* 4/1 (1955) 93-96.

219. "Sermon sur la Divisio Apostolorum attribuable à Gottschalk de Limbourg," in *Sacris erudiri* 7 (1955) 219-228.

220. "Lettres d'Odon d'Ourscamp, cardinal cistercien," in *Studia Anselmiana* 37, *Analecta Monastica* III (Rome, 1955) 145-157.

221. "Le sermon de Grossolano sur le chapître monastique," ibid., 138-144.

222. "La vêture ad succurrendum d'après le moine Raoul," ibid., 158-168.

223. "Lettres de vocation à la vie monastique," ibid., 169-197.

224. "Saint Bernard à Jumbièges," in *Jumièges. Congrès scientifique du XIII^e centenaire* (Rouen, 1955) 791-796. R in *Recueil* . . . II (n. 19).

225. "Un nouveau manuscrit d'Hautmont," in *Scriptorum* 9 (1955) 107-109.

### 1956

226. "Sermons de l'école de S. Bernard dans un manuscrit d'Hauterive," in *Analecta Sacri Ordinis Cisterciensis* 12 (1956) 3-26. R in *Recueil* . . . I (n. 19).

227. "Pierre le Vénérable et les limites du programme clunisien" in *Collectanea Ordinis Cisterciensium Reformatorum* 18 (1956) 84-87. R in *Témoins* (n. 23).

228. "Documents sur la mort des moines," in *Revue Mabillon* 45 (1955) 165-180; 46 (1956) 65-81.

229. "Bénédictions pour les leçons de l'office dans un manuscrit de Pistoie," in *Sacris erudiri* 8 (1956) 143-146.

230. "Littérature et vie mystique," in *Collectana Ordinis Cisterciensium Reformatorum* 18 (1956) 269-302. R in *L'amour des lettres* . . . (n. 13).

231. "Les collections de sermons de Nicolas de Clairvaux," in *Revue bénédictine* 66 (1956) 269-302. R in *Recueil* . . . I (n. 19).

232. "Aspects historiques du mystère monastique," in *Convivium*, N. S., 24 (1956) 641-649; "Epilogo," in *Il monachesimo nell'alto medioevo e la formazione della civiltà occidentale* (Spoleto, 1957) 609-622. R partly in *Témoins* . . . (n. 23).

233. "Saint Antoine dans la tradition monastique médiévale," in *Studia Anselmiana* 38, *Antonius Magnus Eremita*, 356-1956 (Rome, 1956) 229-247.

234. "L'archétype clarévallien des traités de Saint Bernard," in *Scrip-*

*torium* 10 (1956) 229-232, with 2 plates. R in *Recueil*... II (n. 19), without the plates.

235. "Pierre le Vénérable et l'érémitisme clunisien," in *Studia Anselmiana* 40, *Petrus Venerabilis*, 1156-1956 (Rome, 1956) 99-120.

236. "Voyage rétrospectif aux eaux de Vichy et autres lieux," in *Bulletin de la Société d'histoire et d'archéologie de Vichy et des environs* 56 (1956) 171-190.

237. "Maria christianorum philosophia," in *Mélanges de science religieuse* 13 (1956) 103-106.

238. "Les peintures de la Bible de Morimondo," in *Scriptorium* 10 (1956) 23-26, pl. 1-6.

239. "Un homme agréable," in *Cahiers de Saint-André* 13 (1956) 115-118; I in *Vita monastica* 15 (1961) 71-74. R in *Témoins*... (n. 23).

240. "Textes et manuscrits cisterciens dans diverses bibliothéques," in *Analecta Sacri Ordinis Cisterciensis* 12 (1956) 289-310.

1957

241. "Un document sur les débuts des Templiers," in *Revue d'histoire ecclésiastique* 52 (1957) 81-91. R in *Recueil*... II (n. 19).

242. "Comment aborder Saint Bernard," in *Collectanea Ordinis Cisterciensum Reformatorum* 19 (1957) 18-21.

243. "Regula magistri et Règle de Saint Benoît," in *Revue d'ascétique et de mystique* 40 (1957) 101-105.

244. "Les deux rédactions du Prologue de Pierre Lombard sur les Epîtres de S. Paul," in *Miscellanea Lombardiana* (Novara, 1957) 109-112.

245. "Disciplina," in *Dictionnaire de spiritualité*, t. III (Paris, 1957) col. 1291-1302.

246. "Guerric et l'école monastique," in *Collectanea Ordinis Cisterciensium Reformatorum* 19 (1957) 238-248. R partly in *Témoins* ... (n. 23).

247. "Nouvelle réponse de l'ancien monachisme aux critiques des cisterciens," in *Revue bénédictine* 67 (1957) 77-94. R in *Recueil*... II (n. 19).

248. "Inédits de S. Pierre Damien. Un ancien catalogue des Manuscrits de Font Avellane. Sur l'authenticité des poèmes de S. Pierre Damien," in *Revue bénédictine* 67 (1957) 151-174.

249. "Deux opuscules sur la formation des jeunes moines," dans *Revue d'ascétique et de mystique* 33 (1957) 387-399.

250. "Y a-t-il une culture monastique?" in *Il monachesimo nell'alto medioevo e la formazione della civiltà occidentale* (Spoleto, 1957) 339-356. R in *Témoins...* (n. 23).

251. "Saint Pierre Damien poète," in *La vie spirituelle, Supplément* 43 (1957) 423-440.

252. "Pour une histoire humaine du monachisme au moyen âge," in *Studia Anselmiana* 41, *Analecta Monastica* IV (Rome, 1957) 1-7.

253. "Un débat sur le sacerdoce des moines au XIIe siècle," ibid., 8-118 (in collab. with R. Floreville).

254. "Saint Pierre Damien écrivain," in *Convivium*, N.S. 25 (1957) 385-399. R in *S. Pierre Damien...* (n. 16).

255. "Documents sur S. Pierre Damien," in *Rivista di storia della Chiesa in Italia* 11 (1957) 106-113.

256. "Le jugement du Bx Paul Giustiniani sur S. Pierre Damien," in *Rivista di storia della Chiesa in Italia* 11 (1957) 423-426.

257. "Gébouin de Troyes et S. Bernard," in *Revue des sciences philosophiques et théologiques* 41 (1957) 632-640. R in *Recueil...* I (n. 19).

258. "Cluny fut-il ennemi de la culture?" in *Revue Mabillon* 47 (1957) 172-182.

259. "La collection des sermons de Guerric d'Igny," in *Recherches de théologie ancienne et médiévale* 24 (1957) 15-26. R in *Recueil... I* (n. 19).

260. "Deux épîtres de S. Bernard et de son secrétaire," in *Studien und Mitteilungen zur Geschichte des Benediktiner-Ordens* 69 (1957) 227-231. R in *Recueil... II* (n. 19).

261. "S. Bernard en microssillons," in *Collectanea Ordinis Cisterciensium Reformatorum* (1957) 398-402.

262. "Saint-Germain-des-Prés au moyen âge," in *Revue d'histoire de l'Eglise de France* 43 (1957) 3-12; *La vie spirituelle* 99 (1958) 504-514; *Mémorial du XIVe centenaire de l'Abbaye de Saint-Germain-des-Prés* (Paris, 1959), pp. 3-12. R in *Aux sources . . .* (n. 22).

263. "Saint-Germain et les bénédictines de Paris," in *Revue d'histoire de l'Eglise de France* 43 (1957) 223-230; *Mémorial du XIVe centenaire*, 223-230.

264. Review of J. Huijben-P. Debongnie. *L'auteur ou les auteurs de "l'Imitation de Jésus-Christ"* (Louvain, 1957) in *Convivium*, 4 (1957) 757-759.


1958


265. "Saint Bernard et le XIIe siècle monastique," in *Dictionnaire de spiritualité*, IV, fasc. 25 (Paris, 1958) col. 187-194.

266. "Introduction," *S. Bernard. Textes choisis, "Les écrits des saints"* (Namur, 1958) 1-15.

267. "Le cloître est-il un paradis?," in *Le message des moines à notre temps* (Paris, 1958) 141-159.

268. "L'idée de la seigneurie du Christ au moyen âge," in *Revue d'histoire ecclésiastique* 53 (1958) 57-68. R in *L'idée de la royauté . . .* (n. 15).

269. "La vie et la prière des chevaliers de Santiago d'après leur règle primitive," in *Liturgica* 2, *Scripta et Documenta* 10 (Montserrat, (1958) 347-357.

270. "Fragmenta mariana," in *Ephemerides liturgicae* 72 (1958) 292-305.

271. "La crise du monachisme aux XIe et XIIe siècles," in *Bullettino dell'Istituto Storico Italiano per il Medio Evo e Archivio Muratoriano* 70 (1958) 19-41; *Cluniac Monasticism in the Central Middle Ages*, ed. by Noreen Hunt (London, 1971) 217-242. R in *Aux sources . . .* (n. 22).

272. "Nouvelles lettres de Pierre de Celle," in *Studia Anselmiana* 43, *Analecta Monastica* V (Rome, 1958) 160-179.

273.  "Aspects littéraires de l'oeuvre de S. Bernard," in *Cahiers de civi-lisation médiévale* 1 (1958) 425-450, pl. 1-4. R in *Recueil* . . . III (n. 19).

274.  "Virgile en enfer d'après un manuscrit d'Aulne," in *Latomus* 17 (1958) 731-736.

275.  "Les sources chrétiennes," in *La vie spirituelle* 98 (1958) 654-661.

276.  "Les Distinctiones super Cantica de Guillaume de Ramsey," in *Sacris erudiri* 10 (1958) 329-352.

277.  "Le poème de Payen Bolotin contre les faux ermites," in *Revue bénédictine* 68 (1958) 52-86.


                                    1959

278.  "Documents on the Cult of St. Malachy," in *Seanchas Ardmhacha,* Journal of the Armagh Diocesan Historical Society 3 (1959) 318-322. R in *Recueil* . . . II (n. 19).

279.  "Richesses spirituelles du XII^e siècle," in *La vie spirituelle* 100 (1959) 298-306.

280.  "De l'humour à l'amour à l'école de S. Bernard," in *La vie spiri-tuelle* 101 (1959) 182-203; I in *Ecclesia* 18 (1959) 377-383. R in *Témoins* . . . (n. 23).

281.  "Visages de S. Bernard, Notes pour un commentaire du disque S. Bernard," éd. Hachette, *Encyclopédie sonore* (Paris, 1959) 16 pp.

282.  "Le Sacré-Coeur dans la tradition bénédictine au moyen âge," in *Cor Jesu,* t. II (1959) 3-28.

283.  "The Unity of Prayer," in *Worship* 33 (1959) 408-417; *Paroisse et liturgie* 42 (1960) 277-284; *Erbe und Auftrag* 37 (1961) 458-470; *Rivista di ascetica e mistica* 6 (1961) 9-24; *Seminarios* 24 (1964) 401-415; R in *La liturgie* . . . (n. 20); *Cuadernos monasticos* 7 (1972) 79-110.

284.  "Meditation as a biblical reading," in *Worship* 33 (1959) 562-568; *Paroisse et liturgie* 42 (1960) 357-362; R in *La liturgie* . . . (n. 20).

285. Review of M. Pacaut, *La théocratie,* in *Revue belge de philologie et d'histoire* 37 (1959) 474-476.

286. "Une doctrine de la vie monastique dans l'Ecole du Bec," in *Spicilegium Beccense I. Congrès international du IX$^e$ centenaire de l'arrivée d'Anselme au Bec,* (1959) 477-488. R in *Témoins . . .* (n. 23).

287. "Grammaire et humour dans les textes du moyen âge," in *Convivium* 3 (1959) 270-276: *Annales de la Société royale d'archéologie de Bruxelles* 50 (1961) 150-156.

288. "Les Psaumes 20-25 chez les commentateurs du haut moyen âge," in *Richesses et déficiences des anciens psautiers latins* (Rome, 1959) 213-229.

289. "Pour l'histoire des traités de S. Bernard," in *Analecta Sacri Ordinis Cisterciensis* 15 (1959) 56-78. R in *Recueil . . .* II (n. 19).

290. "Textes et manuscrits cisterciens à la Bibliothèque Vaticane," in *Analecta Sacri Ordinis Cisterciensis* 15 (1959) 79-103.

291. "Un missel de Montiéramey," in *Scriptorium* 13 (1959) 247-249, 4 pl.

292. "Anciennes prières monastiques," in *Studia monastica* 1 (1959) 379-392.

293. "Les premières journées vannistes," in *Studia monastica* 1 (1959) 453-454.

294. "Un témoignage sur l'influence de Grégoire VII dans le réforme canoniale," in *Studi Gregoriani* 6 (1959) 173-227.

295. "Vie divine et vie humaine," in *Etudiants catholiques de Nancy* 37 (1959) 28-30.

### 1960

296. "Mérites d'un réformateur et limites d'une réforme," in *Revue bénédictine* 70 (1960) 232-240. R in *Témoins . . .* (n. 23).

297. "Formes anciennes de l'office marial," in *Ephemerides liturgicae* 74 (1960) 89-102.

298. "Une thèse de théologie sur Aelred de Rievaulx," in *Collectanea Cisterciensium Reformatorum* 12 (1960) 49-50.

299. "The Meaning of Life," in *Worship* 34 (1960) 178-184.

300. "Un guide de lecture pour S. Bernard," in *La vie spirituelle* 102 (1960) 440-447.

301. "La spiritualité du VIe au XIIe siècle, de S. Benoît à S. Bernard, Bibliographie organisée," in *La vie spirituelle* 102 (1960) 563-566.

302. "Lettre d'un moine à son abbé," in *Studi médievali* 1 (1960) 687-700.

303. "S. Bernard éditeur d'après les Sermons sur l'Avent," in *Mélanges d'archéologie et d'histoire publiés par l'Ecole francaise de Rome* 72 (1960) 373-396. R in *Recueil. . .* II (n. 19).

304. "Spiritualité vanniste et tradition monastique," in *Revue d'ascétique et de mystique* 36 (1960) 323-335. R in *Témoins . . .* (n. 23).

305. "L'authenticité bernardine du sermon in celebratione adventus," in *Mediaeval Studies* 22 (1960) 214-231. R in *Recueil. . .* II (n. 19).

306. "Sermon sur l'unité dans un manuscrit des Dunes," in *Cîteaux* 11 (1960) 212-213.

307. "S. Liudger, Un témoin de l'évangélisme au VIIIe siècle," in *La vie spirituelle* 102 (1960) 144-160; *Erbe und Auftrag* 37 (1961) 292-305. R in *Témoins. . .* (n. 23).

308. "S. Anschaire, apôtre des scandinaves," in *La vie spirituelle* 103 (1960) 415-431; Saint-Riquier (1960) pp. 21. R in *Témoins . . .* (n. 23).

309. "L'obbedienza religiosa secondo la regola di S. Benedetto," in *Vita monastica* 61 (1960) 51-63; *American Benedictine Review* 16 (1965) 183-193.

310. "Une parenthèse dans l'histoire de la prière continuelle: la *Laus Perennis* du haut moyen âge," in *La Maison-Dieu* 64 (1960) 90-101. R in *La liturgie . . .* (n. 20).

311. "L'abbé Lebeuf, liturgiste," in *Nouvelle Clio* 3 (1960) 157-162.

312. "Mönchtum und Peregrinatio im Frühmittelalter," in *Römische Quartalschrift* 55 (1960) 212-225. Enlarged redaction in *Aux sources* . . . (n. 22).

313. "The Monastic Tradition of Culture and Studies," in *The American Benedictine Review* 11 (1960) 99-131.

314. "Sancta simplicitas," in *Collectanea Ordinis Cisterciensium Reformatorum* 22 (1960) 138-148. R in *Chances* . . . (n. 24).

315. "The Sacraments of the Easter Season," in *Worship* 34 (1960) 296-306.

316. "S. Bruno et le rayonnement de l'idéal cartusien," in *La vie spirituelle* 102 (1960) 652-664. R in *La spiritualité* . . . (n. 17).

317. "Le B^x Paul Giustiniani et les ermites de son temps," in *Problemi di vita religiosa in Italia nel Cinquecento* (Padoue, 1960) 225-240. R in *Témoins* . . . (n. 23).

318. "Spiritualité et culture à Cluny," in *Spiritualità Cluniacense* (Todi, 1960) 103-151. R partly in *Aux sources* . . . (n. 22).

319. "S. Bernard et la tradition biblique d'après les Sermons sur les Cantiques," in *Sacris erudiri* 11 (1960) 225-248. R in *Recueil* . . . I (n. 19).

320. "The liturgical Roots of the Devotion to the Sacred Heart," in *Worship* 34 (1960) 551-566; *La vie spirituelle* 104 (1961) 377-393; *Primer Congreso internacional sobre el culto al Sagrado Corazón de Jesús* (Barcelona, 1961) 351-359; *Beilage zum Kirchlichem Anzeigen* 17 (Luxembourg, 1962) 1-7, 28-29.

321. Review of W. Hafner, *Der Basiliuskommentar zur Regula S. Benedict*, in *Bibliothèque de l'Ecole des chartes* 118 (1960) 209-211.

322. "Liturgy and mental prayer in the life of St Gertrude," in *Sponsa Regis* 22 (1960) 1-5. R in *La liturgie* . . . (n. 20).

323. "Une nouvelle thèse de théologie monastique," in *Collectanea Cisterciensia* 22 (1960) 49-50.

## 1961

324. "Textes et manuscrits cisterciens dans des bibliothèque des Etats-Unis," in *Traditio* 17 (1961) 163-183.

325   "Introduction" to *Lettres choisies de Saint Bernard,* coll. "Les écrits des Saints Ed. du Soleil Levant (Namur, 1961) 9-16.

326.  "Monachesimo ed esilio," in *Vita monastica* 15 (1961) 99-106. R in *Aux sources . . .* (n. 23).

327.  "Le monachisme clunisien," in *Théologie de la vie monastique* (Paris, 1961) 447-457.

328.  "Le monachisme du haut moyen âge (VIIIᵉ-Xᵉ siècles)," in *Théologie de la vie monastique* (Paris, 1961) 437-445; E *Sponsa Regis* 23 (1961) 165-172.

329.  "Sur le statut des ermites monastiques," in *La vie spirituelle, Supplément* 58 (1961) 384-394. R in *Aux sources . . .* (n. 22).

330.  "A la découverte d'Odon de Morimond," in *Collectanea Ordinis Cisterciensium Reformatorum* 23 (1961) 307-313. R in *Témoins . . .* (n. 23).

331.  "La séparation du monde dans le monachisme au moyen âge," in *Problèmes de la religieuse d'aujourd'hui: La séparation du monde* (Paris, 1961) 75-94; *La separación del mundo* (Madrid, 1963) 77-97; *La separazione del mondo* (Alba, 1963) 82-104. R in *Aux sources . . .* (n. 22).

332.  "Monachisme et pérégrination du IXᵉ au XIIᵉ siècles," in *Studia monastica* 3 (1961) 33-52. R in *Aux sources . . .* (n. 22).

333.  "On Monastic Priesthood According to the Ancient Medieval Tradition," in *Studia monastica* 3 (1961) 137-155.

334.  "La theographia de Longuel de Clairvaux," in *Cîteaux* 3 (1961) 212-225.

335.  "Opuscules tirés de manuscrits monastiques," in *Archivum Latinitatis Medii Aevi* 2-3 (1961) 141-143.

336.  "An Itinerary," in *Worship* 8 (1961) 521-527.

337.  "S. Martin dans l'hagiographie monastique du moyen âge," in *S. Martin et son temps. Mémorial du XVIᵉ centenaire des débuts du monachisme en Gaule 361-1961. Studia Anselmiana* 46 (Rome, 1961), 175-188.

338.  "Note sur le devoir d'etat dans la spiritualité ancienne," in *Christus* 29 (1961) 71-74; *The Benedictine Review* 17 (1962) 12-14.

339. "Caratteristiche della spiritualità monastica," in *Problemi e orientamenti di spiritualità monastica, biblica e liturgica* (Rome, 1961) 327-336; S *Cistercium* 87 (1963) 153-156. R in *Aux sources* . . . (n. 22).

340. "Nieuwe stromingen in het oude monachisme," in *Abdij leven* 3 (Achel, 1961) 53-58.

341. "La tradition des sermons liturgiques de S. Bernard," in *Scriptorium* 15 (1961) 240-284 (in collaboration with H. Rochais). R in *Recueil* . . . II (n. 19).

342. "La vie contemplative dans S. Thomas et dans la tradition," in *Recherches de théologie ancienne et médiévale* 28 (1961) 251-268.

343. "Exercices spirituels," in *Dictionnaire de spiritualité* 4, 2 (1961) 1900-1907.

## 1962

344. "Culte liturgique et prière intime dans le monachisme du moyen âge," in *La Maison-Dieu* 69 (1962) 39-55. R in *Aux sources* . . . (n. 22).

345. Review of Maurice Bevenot, *The Tradition of Manuscripts*, in *The Heythrop Journal* 3 (1962) 187-189.

346. "S. Romuald et le monachisme missionnaire," in *Revue bénédictine* 72 (1962) 307-323. R partly in *Témoins* . . . (n. 23).

347. "Pour une histoire de la vie à Cluny," in *Revue d'histoire ecclésiastique* 57 (1962) 386-408; 783-812. R partly in *Aux sources* . . . (n. 22).

348. "Une thèse sur Cîteaux dans la tradition monastique," in *Collectanea Ordinis Cisterciensium Reformatorum* 24 (1962) 358-362.

349. "Deux opuscules médiévaux sur la vie solitaire," in *Studia monastica* 4 (1962) 93-109.

350. "Un congrès sur l'érémitisme," in *Studia monastica* 4 (1962) 404-407.

351. "La flagellazione volontaria nella tradizione spirituale dell'oc-

cidente," F in *Il movimento dei Disciplinati nel Settimo centenario del suo inizio* (Pérouse, 1962) 73-83. R in *Témoins* . . . (n. 23).

352. "Spiritualitas," in *Studi medievali* 3 (1962) 279-296.

353. "Une homélie de Volcuin de Sittichenbach," in *Studi medievali* 3 (1962) 315-339.

354. "Textes et manuscrits cisterciens dans diverses bibliothèques," in *Analecta Sacri Ordinis Cisterciensis* 18 (1962) 121-134.

355. "Theology and Prayer," in *Father Cyril Gaul Memorial Lectures* 2 (St. Meinrad, Ind., 1962) 1-23; *Encounter* 24 (1963) 349-364; *Seminarios* 9 (1963) 466-484; *La preghiera nella Bibbia e nella tradizione patristica e monastica* (Rome, 1964) 951-971. R in *Chances* . . . (n. 24).

356. "Le sacerdoce des moines," in *Bulletin du Comité des études. Compagnie St-Sulpice* 38-39 (1962) 394-422; *Irénikon* 36 (1963) 5-40; *Selecciones de teologia* 3 (1964) 267-272; *Monastic Studies* 3 (1965) 53-86. R in *Chances* . . . (n. 24).

357. "Le nouveau catalogue des manuscrits théologiques de la bibliothèque universitaire de Bâle," in *Scriptorium* 16 (1962) 76-78.

358. "Un traité sur la profession des abbés au XIIe siècle," in *Studia Anselmiana* 50 (1962) 177-191.

359. "Pour une histoire intégrale du monachisme," in *Studia Anselmiana* 50 (1962) 1-3.

360. "Über das Einsiedlerleben im Mittelalter," in *Geist und leben* 35 (1962) 378-382.

361. "La spiritualité des chanoines réguliers," in *La vita comune del clero nei secoli XI et XII* (Milan, 1962) 117-135. R in *Témoins* . . . (n. 23).

362. Review of E. S. Creenhill, *Die geistigen Vorausetzungen der Bilderreihe des "Speculum virginum,"* in *Cahiers de civilisation médiévale* 5 (1962) 477-479.


1963

363. "Les études bernardines en 1963," in *Bulletin de la Société inter-*

*nationale pour l'étude de la philosophie médiévale* 5 (1963) 121-138.

364. "L'*Exordium cistercii* et la *Summa cartae caritatis* sont-ils de Saint Bernard?," in *Revue bénédictine* 73 (1963) 88-89. R in *Recueil* . . . II (n. 19).

365. "*Eremus* et *Eremita*," in *Collectanea Ordinis Cisterciensium Reformatorum* 25 (1963) 8-30. R in *Chances* . . . (n. 24).

366. "Monasticism and St Benedict," in *Monastic Studies* 1 (1963) 9-23. R in *Aux Sources* . . . (n. 22).

367. Review of Demosthenes Savramis, *Zur Siziologie des byzantinischen Mönchtums*, in *The Catholic Historical Review* (1963) 509-510.

368. "Regola benedettina e prezenza nel mondo," in *La bonifica benedettina* (Rome, 1963) 17-25; *Monastic Studies* 2 (1964) 51-63; *Erbe und Auftrag* 40 (1964) 224-233. R in *Aux sources* . . . (n. 22).

369. "Christusnachfolge und Sakrament in der Theologie des Heiligen Bernhard," in *Archiv für Liturgiewissenschaft* 8 (1963) 58-72.

370. "*Umbratilis*. Pour l'histoire du thème de la vie cachée," in *Revue d'ascétique et de mystique* 156 (1963) 491-504. R in *Chances* . . . (n. 24).

371. "Introduction" to Baudouin de Ford, *Le sacrement de l'autel*, in Sources chrétiennes 93 (Paris, 1963) 7-51.

372. "Le monachisme en Islam et en chrétienté," in *Images de Toumiline* (March, 1963) 1-5.

373. "La rencontre des moines de Moissac avec Dieu," in *Annales du Midi* 75 (1963) 405-417; *Moissac et l'Occident au XIᵉ siècle. Actes du Colloque international de Moissac 1963* (Toulouse, 1964) 81-93. R in *Témoins* . . . (n. 23).

374. "Caelestinus de caritate," in *Cîteaux* 3 (1963) 202-217.

375. "Une paraphrase en vers de proverbes bibliques attribuable à Jean de Lodi," in *Studi medievali* 4 (1963) 325-349.

376. "La joie dans Rancé," in *Collectanea Ordinis Cisterciensium Reformatorum* 25 (1963) 206-215. R in *Témoins* . . . (n. 23).

246 *Bibliography*

377. "L'érémitisme en Occident jusqu'à l'an mil," in *Le millénaire du Mont-Athos* 1 (Chevetogne, 1963) 161-180; *L'eremitismo in Occidente nei secoli XI e XII* (Milan, 1965) 27-44.

378. "*Sedere*. A propos de l'hésychasme en Occident," in *Le millénaire du Mont-Athos* 1 (1963) 253-264. R in *Chances . . .* (n. 24).

379. "L'Ecriture Sainte dans l'hagiographie monastique du haut moyen âge," in *La Biblia nell'alto medioevo* (Spoleto, 1963) 103-128.

380. "Problèmes de l'érémitisme," in *Studia monastica* 5 (1963) 197-212.

381. "Une vie de Jérôme d'Ancône par Ludovico Brunori," in *Traditio* 19 (1963) 371-409.

382. "Les études dans les monastères du X$^e$ au XII$^e$ siècle," in *Los monjes y los estudios* (Poblet, 1963) 106-117.

383. "Culture monastique et retour à l'unité," in *Irénikon* 3 (1963) 406-408.

384. "La dévotion médiévale envers le Crucifié," in *La Maison-Dieu* 75 (1963) 119-132.

385. "Note sur la manière de citer Mabillon," in *Studia monastica* 5 (1963) 423-424.

### 1964

386. "Il ritiro come esercizio di vita solitaria," in *Vita monastica* 77 (1964) 55-62. R in *Chances . . .* (n. 24).

387. "Spiritualité monastique du VI$^e$ au XII$^e$ siècle," in *Dictionnaire de spiritualité*, art. "France," 5 (1964) 805-806, 818-847; *Histoire spirituelle de la France* (Paris, 1964) 64-110.

388. "Théologie traditionnelle et théologie monastique," in *Irénikon* 37 (1964) 50-74; *Seminarios* 25 (1965) 203-223; S in *Cistercium* 24 (1972) 23-46. R in *Chances . . .* (n. 24).

389. "Un traité de Jérôme de Matelica sur la vie solitaire," in *Rivista di storia della Chiesa in Italia* 18 (1964) 13-22.

390. "Préface" to J. Hourlier, *S. Odilon, abbé de Cluny* (Louvain, 1964) 5-7.

391. "Méditations d'un moine de Moissac au XI$^e$ siècle, Présentation," in *Revue d'ascétique et de mystique* 40 (1964) 197-200.

392. "Méditations d'un moine de Moissac au XI$^e$ siècle. Textes," ibid., 201-210.

393. "Ancien sermon monastique dans le manuscrit Palat. Lat. 295," in *Mélanges Eugène Tisserant* 6 (1964) 577-582.

394. "Aspects spirituels de la symbolique du livre au XII$^e$ siècle," in *L'homme devant Dieu. Mélanges H. de Lubac* (Paris, 1964) 63-72.

395. "De quelques procédés du style biblique de S. Bernard," in *Cîteaux* 5 (1964) 330-346. R in *Recueil* . . . III (n. 19).

396. "Marie reine dans les sermons de S. Bernard," in *Collectanea Cisterciensia* 26 (1964) 265-276; *Ora et labora* 21 (1966) 70-79.

397. "Problèmes et orientations du monachisme," in *Etudes* (May, (1964) 667-684; S in *Cistercium* 16 (1964) 163-177; I in *Ora et labora* 19 (1964) 162-177; *Tijdschrift voor geestelijk leven* 10 (1964) 730-754. R in *Chances* . . . (n. 24).

398. "Un réformateur, S. Bernard," in *Lettre de Ligugé* 104 (1964) 7-9.

399. "S. Bernard écrivain d'après d'Office de S. Victor," in *Revue bénédictine* 74 (1964) 155-169. R in *Recueil* . . . II (n. 19).

400. "Überlegung und Neubesinnung im heutigen Mönchtum," in *Das Wagnis der Nachfolge* (Paderborn, 1964) 59-94. R in *Chances* . . . (n. 24).

401. "Nouveau sermon d'Isaac de l'Etoile," in *Revue d'ascétique et de mystique* 40 (1964) 277-288.

402. In collab. with J. Figuet: "La Bible dans les homélies de S. Bernard sur *Missus est,*" in *Studi medievali* 5 (1964) 3-38. R in *Recueil* . . . III (n. 19).

403. "Notes sur la tradition des épîtres de S. Bernard," in *Scriptorium* 18 (1964) 198-209, pl. 23-24. R in *Recueil* . . . III (n. 19).

404. "Un dialogo riuscito," in *Studi cattolici* 45 (1964) 102-105.

405. "Textes et manuscrits cisterciens dans diverses bibliothèques," in *Analecta Sacri Ordinis Cisterciensis* 20 (1964) 218-231.

406. Review of R. W. Southern, *St Anselm and his Biographer*, in *Medium Aevum* 33 (1964) 222-227.

407. "L'assemblée locale dans la communion de l'Eglise universelle," in *La Maison-Dieu* 79 (1964) 81-105.

408. In collaboration with R. Grégoire: "Review of Corpus consuetudinum monasticarum, t. I et II," F in *Studi medievali* 5 (1964) 658-668.

409. "Présent et avenir du monachisme africain," in *Christus* 44 (1964) 567-574; I in *Ora et labora* 20 (1965) 97-103. R in *Chances . . .* (n. 24).

410. "Une lettre de l'abbé de Pontigny à un bourgeois de Provins au XIIIᵉ siècle," in *Bulletin de la Société d'histoire et d'archéologie de l'Arrondissement de Provins (Seine-et-Marne)* (1964) 67-68.

411. "Préface" to D. Farkasfalvy, *L'Inspiration de l'Ecriture Sainte dans la théologie de Saint Bernard*, Studia Anselmiana, 53 (Rome, 1964) 7-9.

1965

412. "Deux questions de Berthaud de Saint-Denys sur l'exemption fiscale du clergé," in *Etudes d'histoire du droit canonique dédiées à G. Le Bras* (Paris, 1965) 607-617.

413. "Pétulance et spiritualité dans le commentaire d'Hélinand sur le Cantique des Cantiques," in *Archives d'histoire doctrinale et littéraire du moyen âge* 31 (1964), 37-59.

414. "Culte et pauvreté à Cluny," in *La Maison-Dieu* 81 (1965) 33-50. R in *Témoins . . .* (n. 23).

415. "Le monachisme africain d'aujourd'hui et le monachisme antique," in *Irénikon* 28 (1965) 33-56; *Monastic Studies* 4 (1966) 137-160; I in *Ora et labora* 20 (1965) 97-103, 172-177; 21 (1966) 11-22. R in *Chances . . .* (n. 24).

416. "Les relations entre le monachisme oriental et le monachisme occidental dans le haut moyen âge," in *Le millénaire du Mont-Athos* II (Chevetogne, 1965) 49-80.

417. "Problems Facing Monachism Today," in *The American Benedictine Review* 16 (1965) 47-60; *Geist und Leben* 38 (1965) 214-223. R in *Chances . . .* (n. 24).

418. "Pour l'histoire de l'obéissance au moyen âge," in *Revue d'asceti-que et de mystique* 41 (1965) 125-143.

419. "L'érémitisme et les Cisterciens," in *L'eremitismo in Occidente nei secoli XI e XII* (Milan, 1965) 573-576. R in *Témoins . . .* (n. 23).

420. "Epilogue," in *L'Eremitismo in Occidente nei secoli XI et XII,* ibid. 593-595.

421. "Compte-rendu de voyage en Afrique 1965," in *Bulletin de liaison des Monastères d'Afrique* 2 (1965) 23-29.

422. "L'obéissance, éducatrice de la liberté, dans la tradition monas-tique," in *La liberté évangélique, principes et pratique* (Paris, 1965) 55-85.

423. "The Role of Monastic Spirituality Critically Discussed," in *Worship* 39 (1965) 583-596; *Protestants and Catholics on the Spiritual Life* (Collegeville, Minn., 1966) 20-33; *La vie spirituelle* 114 (1966) 623-644; *Cuadernos monasticos* 2 (1966) 1-31. R in *Aspects du monachisme* (n. 26).

424. "Prières médiévales pour recevoir l'Eucharistie, pour saluer et pour bénir la croix," in *Ephemerides liturgicae* 79 (1965) 327-340.

425. "Charlemagne et les moines," in *Collectanea Cisterciensia* 27 (1965) 242-245; *Vita monastica* 20 (1966) 43-48. R in *Chances . . .* (n. 24).

426. "Postface," in *La notion de mépris du monde dans la tradition spirituelle occidentale, Revue d'ascétique et de mystique* 41 (1965) 287-290; *Le mépris du monde,* Problèmes de vie religieuse (Paris, 1965) 55-58.

427. "La vie monastique est-elle une vie contemplative?," in *Collectanea Cisterciensia* 27 (1965) 108-120; S in *Schola caritatis* 42 (1967) 141-145. R in *Chances . . .* (n. 24).

428. "Deux nouvelles revues monastiques," in *Studia monastica* 7 (1965) 201-206.

429. "Sermon de Philippe le Chancilier sur S. Bernard," in *Cîteaux* 16 (1965) 205-213; R in *Recueil . . .* III (n. 19).

430. "Documents sur les fugitifs," in *Analecta monastica* 7, *Studia Anselmiana* 54 (Rome, 1965), 87-145.

431. "De la tradition comme ouverture au présent," in *Rythmes du monde* 39 (1965) 5-15; *Monastic Studies* 4 (1966) 1-15. R in *Chances* . . . (n. 24).

432. "Presentation" (with E. Francechini) of Jonas. *Vita Columbani et discipulorum eius*, éd. by M. Tosi, E. Cremona, M. Paramidani (Piacenza, 1965), p. XIV-XV.

433. "Orientations du monachisme en Afrique," in *Rythmes du monde* 39 (1965) 19-20.

434. "Problèmes et perspectives du monachisme africain," in *Christus* 49 (1965) 120-135; I in *Ora et labora* 21 (1966) 101-113.

435. "Hélinand de Froidmont ou Odon de Cheriton? ," in *Archives d'histoire doctrinale et littéraire du moyen âge* 32 (1965), 61-69.

436. "Textes contemporains de Dante sur des sujets qu'il a traités," in *Studi medievali* 6 (1965) 491-535.

437. In collab. with G. Gärtner:" S. Bernard dans l'histoire de l'obeissance monastique," in *Anuario de estudios medievales* 2 (1965) 31-62; *Cistercian Studies* 3 (1968) 207-234. R in *Recueil* . . . III (n. 19).

438. "Cultura spirituale e ideale riformatore dell'abbazia di Pomposa nel sec. XI," in *Analecta Pomposiana* 1 (1965) 73-88. R in *Témoins* . . . (n. 23).

439. "Nouveaux aspects littéraires de l'oeuvre de S. Bernard," in *Cahiers de civilisation médiévale* 8 (1965) 299-326. R in *Recueil* . . . III (n. 19).

440. "Comment vivaient les frères convers," in *Analecta Cisterciensia* 21 (1965) 239-258; *I laici nella società religiosa del secoli XI e XII* (Milan, 1967) 152-182.

441. "Gilbert Crispin," in *Dictionnaire de spiritualité*, 6, fasc. 39-40 (1965) 369-370.

442. "Giustiniani Paul," ibid. 414-417.

443. "Prières attribuées à Guillaume et à Jean de Fruttuaria," in *Monasteri in Alta Italia* (Turin, 1966) 157-166.

444. "Clôture et ouverture," in *"In Unitate"* 7 (1965) 1-2.

1966

445. "L'univers religieux de S. Colomban et de Jonas de Bobbio," in *Revue d'ascétique et de mystique* 42 (1966) 15-30. R in *Aspects du monachisme* (n. 26).

446. "A propos d'un séjour de S. Ignace à Montserrat," in *Christus* 50 (1966) 161-172. I in *Ora et labora* 26 (1971) 129-137. R in *Aspects du monachisme* (n. 26).

447. "La vie contemplative et le monachisme d'après Vatican II," in *Gregorianum* 47 (1966) 495-516; *Ecoute,* n. 151 (1966) 1-27; I in *Ora et labora* 22 (1967) 18-35; *Cistercian Studies* 2 (1967) 53-75; R by *Asirvanam Monastery, Kengeri* (Bangalore, 1967), 16 pp.; *Cuadernos monasticos* 3 (1967) 51-91; R in *Aspects du monachisme* (n. 26).

448. "Jérôme de Matelica et Aegidius Ghiselini," in *Rivista di storia della Chiesa in Italia* 20 (1966) 9-17.

449. "Le formulaire de Pontigay," in *Miscellanea Populetana* (Poblet, 1966) 229-265.

450. "L'art de la composition dans les sermons de S. Bernard," in *Studi medievali* 7 (1966) 128-153. R in *Recueil . . .* III (n. 19).

451. "Petrus Venerabilis," in *Die Heiligen in ihrer Zeit* (Main, 1966) 1-4.

452. "Petrus Damiani," ibid. 540-541.

453. "Sur le caractère littéraire des sermons de S. Bernard," in *Studi medievali* 7 (1966) 701-744. R in *Recueil . . .* III (n. 19).

454. "Un formulaire écrit dans l'Ouest de la France au XIIe siècle," in *Mélanges offerts à René Crozet* (Poitiers, 1966) 765-775.

455. "Livres et lectures dans les cloîtres du moyen âge," in *Nouvelle revue luxembourgeoise* 3 (1966) 243-252; I in *Vita monastica* 19 (1965) 122-134; R in *Aspects du monachisme* (n. 26).

456. "Nouvel itinéraire en Afrique," in *Bulletin de liaison des monastères d'Afrique* 5 (1966) 66-72.

457. "La royauté du Christ. Les Pères," in *Assemblées du Seigneur* 88 (Saint-André, 1966) 64-79.

458. "Bible et réforme grégorienne," in *Concilium* 17 (1966) 57-68; Spanish ed. 404-420; Dutch ed. 61-76; Portugese ed. 56-68; American ed. 63-77; English ed. 34-41; German ed. 507-514.

459. "Liturgie monastique ou liturgie des monastères?," in *Liturgie et monastères. Etudes* 1 (Saint-André, 1966) 11-18.

460. "Galvano di Levanto e l'Oriente," in *Venezia e l'Oriente fra Medioevo e Rinascimento* (Florence, 1966) 403-416.

461. "Sur le rôle des contemplatifs dans la société de demain," in *Collectanea Cisterciensia* 28 (1966) 125-137; *Cistercian Studies* 1 (1966) 117-129. R in *Chances . . .* (n. 24).

462. "L'art de la composition dans les traités de S. Bernard," in *Revue bénédictine* 76 (1966) 87-115. R in *Recueil . . .* III (n. 19).

463. "Cluniazensische Reforms," in *Sacramentum Mundi. Theologisches Lexikon für die Praxis* 1 (1966) 795-799.

464. "Un trappiste malgache au XVIIᵉ siècle?," in *Collectanea Cisterciensia* 28 (1966) 68-70.

465. "Preface" to R. Grégoire, *Les homéliaires du moyen âge. Inventaire et analyse des manuscrits* (Rome, 1966) V-VII.

466. "Notes Abélardiennes," in *Bulletin de philosophie médiévale* 8-9 (1966-1967) 59-62.

1967

467. "Les leçons d'un millénaire monastique," in *La vie spirituelle* 116 (1967) 91-107. R in *Aspects du monachisme* (n. 26).

468. "Contemplant sur la montagne," ibid., 377-387. R ibid.

469. "L'érémitisme en Occident," in *Lettre de Ligugé* 121 (1967) 10-19.

470. "La professione secondo battesimo," in *Vita religiosa* 3 (1967) 3-8.

471. "Témoignages contemporains sur la théologie du monachisme," in *Gregorianum* 48 (1967) 49-76; I in *Ora et labora* 22 (1967) 78-87; *Cistercian Studies* 2 (1967) 189-220. R in *Aspects du monachisme* (n. 26).

472. "La récréation et le colloque dans la tradition monastique," in *Revue d'ascétique et de mystique* 43 (1967) 3-20.

473. *"Lectulus.* Variazioni su un tema biblico nella tradizione monastica," in *Bibia e Spiritualità* (Rome, 1967) 417-436. R in *Chances* . . . (n. 24).

474. "Une bibliothèque vivante," in *Millénaire monastique du Mont Saint-Michel* II (Paris, 1967) 247-255; *Vita monastica* 20 (1966) 217-230.

475. "Prières d'apologie dans un sacramentaire du Mont-Saint-Michel. Jean de Fécamp au Mont Saint-Michel," in *Millénaire monastique du Mont Saint-Michel* II (Paris, 1967) 357-361.

476. "Vita contemplativa e monachesimo secondo il Concilio Vaticano II" (Sorrento, Monastero San Paolo, 1967), 32 pp. (translation of n. 425 and of part of n. 447).

477. "S. Bernard prêcheur d'après un exemple inédit," in *Mélanges offerts à M. D. Chenu,* (Paris, 1967) 345-362.

478. "Genèse et évolution de la vie consacrée," in *Revue diocésaine de Tournai,* 7 (Tournai-Paris, 1967) 2-27; *Monastic Studies* 5 (1968) 59-85; *Theology Digest* 28 (1968) 212-228; R in *Aspects du monachisme* (n. 26).

479. "Le monachisme contesté," in *Nouvelle Revue théologique* 99 (1967) 607-618; I in *Ora et Labora* 22 (1967) 164-173; *Cistercian Studies* (1967); R in *Aspects du monachisme* (n. 26).

480. "Eucharistie et monachisme d'après un ouvrage récent," in *Collectanea Cisterciensia* 29 (1967) 116-118.

481. "Impressions sur le monachisme africain et malgache," in *Parole et mission* 10 (1967) 480-499; *Rythmes du monde* 14 (1966), 165-176; I in *Vita monastica* 21 (1967) 38-47, 97-106. R in *Aspects du monachisme* (n. 26).

482. "Monasticism and angelism," in *The Downside Review* 85 (1967) 127-137. R in *Aspects du monachisme* (n. 26).

483. "St. Bernard and the Church," ibid., 274-294.

484. "Dévoloppement de la liturgie du Sacré-Coeur," in *Assemblées du Seigneur* 56 (Paris, 1967) 7-12.

485. "Saint Bernard et l'expérience chrétienne," in *La vie spirituelle* 117 (1967) 182-198; *Worship* 41 (1967) 222-233; *Grosse Gestalten christlicher Spiritualität*, hsgb v., J. Sudbrack. J. Walsh (Wurzburg, 1969), 122-136; R in *Aspects du monachisme* (n. 26).

486. "L'avenir des moines," in *Irénikon* 40 (1967) 189-220; *Cistercian Studies* (1967); I in *Ora et Labora* 23 (1968) 49-58, 324-328. R in *Aspects du monachisme* (n. 26).

487. "Fragmenta monastica," I in *Benedictina* 14 (1967) 23-26.

488. "Pour l'histoire du vocabulaire latin de la pauvreté," in *Melto* 3, Mélanges Mgr Pierre Dib (Beyrut, 1967), 293-308.

489. "Observations sur les sermons de S. Bernard pour le Carême," in *Cîteaux* 18 (1967) 119-129.

490. "Benedictine spirituality," in *New Catholic Encyclopedia* 2 (1967) 285-288, 491.

491. "Gilbert Crispin," ibid., 6, 477.

492. "Ivo of Chartres," ibid., 7, 777-778.

493. "Monastic Schools," ibid., 9, 1031-1032.

494. "Theology and Prayer," ibid., 14, 64-65.

495. "Itinéraire monastique à Madagascar," in *Bulletin de liaison des monastères d'Afrique* 6 (1967) 30-33.

496. "Questions des XIIIe et XIVe siècles sur la juridiction de l'Eglise et le pouvoir séculier," in *Studia Gratiana* 12, *Collectanea Stephan Kuttner*, 2 (1967), 309-324.

497. "Il s'est fait pauvre," in *La vie spirituelle* 117 (1967) 501-518. R in *Aspects du monachisme* (n. 26).

498. "S. Bernard écrivain d'après les Sermons sur le Psaume *Qui habitat,*" in *Revue bénédictine* 77 (1967) 364-374.

499. "Le cheminement biblique de la pensée de S. Bernard," in *Studi Medievali* 8 (1967) 835-856.

500. "Maria contemplativa ed attiva," in *Miles Immaculatae* 3 (1967) 425-429; *Mount Carmel* 16 (1968) 87-91; R in *Vie religieuse* (n. 27).

501. "Tradition et évolution dans le passé et le présent de la vie religieuse," in *Revue diocésaine de Tournai* 22 (1967) 398-420; *Vivre ensemble l'aujourd'hui de Dieu. La vie religieuse, signe du royaume pour tous les hommes, 3-8 avril 1967* (Ramegnies-Chin-lez-Tournai, 1968) 79-98; *Strukturen christlicher Existenz. Beiträge zur Erneuerung des christlichen Lebens Pater Friedrich Wulf zum sechzigsten Geburtstag* (Würzburg, 1968) 263-281; *Rinnovamento della vita religiosa* (Rome, 1970), 27-58; R in *Vie religieuse* (n. 27).

502. "Jean de Gorze et la vie religieuse au X<sup>e</sup> siècle," in *Saint Chrodegang* (Metz, 1967) 133-151. R in *Aspects du monachisme* (n. 26).

503. "L'eremitisio ieri e oggi," in *Vita religiosa* 3 (1967) c 243.

504. "Un fondateur monastique au XIII<sup>e</sup> siècle. Pour un portrait spirituel de S. Silvestre Guzzolini," in *Inter fratres* 27 (1967) 10-24; I in *Ora et Labora* 24 (1969), 68-79; *Downside Review* 87 (1969) 1-10.

## 1968

505. "Monastic Life after the Second Vatican Council," in *Downside Review* 282 (1968) 13-30.

506. "Chronique de l'actualité contemplative," in *Nouvelle Revue théologique* 90 (1968) 66-78. R in *Vie religieuse* (n. 27).

507. "Un témoin de la dévotion médiévale envers S. Pierre et les Apôtres," in *Gregorianum* 49 (1968) 134-154.

508. "Alle origini della vita religiosa e dei voti," in *Vita religiosa* 4 (1968) 3-10.

509. "Variazioni sui millenari monastici," in *Bollettino della Deputazione di Storia patria per l'Umbria* (Perugia, 1968) 186-191.

510. "Les formes successives de la lettre-traité de S. Bernard contre Abélard," in *Revue bénédictine* 78 (1968) 87-105.

511. "Preface" to W. Tunynk, *Vision de paix* (Paris, 1968) 5-15.

512. "Le rôle des moines dans le mouvement liturgique," in *Paroisse et liturgie* 3 (1968) 248-255.

513. "S. Bernard et les jeunes," in *Collectanea Cisterciensia* 30 (1968) 147-154. R in *Vie religieuse* (n. 27).

514. "Le monachisme en marche," in *Vivante Afrique* 256 (1968) 1-4.

515. "Contemplation et vie contemplative hier et aujourd'hui," in *Vie consacrée* 40 (1968) 193-226; *Ecoute* 170 (1969) 1-19. R in *Vie religieuse* (n. 27).

516. "Fragmenta monastica. II. Oraisons á S. Pierre et aux Apôtres," in *Benedictina* 15 (1968) 14-18.

517. "Relation de voyage dans les monastères d'Asie," in *Bulletin de liaison des monastères d'Afrique* 7 (1968) 7-21; *The Examiner,* (6 April, 1968) 5-9.

518. "Un renouveau après bein d'autres," in *Informations catholiques internationales* (15 December 1968), 38-40. Dutch and Spanish edition, ibid.

519. "An Experiment in Indianizing the Church," in *The Examiner* (6 April 1968); *Cistercian Studies* 3 (1968) 183-186.

520. "Le monachisme en marche," in *Vivante Afrique,* (May-June, 1968), 1-4.

521. "Essais sur l'esthétique de S. Bernard," in *Studi medievali* 9 (1968) 688-728.

522. "Problèmes monastiques d'Extrême-Orient," in *Rythmes du monde* 42 (1968) 214-232; *A New Charter for Monasticism* (Notre Dame-London, 1970) 280-300.

523 "Die Mönche," in *Der grosse Entschluss* 24 (1968-1969) 28-31, 119-121, 224-226, 372-374, 532-535; *Entschluss* 25 (1970) 177-180, 416-418.

524. "La confession louange de Dieu," in *La vie spirituelle* 118 (1968) 253-265; *Worship* 42 (1968) 159-176; *Cistercian Studies* 4 (1969) 192-212. R in *Vie religieuse* (n. 27).

525. "Continuité et vérité," in *La Maison-Dieu,* n. 95 (1968) 131-141; *El oficio divino hoy* (Barcelona, 1969), 191-205; *Erbe und Auftrag* 45 (1969) 280-288. R in *Le défi* (n. 28).

526. "Le chapitre des coulpes," in *La vie des communautés religieuses* 26 (1968) 108-117; I in *Vita religiosa* 4 (1968) 439-447. R in *Le défi* (n. 28).

527. Review of B. de Gaiffier, *Etudes critiques d'hagiographie et d'iconologie* in *Studi medievali* 9 (1968) 235-240. F.

528. "Mönchtum in den jungen Kirchen," in *Liturgie und Mönchtum* 43 (1968) 69-76.

529. "Problèmes du monachisme chrétien en Asie," in *Collectanea Cisterciensia* 30 (1968) 15-52; *Parole et mission* 11 (1968) 437-465; I in *Ora et Labora* 24 (1969) 2-32; I in *Vita monastica* 22 (1968) 147-159. R in *Vie religieuse* (n. 27).

530. "L'humanisme littéraire de S. Bernard," in *Entretiens sur la renaissance du XIIᵉ siècle*, éd. par M. de Gandillac-E Jeauneau (Paris-La-Haye, 1968) 295-308.

1969

531. "Vie monastique," in *Orval. Neuf siècles d'histoire 1069-1969* (Orval, 1969) 217-222.

532. Review of M. D. Knowles - D. Obolensky, *Nouvelle histoire de l'Eglise, II: Le moyen âge*, in *Cahiers de civilisation médiévale* 12 (1969) 84-86.

533. "Une rédaction en prose de la *Visio Anselli* dans un manuscrit de Subiaco," in *Benedictina* 16 (1969) 188-195.

534. "Humanisme des moines au moyen âge," in *Dictionnaire de spiritualité* 7 (1969) 960-970.

535. "*Ad ipsam sophiam Christus*. Le témoignage monastique d'Abélard," in *Sapienter ordinare. Festgabe für Erich Kleineidam* (Leipzig, 1969), 179-198; *Revue d'ascétique et de mystique* 46 (1970) 161-182.

536. "Lettres d'Amérique latine," in *Bulletin de l'A.I.M.* 10 (1969) 21-34; I in *San Benedetto* 14 (1970) 72-78.

537. Review of D. E. Luscombe, *The School of Peter Abelard*, in *The Ampleforth Journal* 74 (1969) 411-412. F.

538. "Foreword" to A. Hallier, *The Monastic Theology of Aelred of Rievaulx* (Spencer, 1969) XV-XVII.

539. "Les lettres de Guillaume de Saint-Thierry à S. Bernard," in *Revue bénédictine* 9 (1969) 375-391.

540. "The Exposition and Exegesis of Scripture from Gregory the Great to Saint Bernard," in *Cambridge History of the Bible. The West from the Fathers to the Reformation* (Cambridge, 1969) 183-197.

541. "San Maiolo fundatore e riformatore di monasteri a Pavia," in *Atti nel 4º convegno internazionale di studi sull'alto mediaevo* (Spoleto, 1969), 155-173. R partly in *Aspects du monachisme* (n. 26).

542. "Producción y consumo según Isaac de Stella," in *Cistercium* 20 (1969) 211-220; F in *Collectanea Cisterciensia* 31 (1971) 159-166; *Cistercian Studies* 4 (1969) 267-274.

543. "Tâtonnements du monachisme dans le tiers-monde," in *Parole et mission* 12 (1969) 587-591.

544. "Humanisme et foi chrétienne," in *Parole et mission* 12 (1969) 623-627.

545. "Actualité de l'humour," in *La vie spirituelle* 121 (1969) 263-271; I in *Monastica* 12, n. 3 (1971) 42-47. R in *Le défi* (n. 28).

546. "Derniers souvenirs de Thomas Merton," in *Bulletin de l'A.I.M.* 9 (1969) 17-21; *Collectanea Cisterciensia* 39 (1969) 9-14; I in *Ora et Labora* 24 (1969) 121-125.; R in *Le défi* (n. 28).

547. "Le monachisme dans un monde en transformation," in *La vie spirituelle* 121 (1969) 5-31; *Geist und Leben* 42 (1969) 118-137); *American Benedictine Review* 22 (1971) 187-207. R in *Le défi* (n. 28).

548. "Confession et louange de Dieu chez S. Bernard," in *La vie spirituelle* 120 (1969) 588-605; *Cistercian Studies* 4 (1969) 199-212; S in *Cistercium* 21 (1969) 211-220.

549. "Prière et vitesse," in *La Vie spirituelle* 120 (1969) 191-224; ed. C. Mooney, *Prayer. The Problem of Dialogue with God* (Paramus-London, 1969), 23-46; I in *Monastica* 12, n. 2 (1971) 54-78. R in *Le défi* (n. 28).

550. "Espérance et esthétique," in *Lettre de Ligugé*, n. 138 (1969) 5-7; I in *Monastica* 11 (1970) n. 1, 30-33.

551. "Ugo di Cluny," in *Bibliotheca sanctorum* 12 (1969) 752-755.

552. "Les intentions des fondateurs de l'Ordre cistercien," in *Collectanea Cisterciensia* 30 (1968) 233-371; *Cistercian Studies* 4 (1969) 21-61; *The Cistercian Spirit. A Symposium* (Spencer, 1970) 88-133; S in *Cistercian* 22 (1970) 285-299.

553. "Impressions sur le monachisme en Inde," in *Parole et mission* 12 (1969) 405-424. R in *Le défi* (n. 28).

554. "La rencontre des moines d'Asie à Bangkok," in *Parole et mission* 12 (1969) 390-404; *Collectanea Cisterciensia* 31 (1969) 91-96; I in *Ora et Labora* 24 (1969) 163-170; *Il tetto* 7 (1970) 78-88; *Erbe und Auftrag* 47 (1971) 68-74. R in *Le défi* (n. 28).

555. "Present Day Problems in Monasticism," in *Downside Review* 87 (1969) 135-156; *Rythmes du monde* 45 (1969) 7-23; *A New Charter for Monasticism* (Notre Dame-London, 1970) 23-44. R in *Le défi* (n. 28).

556. "Pour une spiritualité de la cellule," in *Collectanea Cisterciensia* 3 (1969) 74-82; I in *Ora et Labora* 25 (1970) 103-110. R in *Le défi* (n. 28).

557. "Problèmes de la prière dans les communautés religieuses," in *La vie des communautes religieuses* 27 (1969) 2-13. R in *Le défi* (n. 28).

558. "Monastic Culture as a Link with Antiquity," in *The Twelfth-Century Renaissance*, ed. Charles R. Young (Holt, Rinehart and Winston, 1969), pp. 41-50.

1970

559. "Introduction" to *Bernard of Clairvaux, I. Treatise. I:* "Apologia to Abbot William" (Spencer, 1970) 3-22.

560. "Introduction" to "St Bernard's Book on Precept and Dispensation," ibid., 73-102.

561. Review of S. Giuliani, *Profilo di un santo. S. Silvestro abate,* in *Rivista di storia della Chiesa in Italia* 24 (1970) 244. F.

562. Review of G. Sprunk, *Kunst und Glaube in der lateinischen Heiligenlegende* (München, 1970) ibid., 25 (1970) 240-242. F.

563. "Qu'est-ce que vivre selon une règle?," in *Collectanea Cisterciensia*

*Bibliography*

32 (1970) 155-163; I in *Ora et Labora* 25 (1970) 145-151. R in *Moines et moniales* (n. 29).

564. "Deux nouveaux Docteurs de l'Eglise," in *La vie spirituelle*, 123 (1970) 135-146; I in *Monastica*, 12, n. 1 (1971) 49-57.

565. "Le diverse forme di vita religiosa," in *Studi Francescani* 67 (1970) 105-115. R in *Moines et moniales* (n. 29).

566. "Les contemplatives peuvent-elles se gouverner elles-mêmes?," in *vie consacrée* 42 (1970) 3-28; *Cistercian Studies* 5 (1970) 111-130; I in *Vita monastica* 24 (1970) 78-103. R in *Moines et moniales* (n. 29).

567. "Attualità della communità apostolica," in *Servizio della parola*, n. 21 (1970) 10-14. R in *Moines et moniales* (n. 29).

568. "A Sociological Approach to the History of a Religious Order," in *The Cistercian Spirit. A Symposium* (Spencer, 1970) 134-143.

569. "Bref traité sur la confession dans un manuscrit d'Orval," in *Recherches de théologie ancienne et médiévale* 27 (1970) 142-147.

570. "Profession According to the Rule of St Benedict," *Cistercian Studies* 5 (1970) 252-277; *Rule and Life. An Interdisciplinary Symposium* (Spencer, 1971) 117-150.

571. "The Priesthood in the Patristic and Medieval Church," in *The Christian Priesthood* (London-Denville, N.J., 1970) 53-75.

572. "La rencontre des moines d'Extrême-Orient," in *Bulletin de l'A. I.M.* 11 (1970) 29-35. English edition, ibid.

573. "Un témoin de l'antiféminisme au moyen âge," in *Revue bénédictine* 80 (1970) 304-309.

574. "Monastic Historiography from Leo IX to Callistus II," in *Studia monastica* 12 (1970) 57-86; F in *Il monachesimo e la riforma ecclesiastica (1949-1122)* (Milan, 1971) 271-301.

575. "Violence and the Devotion to S. Benedict in the Middle Ages," in *Downside Review* 88 (1970) 344-360; *Mélanges de science religieuse* 28 (1971) 3-15.

576. "Attualità di una crisi mediaevale." Préface to G. Lunardi, *L'ideale monastico nelle polemiche del Seculo XII sulla vita religiosa* (Noci, 1970) 5-8.

577. "Vieni e Seguimi," in *Monastica* 11 (1970) n. 1, 3-10.

578. "L'humanisme des moines au moyen âge," in *A Giuseppe Ermini, I, Studi mediaevali* (1970) 69-113.

579. "Thèmes pour une réflexion chrétienne sur l'Expo 70," in *Nouvelle revue théologique* 102 (1970) 634-648; *The Japan Missionary Bulletin* 24 (1970) 347-353, 413-418; I in *Monastica* 11 (1970) 31-46.

580. "Il monachesimo cristiano e gli altri," in *Vita religiosa* 6 (1970) 180-184. R in *Moines et moniales* (n. 29).

581. "Existe-t-il une prière contemplative?," in *La vie des communautés religieuses* 28 (1970) 194-199; I in *Ora et Labora* 28 (1970) 1-5; *Spiritual Life* 17 (1971) 34-39.

582. "Presentazione," in Ed. Ferruccio Gastaldelli, *Goffredo di Auxerre "Super Apocalypsim"* (Roma, 1970) 7-8.

583. "Teologia de la vida monastica, estratto e Conferencia de D. Jean Leclercq à Montreal," in *La Saulsaie* 4 (1970) n. 14, pp. 19-60.

**1971**

584. "La rencontre des monachismes," in *Parole et mission* 14 (1971) 340-348.

585. "St Bernard and the Rule of St Benedict," in *Rule and Life. An Interdisciplinary Symposium* (Spencer, 1971) 151-168.

586. "Teologia de la vida monastica," in *Cuadernos monasticos* 6 (1971) 9-60.

587. "Monachesimo femminile," in *Dizionario degli instituti di perfezione* (Rome, 1971) 31-36.

588. "Recherches sur la collection des épîtres de S. Bernard," in *Cahiers de civilisation médiévale* 14 (1971) 205-219.

589. "Lettres de S. Bernard: histoire ou littérature?," in *Studi medievali* 12 (1971) 1-74.

590. "Le cloître est-il une prison?," in *Revue d'ascétique et de mystique* 47 (1971) 407-420.

262     Bibliography

591. "Prière monastique et accueil," in *Collectanea Cisterciensia* 33 (1971) 379-400; *Vita Monastica* 26 (1972) 96-125.

592. "Marginalité et accueil," ibid., 401-405.

593. "L'encyclique de S. Bernard en faveur de la croisade," in *Revue bénédictine* 81 (1971) 282-308.

594. "Multipluralism. Benedictine Life in the Church To-day," in *The Ampleforth Journal* 76 (1971) 75-83; I in *Ora et Labora* 26 (1971) 158-166; *Cistercian Studies* 7 (1972) 77-84.

595. "Une réunion de contemplatives à Obout," in *Bulletin de l'A.I.M.* 12 (1971); 26-31 English ed., ibid.

596. "Une expérience pascale," in *Collectanea Cisterciensia,* 33 (1971) 120-123.

597. "Note sur la tradition monastique d'Occident," in *Collectanea Cisterciensia* 33 (1971) 102-104.

598. "Consécration religieuse et vie contemplative," in *La vie des communautés religieuses* 29 (1971) 2-19.

599. "Vie monastique masculine et vie monastique féminine," in *Supplément à la Lettre de Ligugé* 149 (1971) 3-9; *Cistercian Studies* 6 (1971) 327-333; I in *Ora et Labora* 27 (1972) 3-8.

600. "Le Commentaire d'Etienne de Paris sur la Règle de S. Benoît," in *Revue d'ascétique et de mystique* 47 (1971) 129-144.

601. "Introduction" to Thomas Merton, *Contemplation in a world of Action* (New York, 1971) IX-XX.

602. "Culture and the Spiritual Life," in *Review for Religious* 30 (1971) 167-178.

603. "Un formulaire de chancellerie de l'abbaye d'Orval," in *Cîteaux* 21 (1970) 300-301.

604. "S. Gérard de Csanád et le monachisme," in *Studia monastica* 13 (1971) 13-30.

605. "La figura di Pier Damiano. Ermite et homme d'Eglise," in *Testi e documenti di vita sacerdotale e di arte pastorale XVII* (Rome, 1971) 105-113.

606. "Deux témoins de la vie des cloîtres au moyen âge," in *Studi medievali* 12 (1971) 987-995.

607. "Prière des heures et civilisation contemporaine," in *La Maison-Dieu*, n. 105 (1971) 34-45.

1972

608. "Notes abélardiennes," in *Bulletin de Philosophie médiévale* 13 (1972) 71-74.

609. Review of Richard E. Weingart, *The Logic of Divine Love* (Oxford, 1970) in *Medium Aevum* 41 (1972) 59-61. F.

610. "Evangile et culture dans la tradition bénédictine," in *Nouvelle revue théologique* 104 (1972) 171-182; *Revue historique ardennaise* 7 (1972) 143-149.

611. "St Bernard of Clairvaux and the Contemplative Community," in *Contemplative Community*, Cistercian Studies Series 21 (Spencer, 1972) 61-113; *Cistercian Studies* 7 (1972) 97-142; *Collectanea Cisterciensia* 34 (1972) 36-84. F.

612. "Per un ritratto spirituale del b. Bernardo Tolomei," in *Saggi e ricerche nel VII Centenario della nascita del b. Bernardo Tolomei (1272-1972)*, Studia Olivetana 1 (Monte Oliveto Maggiore, 1972) 11-21. F.

613. "Pédagogie et formation spirituelle du VIe au XIIe siècle," in *La scula dell'Occidente latino nell'alto medio evo* (Spoleto, 1972) 42-72.

614. Review of H. Steger, *Philologia Musica*, in *Rivista di storia della Chiesa in Italia* 26 (1972) 176-177. F.

615. "Experience and Interpretation of Time in the Early Middle Ages," in *Studies in Medieval Culture* (not yet published); *Ora et Laboro* 27 (1972) 49-58. I.

616. "Un tour du monde monastique par les Mers Sud," in *Bulletin de l'A.I.M.* 13 (1972) 7-17; English ed., 7-17.

617. "Scopis mundatum (Matth. 12,44; Mc 11, 25). La balai dans le Bible et dans la liturgie d'après la tradition latine," in *Epektasis. Mélanges offerts au Cardinal Jean Daniélou* (Paris, 1972) 129-137.

618. "L'ascèse de la prière," in *Seminarium* 12 (1972) 12-25; *Monastic Studies* 8 (1972) 89-102; Monastica 13 (1972) 38-48. I.

619. "New Forms of Contemplation and of the Contemplative Life," in *Theological Studies* 33 (1972) 307-319.

620. "Les chapîtres généraux de Cîteaux, de Cluny et des Dominicains," in *Concilium* 7 (1972) 91-97.

621. "The Definitive Character of Religious Commitment," in *American Benedictine Review* 23 (1972) 181-205.

622. "Jean de Fécamp," in *Dictionnaire de spiritualité* 8 (1972) 445-448.

623. Review of F. C. Gardiner, *The Pilgrimage of Desire*, in *Cahiers de civilisation médiévale* 15 (1972) 82-83.

624. Review of M. Aubran, *La vie de S. Etienne d'Obazine*, in *Medium Aevum* 41 (1972) 143-144.

625. "The Relevance of Prayer Today," *Encounter* 17 (1972) 3-13.

626. "Pour l'histoire du canif et de la lime," in *Scriptorium* 26 (1972) 46-52.

627. Preface to Francis Acharya, *Kurisumala Ashram. Chronique de Douze Années* (Vanves, 1972) 1-6.

628. "The Experience of God and Prayer for Christians of our Time," in *Spiritual Life* 18 (1972) 246-255.

629. "Lecture, culture et vie spirituelle," in *La vie des communautés religieuses* 30 (1972) 205-218.

# CISTERCIAN FATHERS SERIES

Under the direction of the same Board of Editors as the *Cistercian Studies Series,* the *Cistercian Fathers Series* seeks to make available the works of the Cistercian Fathers in good English translations based on the recently established critical editions. The texts are accompanied by introductions, notes and indexes prepared by qualified scholars.

CF   1:  Bernard of Clairvaux, Vol. 1: *Treatises I*
           Introductions: Jean Leclercq OSB
CF   2:  Aelred of Rievaulx, Vol. 1: *Treatises, Pastoral Prayer*
           Introduction: David Knowles
CF   3:  William of St Thierry, Vol. 1: *On Contemplating God, Prayer, Meditations*
           Introductions: Jacques Hourlier OSB
CF   4:  Bernard of Clairvaux, Vol. 2: *On the Song of Songs I*
           Introduction: Corneille Halflants OCSO
CF   5:  Aelred of Rievaulx, Vol. 2: *Spiritual Friendship*
           Introduction: Douglas Roby
CF   6:  William of St Thierry, Vol. 2: *Exposition on the Song of Songs*
           Introduction: J. M. Déchanet OSB
CF   7:  Bernard of Clairvaux, Vol. 3: *On the Song of Songs II*
           Introduction: Jean Leclercq OSB
CF   8:  Guerric of Igny: *Liturgical Sermons I*
           Introduction: Hilary Costello and John Morson OCSO
CF   9:  William of St Thierry, Vol. 3: *The Enigma of Faith*
           Introduction: John Anderson
CF 12:  William of St Thierry, Vol. 4: *The Golden Epistle*
           Introduction: J. M. Déchanet OSB
CF 13:  Bernard of Clairvaux, Vol. 5: *Treatises II*
           Introduction: M. Basil Pennington OCSO
CF 24:  *Three Treatises on Man: A Cistercian Anthropology*
           Introduction: Bernard McGinn
CF 32:  Guerric of Igny: *Liturgical Sermons II*

CISTERCIAN PUBLICATIONS
CONSORTIUM PRESS
Washington D.C.